Walking Wisely

Walking Wisely

WALKING WITH JESUS
VOLUME SIX

*An Expository Commentary
based upon Paul's Letter to the Ephesians*

(CHAPTER FIVE VERSES 1–33)

ROBERT B. CALLAHAN SR.

RESOURCE *Publications* • Eugene, Oregon

WALKING WISELY
An Expository Commentary based upon Paul's Letter to the Ephesians
(Chapter Five Verses 1–33)

Copyright © 2013 Robert B. Callahan Sr. All rights reserved. Except for brief quotations in critical publications or reviews, no part of this book may be reproduced in any manner without prior written permission from the publisher. Write: Permissions, Wipf and Stock Publishers, 199 W. 8th Ave., Suite 3, Eugene, OR 97401.

Resource Publications
An Imprint of Wipf and Stock Publishers
199 W. 8th Ave., Suite 3
Eugene, OR 97401
www.wipfandstock.com

ISBN 13: 978-1-60899-650-6
Manufactured in the U.S.A.

All scripture quotations, unless otherwise indicated, are taken from the Holy Bible, The King James Study Bible, Copyright ©1983, 1988. (Previously published as the Liberty Annotated Study Bible and as The Annotated Study Bible, King James Version) Copyright © 1988 by Liberty University. Thomas Nelson Publishers.

*For my wife, Ginger,
whose encouragement, faith,
love, and objectivity contributed
significantly to Walking with Jesus*

Topical Categories in Walking with Jesus
(An Expository Commentary)

Volume One	Volume Two	Volume Three	Volume Four
The Triune God Speaks to the Saints	*Sin and Redemption*	*Christ's Prisoner*	*Walking As Mature Christians*
To the Faithful in Christ Jesus	Sin and God's Wrath	For This Cause— God's Glory	Living in Harmony With Christ
God's Will— Spiritual Blessings	God, Rich in Mercy and Grace	Revealing God's Hidden Truths	Unity in the Triune God The Holy Spirit
Trusting in Him	A Right Relationship With God	Praying to the Father	The Lord Jesus Christ
Praying for Christians	Reconciliation	Believing God's Power	God, the Father
	Praying Through the Holy Spirit		Grace According to Christ's Gifts
	God's Foundation (Apostles and Prophets)		Maturing in Christ

Topical Categories in Walking with Jesus

(An Expository Commentary)

Volume Five	Volume Six	Volume Seven	Volume Eight
Following Christ	*Walking Wisely*	*Satan and God's Armor*	*Christ's Ambassadors*
Alienated from God	Christ-Like Conduct	Family Relationships	A Call to Discipleship
Ye Have Not So Learned Christ	No Inheritance in the Kingdom of God and Christ	Life's Basic Relationship	Wearing God's Armor
Christ-Like Conduct	Walking in the Light	The Whole Armor of God	Christ's Ambassadors
	Walking Circumspectly	Satan and His Evil Forces	
	The Marriage Relationship		
	Christ and His Church		

Ephesians "brings one into an atmosphere of unbounded spiritual affluence that creates within one's heart deepest peace and assurance. It is impossible to live habitually in Ephesians and be depressed."

RUTH PAXSON

Contents

Volume Six: Topical Categories xi
Foreword xiii
Preface xv
Acknowledgments xvii
The Question of Authorship xix
Introduction xxi

1 Be Followers of God 1

2 God's Love 9

3 Walking in the Light 16

4 No Inheritance in God's Kingdom 24

5 God's Wrath 32

6 Children of Light 39

7 Knowing the Will of God 47

8 What Is Acceptable 55

9 Not as Fools, But as Wise 64

10 Walking Circumspectly 72

11 The Reality of the Spirit 81

12 Being Filled With the Spirit 88

13 Giving Thanks Always 95

14 Walking in Harmony 105

15　A Relationship as That of Christ to the Church　112

16　Wives . . . Unto Your Own Husbands　121

17　Husbands, Love Your Wives　130

18　Marriage: The Husband and Wife Relationship　138

19　Christ Nourishes and Cherishes　147

20　Christ and the Ecclesia　156

21　The Mystery　165

22　Old and New Blessings　173

Outline Questions　183
Bibliography　229
Index of Scripture References　231

Volume Six: Topical Categories

Category	Scripture	Chapters
Christ-like Conduct	Eph. 5:1–2	1–2
No Inheritance in the Kingdom of God and Christ	Eph. 5:3–5	3–4
Walking in the Light	Eph. 5:6–14	5–8
Walking Circumspectly	Eph. 5:15–21	9–14
The Marriage Relationship	Eph. 5:22–23	15–19
Christ and His Church	Eph. 5:26, 32–33	20–22

Foreword

Robert Callahan's multi-volume work of Paul's Letter to the Ephesians is both a welcomed and long-overdue guide for Christian living today. The Apostle's sense of the eternity and greatness of God, his emphasis on the living reality and exaltation of Christ, his devotion to God's grace as an unearned gift of enduring love, and his call to an ardent and faithful discipleship all witness to an urgency and renewal critically needed in our time. Callahan's heart and style rise to meet this challenge and to convey God's message of hope and promise, of presence and courage, to Christian souls of any and every contemporary Christian tradition.

Callahan's format allows for both a devotional and studious usage. One can permit one's soul to savor every spiritual nuance the author uncovers, verse by verse, mark the passage, and return later for further nourishment. Or one can linger from text to text, gleaning with the author both theological and spiritual insight for enhancing personal discipleship, equally applicable in the arena of church and society.

The author draws on an array of insightful theological and spiritual wisdom, garnered from scholars and saints alike, theologians and missionaries. Calvin's Institutes guide Callahan's expositions, as well as the work of Markus Barth—known for his commentary on Ephesians and his delineation of Pauline theology. The author cites frequent and astute observations from Barth's exegesis of this nature. In addition, Callahan makes wise usage of Martyn Lloyd-Jones' emphasis on "experiencing the living Christ." For Lloyd-Jones, as well as the author, mere intellectual knowledge of the Christ fails to undergird one's faith or discipleship, when life's journey truly becomes sore bestead. Callahan also draws from the great 17th century theologian William Gurnall's delightful work: The Christian in Complete Armour. Perhaps students of Church history remember how both John Newton and Charles Spurgeon prized Gurnall's approach and piety and preferred it to many perspicacious studies available in their time. Gurnall's Complete Armour is known for its pithy, fervent, and wise counsel that confronts human vagaries with the truth about the self. In that respect, so too does Robert Callahan's gentle but firm counsel enrich the Christian heart and inspire one to a higher level of discipleship. No one can fail to sense this in Walking with Jesus. Whether encouraged to venture this methodology owing to his own years as a Presbyterian elder, or as an avid member and participant of the bi-annual Calvin's Colloquiums for the past 30 years, or as a fond reader of Ruth Paxson's The Wealth, Walk and Warfare of the Christian, the result is the same: a powerful, inspirational, and theologically heart-warming guide to discipleship today.

Ministers, Christian educators, seminary students, laypersons, and lovers of Jesus' life will find Callahan's work immensely valuable. His volumes deserve our grateful and sincere attention, as we too seek to walk with Jesus.

Benjamin W. Farley
Younts Professor Emeritus of Bible, Religion, and Philosophy
Erskine College, Due West, South Carolina

Preface

Paul's Epistle to the Ephesians shows us the joy and challenge of being united to Christ in his death and resurrection. It takes us from being seated with Him in the heavenlies (chapter 2), down to the battles we must wage, in His armor, with powers of evil (Eph. 6). In a balanced and judicious manner, longtime Presbyterian elder, Bob Callahan, exercises remarkable insight in opening to believers the vital truths of Ephesians; truths that once taken in, transform the attitude towards life, and often set the soul singing!

As a professor of theology, I have carefully worked through one of his multivolumed series, and found it to be theologically sound: evangelical and scholarly at the same time. It has spiritual depth and is extremely practical; it is accessible in good, clear English. It is neither a commentary, nor a series of sermons. In some ways it reminds me of some of the ancient Patristic engagements with a series of texts of Holy Scripture. It brings the reader into the presence of the Most High, and—if considered thoughtfully and prayerfully, is likely to cause him to sit down under the canopy of God's love.

The journey of Christians in today's world is very demanding indeed, and Bob's work is intended to be a guide to help every pilgrim 'Walking with Jesus.' It will be a rich resource for Sunday Schools, Bible studies, as well as for individual devotions.

Douglas F. Kelly
Reformed Theological Seminary
Charlotte, NC

Acknowledgments

The crafting of Walking with Jesus was not a "one man show" but numerous people working together to present a formidable work. Three guiding lights have been paramount in the minds of those making significant contributions: one, presenting the theology in accord with the tenets of the Reformed Faith; two, employing language that presents the Gospel in a meaningful and understandable light; and, three, expounding upon Scripture in a clear, concise, and forthright manner.

It has been God's blessing that the following ministers and theologians have enthusiastically and willingly provided their time and talents to enhance this work. They are:

Dr. Frank Barker, Founder and Pastor Emeritus of the Briarwood Presbyterian Church, Birmingham, AL

Dr. Benjamin W. Farley, Younts Professor Emeritus, Bible, Religion, and Philosophy, Erskine College, Due West, SC

Dr. James C. Goodloe, IV, Executive Director, Foundation for Reformed Theology, Richmond, VA

Dr. Todd Jones, Senior Minister, First Presbyterian Church, Nashville, TN

Dr. Douglas Kelly, Richard Jordan, Professor of Theology, Reformed Theological Seminary, Charlotte, NC

Dr. Norman McCrummen, Senior Pastor, Spring Hill Presbyterian Church, Mobile, AL

Dr. Mark Mueller, Senior Pastor, First Presbyterian Church, Huntsville, AL

Dr. Richard Ray, Former Managing Director of John Knox Press, Montreat, NC

Without the knowledge, wisdom, and encouragement of these individuals this work would neither have become a reality nor available to individuals seeking a better understanding of the teachings of the Scripture and the joy of walking daily with the Lord Jesus.

Several others have labored diligently to create this work, and to produce the finished product. Our daughter, Karen Callahan Myrick, made significant contributions during the drafting process through her knowledge of grammar. Ms. Lynn Sledge, as the copy editor, judiciously reviewed the manuscript and made valuable contributions for improving it. Four ladies, Helen Marshall, D'Anne Dendy, Kelly Comferford, and Elizabeth Annan, worked tirelessly, with dedication, to prepare draft after draft and to make positive contributions to the project. In addition, Wick Skinner made invaluable contributions through his attention to details, grammar, and vocabulary.

It is not possible to thank them sufficiently for their dedication to making this volume a desirable repository of Christian truths, and in so doing to cheerfully work on draft after draft, to recommend enhancements, and to make appropriate changes in the text. Their unselfish contributions are too many to enumerate. May God bless them.

The Question of Authorship

Recent scholars have questioned the authorship of the letter to the Ephesians and have been less convinced that it was the Apostle Paul. However, for the sake of simplicity of expression we will abide by the traditional view and refer to Paul as its author.

Introduction

The creation of this work was the result of unusual developments which some would attribute to happenstance and others to God's providence. You may be the judge after considering the following.

During May 2000 a friend invited my wife and me to visit the Spring Hill Presbyterian Church in Mobile and hear their new minister, Norman McCrummen. We accepted his invitation.

The following March, Dr. McCrummen was preaching on anything but Ephesians when he interrupted his sermon, paused long enough to slowly scan the congregation twice, and said, "I want everyone to read the first and second chapters of Ephesians by next Sunday" and promptly returned to his sermon. The next day I called him and said, "I can't do it" a few times. Finally, his light went on and he said, "What can't you do?" I said, "I can't read the first and second chapters of Ephesians by next Sunday." He asked, "Why can't you? It will only take ten to fifteen minutes." I responded, "I have fifty-eight to sixty expository messages on the first two chapters of Ephesians that took thirty to thirty-five minutes to present." His response was, "I want to read all those and everything else you have on Ephesians." Thus began the long, arduous, and heartwarming journey of converting handwritten notes along with printed ones into the written word. It has been a joyful, though demanding experience.

Paul's Letter to the Ephesians has been described as "The holiest of the holies." My love affair with it began in the 1980's when I read a book containing great sermons of the twentieth century. The most impressive one was written by Martyn Lloyd-Jones. As a result, I read other works of his including his exposition of Ephesians. Thereafter, unexpectedly, I was asked to teach an adult Bible Study Group. They said they would provide the material, but I demurred and said, "I would gather my own material." This set in motion the process of acquiring knowledge through the best expository works available at the time on Ephesians including Martyn

Lloyd-Jones, William Gurnall, Ruth Paxson, Markus Barth, John Calvin, Otto Weber, and others.

The objective was to present the essence of Paul's letter as it was presented to him by the Lord Jesus and the Holy Spirit. Further, to mine the gold available in the fruitful works of those fertile minds that God had cultivated and enabled to expound upon the truths that His only begotten Son had revealed to His apostles and disciples. Therefore, it was a paramount obligation to express God's truths in a simple, straightforward manner according to the dictates of the Holy Spirit so that the reader may grasp it and interpret it according to the will of our Lord and Saviour Jesus Christ.

The need for the truths of the Gospel is as great today as it was in the first century. The conditions are similar and the challenges facing our culture reveal the need for knowing the living God and His Son. Today, the people of faith require the same spiritual nourishment as those brave souls of the early days after the Resurrection, who would rather face death than deny their Lord and Saviour.

There are people in responsible positions in Christ's church who deny Him by: their passivity; seeking secular acceptance; and failing to honor Him in public. These apostasies negatively impact members of organized Christian churches as well as non-believers.

They create an environment in which unrighteousness flourishes. This results in irreverence as aptly described by R.W. Dale, "Where there is irreverence for the divine law the vision of God becomes fainter; as the vision of God becomes fainter the restraints of the Divine Righteousness are lessened and at last the vision of God is lost altogether." May God enlighten us regarding His infallible Word so that we will hunger and thirst for righteousness, and for the vision of God to shine brighter and brighter as we serve Him with courage, wisdom, justice, and self-control.

This expository commentary is designed to bring individuals, whether they are spiritually children, adolescents or adults into a closer, more mature relationship with the Lord Jesus Christ. It begins with the Triune God; presents the doctrines of the Christian faith; reminds us "that we henceforth be no more children, tossed to and fro . . . but speaking the truth in love, may grow up into Him in all things, . . . even Christ." It continues by emphasizing the importance of being renewed in the spirit of your mind; putting on the new man, which after God is created in righteousness and true holiness; using the whole armor of God to thwart the manifold attacks of Satan; and concluding with the admonition to conduct ourselves as Christ's ambassadors.

The spiritual food contained ranges from milk and honey to tough meat. The flavor of this exposition encompasses all varieties—sweet, sour, pleasant, bitter, tart, tasteless, dry, burned, and succulent. Do not reject the nourishment because of its texture or flavor, but seek to understand it despite your preferences, since it provides food for good health and strength for joyful living. May God's truths flourish in your heart and mind, and enable you to withstand the tests, trials, and tribulations that come your way as you are "Walking with Jesus."

In presenting this work, I realize everyone has different challenges. The fascinating part of God's Word is that it meets us where we are. The question is, will we meet Him there, hear what He has to say, and accept the nourishment He offers?

The words of William Gurnall are appropriate and enlightening in contemplating God's Word. He said prior to expounding upon Ephesians, "The fare that I shall be serving during the coming weeks will be from God's own table. If perchance it does not go down well or should not have the flavor that you desire, please do not despise the provider of the food, but blame the cook who has prepared it and is serving it." To that I say, Amen!

The courses being served by this cook are described herein. May they provide the taste and nourishment you are seeking.

Robert B. Callahan, Sr.

1

Be Followers of God

> *BE ye therefore followers of God, as dear children;*
> *And walk in love, as* (or even as) *Christ also hath loved us, and hath given himself for us an offering and a sacrifice to God for a sweet-smelling savor* (aroma) [Eph. 5:1–2].

The scholars have a good time trying to determine if the first and second verses of this fifth chapter belong to the fourth chapter or to the fifth one. However, they appear to agree that these two verses are important and serve as an excellent bridge between the latter half of the fourth chapter through the twentieth verse of the fifth chapter.

Once again, we must recognize the context in which these verses appear, the key points immediately preceding and following them, and the primary thoughts, which are:

> *Be ye therefore followers of God, as dear children;*
> *Walk in love, as Christ also hath loved us;*
> *Hath given himself for us an offering and a sacrifice to God, for a sweet-smelling savor* (aroma).

The Apostle provided specific injunctions and reasons after stating we are to *put off* the old and *put on the new man.* Then he went to the heart of the matter in Ephesians 4:32 saying that we are to become *kind, tenderhearted,* and *forgiving even as God for Christ's sake hath forgiven you.*

Paul continues with a positive injunction saying, *Be ye therefore followers of God, as dear children; And walk in love, as* (or even as) *Christ also hath loved us, . . .* and then he gives the motivating reason that (Christ) *hath given himself for us an offering and a sacrifice to God for a sweet-smelling savor* (aroma). Think of that injunction and the reason for it. Then let someone tell you being a Christian or a member of Christ's body is easy. Then let someone say let's skip over the details, let's just cover the high spots, let's move on.

I doubt there are very many sermons available on the last half of Chapter 4 and the first half of Chapter5 in Ephesians. Undoubtedly there are even less on the first and second verses of this chapter and the last two verses of Chapter 4.

Yet Paul thought they were important. You will recall his letter to the Ephesians concentrated on the highlights, the important matters he had discussed, taught, and preached during his three year ministry among them. We need to remember Paul's words to the Ephesians in Chapter 20 of Acts regarding his ministry in Ephesus:

> he kept nothing back as he taught publicly from house to house;
>
> Paul testified to the Gospel and God's grace as he declared the full counsel of God, and stated that is the way for the community of believers;
>
> Paul was not hesitant declaring to the Ephesian elders that grievous wolves would enter in and not spare the flock; and
>
> Therefore, he exhorted them to watch and remember Christ's teachings, and commended them to God: to the Word of God strengthening them; and endowing them with the inheritance provided to those receiving salvation.

Then he knelt down and prayed with them. Paul taught the Ephesians! He taught them the ABC's of the Gospel, the truths as they are in Christ Jesus. He did not gloss over them, but provided details and insight.

No wonder John Knox said, in his last days, to his wife and manservant, "Read Isaiah 53, John 17, or something from Ephesians." No wonder some scholars call the Epistle to the Ephesians, "The Holy of Holies."

Paul builds point by point and step by step. He starts with the relatively easy, then proceeds to the more difficult. He wants us to: see our own weaknesses; turn from ourselves to the Lord Jesus Christ; focus on Him; dwell with Him; and learn from Him. We are to know the power available from Christ, what He has done for us, and what we are to become as members of His body, as we have professed to be.

There are definite challenges *as dear children* of God. We are to *walk in love, as Christ also hath loved us*. What does it mean to be *fol-*

lowers of God and to *walk in love*? These are not just nice flowery words that can be ignored or passed over. They are to grab us and cause us to ponder them. Why? Because, Paul, under the influence of the Holy Spirit has given us two important commands to follow all the days that God gives us. They are to be our guiding lights. First, we are to be, become, *followers of God, as dear children*. This means that we are to: know God; learn all we can about Him; love Him, truly love Him; and be obedient to His commands. This is not easy. It requires a strong commitment accompanied by considerable effort and time plus determined resiliency when encountering the obstacles and pitfalls of daily living.

Second, if the first command is not difficult enough, we are to *walk in love, as Christ also hath loved us, and hath given himself for us an offering and a sacrifice to God . . . .* How do you like that for a challenge? Who said being a follower of God and Christ would be easy? How can we obey these commands? By being obedient disciples of His will? Yes! But primarily by the power of the Holy Spirit and trusting Him. This means being Christ centered and losing all traces of being self-centered. What happens when we do this? We will know the joy, peace, and love of being in Christ. Yes, there may be difficulties in receiving these blessings, but there is nothing, no nothing, more worthwhile in this life.

What does Paul mean by the injunction, *Be ye therefore followers of God, as dear children; And walk in love, as* (or even as) *Christ also hath loved us*? The first words should be translated "become imitators of God." We are not just to follow along after God. Some of us have had dogs for pets. I have had several of which I have been very fond. They would follow along when I would take a walk or run. They would also do their own thing. They would chase squirrels or birds or just go off and investigate various and sundry things. Then they would catch up and follow along.

According to Webster, *follow* means to "come after in time, position or logical sequence." That is not what the Apostle means. We are not to follow one after another into the church house, or in reciting creeds, or in responsive readings. The meaning is much more than that. The Greek word Paul uses is *mimētēs*, which is translated "imitator." It means we are to "become imitators" of God. We are to imitate Him. More to the point, we are to become like Him, copy Him, reproduce within ourselves those traits or characteristics that can be adopted, appear like Him, and resemble Him. "He who is to be imitated determines the nature of the imitation," as Markus Barth said.

Now, what do you think about those comments or statements that it is easy to be a Christian or a member of Christ's body? We are to become imitators of God. Naturally, questions arise at a time like this. Is Paul serious? Is this a gross exaggeration? Is Paul talking to people who live, work, and play in the real world? Is this injunction directed toward people confronted by temptations and surrounded by evil?

I think you know the answers to these questions. It is apparent that if we are to imitate God, then we must know Him. This is important. It is not that we are to know something about Him. It is that we are to know Him! That is very different from knowing about Him. We are to know Him!

How are we to know Him? Through His Son, Jesus Christ, through the Word of God as provided in the Scriptures, and through the presence and power of the Holy Spirit.

What are we to imitate? There are certain attributes of God that we cannot imitate. They belong to Him and Him alone, such as His glory, majesty, eternity, omnipotence, omnipresence, and omniscience.

However, there are some traits that we are to imitate, to adopt, and to practice. They are holiness, *be ye holy for I am holy*; righteousness, justice, goodness, mercy, love, compassion, loving kindness, and faithfulness. And, as pointed out previously, we are to radiate kindness, tenderheartedness, and forgiveness.

These are communicable attributes of God. They should be imitated and practiced. "If we are children of God, we ought to be imitators of Him," as clearly stated by John Calvin.

What does Jesus say about this?

> *But I say unto you, Love your enemies, bless them that curse you, do good to them that hate you, and pray for them which despitefully* (spitefully) *use you, and persecute you;*
> *That ye may be the children* (sons) *of your Father which is in heaven: for he maketh his sun to rise on the evil and on the good, and sendeth rain on the just and on the unjust* [Matt. 5:44–45].

Paul makes it very clear [Eph. 4:32, 5:2] that we are to be imitators of Christ as well as of God. We are to imitate and to practice what the Father and Son have given unto us. Paul's teachings in these verses reveal two important points. First, His exhortation to be imitators is based upon the Gospel of the Lord Jesus Christ and the good news of God's grace presented to and known by the members of Christ's body. Second, the grace of God is so complete that its impact upon the followers can neither be subdued nor eliminated. Also, this is true of His love, discipline, and wisdom.

Why are we to be imitators of God? Because first and foremost we are His children. If we are His children, we should strive to be like Him. We should imitate Him, obey Him, and walk after Him in His ways.

There are two thoughts to exhibit when imitating God: first, to be obedient, realistic, relevant, and accurate; and second, visible action should reflect and exhibit the invisible patterns revealed by God.

Becoming imitators of God allows a great deal of freedom if it is in accord with the revealed Word and the truth as it is in Jesus. This verse should enable us to have a better understanding with respect to the following: the references to Christ in the preceding and following verses make us realize that becoming imitators of God is dependent upon the Lord Jesus Christ. Scripture says,

> . . . *even as God for Christ's sake hath forgiven* (in Christ forgave) *you* [Eph. 4:32].
> *And walk in love, as* (or even as) *Christ also hath loved us, and hath given himself for us an offering and a sacrifice to God for a sweet-smelling savor* (aroma) [Eph. 5:2].

The imitation of God is directly related to God's forgiveness, to Christ offering Himself as a sacrifice, and to our becoming what God would have us become. The crucified Lord Jesus Christ is the one and only mediator between God and man. This point can neither be ignored nor forgotten.

Being imitators of God does not mean living moral and upright lives according to our own mindsets or the standards of the secular world. That type of conduct can be described as goodness for goodness sake. There are people who exhibit certain moral standards and codes, but that does not mean they are members of Christ's body. It is because we are children of God that we either do things or refrain from doing them, and for no other reason.

This is seen in the first chapter of Ephesians when Paul says under the influence of the Holy Spirit, *Having predestinated us unto the adoption of children* (sons) *by Jesus Christ to himself, according to the good pleasure of his will* [Eph. 1:5]. Also, it is seen in the following: *For we are his workmanship* (creation), *created in Christ Jesus unto* (for) *good works, which God hath before ordained* (prepared) *that we should walk in them* [Eph. 2:10].

When examining these truths there are additional facts to remember. When we are believers, we are active, we are not passive. When we are forgiven, it is a reality, it is active. When we are reborn, we become new creatures. *Therefore if any man be in Christ, he is a new creature* (creation)*: old things are passed away; behold, all things are become new* (in us) [2 Cor. 5:17]. When we have *put on* the new man, we are created in righteousness and holiness in the truth; we *put off* the old character, conduct, and conversation; we become partakers of the divine Spirit; we reject the things of the flesh and secular world; and we become imitators of God because we are His children.

Not only are we His children, but as Scripture says, we are His *dear children*. A more accurate translation is that we are His "beloved children." He loves us, He is interested in us, and He wants us to walk with Him and to do things with Him. He does not want us to ignore Him.

What should our response be to God's love for us as "beloved children"? To show our love for Him by pleasing and obeying Him, by serving Him seven days a week. We are members of His family and are to conduct ourselves accordingly. We are not to bring reproach to God's family, only honor and respect. We are to be imitators of God the Father. This is seen in the teachings of Jesus, who said, *A new commandment I give unto you, That ye love one another; as I have loved you, that ye also love one another* [John 13:34].

Jesus calls His disciples *little children* in a caressing manner. He cares for them and wants them to know it. Further, he gives them the new commandment so that while He is absent from them they will conduct themselves according to His teachings, they will exhibit the fact they have not been taught in vain, and they will meditate upon this commandment and His manner of living.

Christ wanted to inscribe this commandment, *That ye love one another; as I have loved you,* . . . on the hearts of His disciples and the members of His body. Basically, He is saying, according to Calvin, "I wish you to remember this commandment always, as if it were a law recently made."

Why does Jesus do this? He does not want us to lose sight of this commandment, or to allow our hearts and minds to fade away and not pursue it with diligence. Jesus realized it was and is hard to keep loving. We want to inject ourselves, our feelings, and our mindsets. We want to lay that commandment aside and obey Him in other ways.

God's love is extended to those who are outside Christ's body as well as to those who are members of it. However, since God's image shines more brightly on the members, the true members of the body, it is only proper and fitting that the bond of love should be much more evident among Christ's disciples. Love originates with God. It has its roots in Him. It is to be directed to Him.

A mutual attitude of love can exist only among those governed by the same Spirit. Christ speaks of an extremely high degree of love. We recognize and accept the fact that God sends the rain on the just and the unjust, and that His goodness is extended to everyone. Therefore, we should love everyone, even those who hate us.

Why does Christ set this example? Not because we can attain it and exemplify it in our conduct, but that we might exert ourselves in striving to achieve the same mark. We are to be imitators of God. Christ says, *By this shall all men know that ye are my disciples, if ye have love one to another* [John 13:35]. By this he is confirming that they have not been taught in vain. This is to be His disciples distinguishing mark. They are to love His other disciples.

There are some things that do not mix, like fire and water. Among these are the love of God and love of self, and the love of self and the love of neighbor. Self-love restricts love and results in it eroding away. It is such an insidious thing that it feeds upon itself and banishes or destroys the love of neighbor and love of God.

Whoever wishes to belong to Christ and to be one of the beloved children must direct his life toward loving the brethren. In doing this, we are to be imitators of God. As Jesus says, *Let your light so shine before men, that they may see your good works, and glorify your Father which is in heaven* [Matt. 5:16].

Martyn Lloyd-Jones asks "how are we to imitate God?" By walking in love, as Christ hath also loved us. Jesus says, *Be ye therefore perfect, even as your Father which is in heaven is perfect* [Matt. 5:48]. That is to be our goal. We are to live as children of God the Father.

Remember, Jesus said,

> *For if ye love them which love you, what reward have ye? do not even the publicans* (tax collectors) *the same?*

> *And if ye salute* (greet) *your brethren only, what do ye more than others? do not even the publicans* (tax collectors) *so* [Matt. 5:46–47]?

What is unusual about that? Certainly there is nothing wonderful about it. That is not how a member of Christ's body is to act. He or she is to become an imitator of God and to act as a beloved child of God's, *And walk in love, as* (or even as) *Christ also hath loved us, and hath given himself for us an offering and a sacrifice to God* [Eph. 5:2].

Yes, it gets more and more difficult as we study the teachings of the Master and try to practice them. However, it is also more rewarding, joyful, and exhilarating to study His commands and teachings and to endeavor to practice them. We are to become imitators of God, through His Son!

Remember, we are to be *followers of God*, we are to *walk in love as Christ also hath loved us.*

Amen!

2

God's Love

And walk in love, as (or even as) *Christ also hath loved us, and hath given himself for us an offering and a sacrifice to God for a sweet-smelling savor* (aroma) [Eph. 5:2].

And walk in love, as (or even as) *Christ also hath loved us, and hath given himself for us an offering and a sacrifice to God for a sweet-smelling savor* (aroma) is another of those magnificent gems for which Paul is noted. It contains several messages that cannot be ignored.

I have a confession to make. Recently, while my wife and I were in the midst of digging up and removing old plants, eliminating weeds and planting new shrubs and bushes, I said to her, "You know I just may skip some material and move on. There is some material I want to get to and examine." So guess what? When starting to prepare the other material, I reread this verse and instantly realized it contained truths that cannot be bypassed.

What are they? First, a phrase that definitely appeals to each and every one, *And walk in love*. If there is any word that has been more maligned or misinterpreted than the word *love* in Scripture I do not know what it is. Love is not a sentimental or physical attraction. It is not something fleeting or passing. It is not easy or fanciful.

What are the characteristics of love? Love is tough, strong, elastic. It has unlimited resources and shows itself in obedience, in serving others, in denying oneself, and above all, in forgiving others. These truths are different from those commonly described, encountered, or observed.

What does the word *love* mean as it is used in this context? It is from the Greek word *agape*.

Agape is used to describe the attitude of God toward His Son, the Lord Jesus Christ. You will recall, on the mount during the transfiguration, God said, *This is my beloved Son, in whom I am well pleased; hear ye him* [Matt. 17:5].

Agape conveys God's will for His children regarding their attitude toward one another. It is stated in Jesus' command, *A new commandment I give unto you, That ye love one another; as I have loved you, that ye also love one another* [John 13:34].

Agape shows God's love toward all people as revealed by Paul under the influence of the Holy Spirit, *And the Lord make you to increase and abound in love one toward another, and toward all men, even as we do toward you* [1 Thess. 3:12].

Agape expresses the essential nature of God. John does this in a simple, but wonderful way saying, *He that loveth not knoweth not God; for God is love* [1 John 4:8]. Love shows itself by helping and doing for its object rather than desiring to possess and enjoy for itself.

The love of God to men and women is expressed in two words, Jesus Christ. What we know of God's love is known through Him. That is why it is so important to acquire knowledge and an understanding of Christ. Jesus reveals God's love by action, by what He did, by what He does, and by who He is. He reveals to us a loving faith. A love that is not a rose garden, or easy, or without its difficulties, but a love that is strong, refreshing, and irresolute.

For Paul, the love of God and the love of Christ were one and the same. Romans substantiates this stating, *For I am persuaded, that neither death, nor life, nor angels, nor principalities, nor powers, nor things present, nor things to come, Nor height, nor depth, nor any other creature, shall be able to separate us from the love of God, which is in Christ Jesus our Lord* [Rom. 8:38–39]. The love of God is seen in numerous ways.

It is important to know how God shows His love if we are to walk in it, and that is what we are required to do. We are to grasp and cling to the attributes of His love as revealed in the Holy Trinity and provided for the elect of God, the real church, and the world.

These attributes are for our comfort, illumination, and strength as we continue walking with Jesus. They are evident in His Person and include the realization that God's love: is not dependent upon how we act or react; is spontaneous and limitless; fulfills His promises, irregardless of our conduct; is revealed in Christ's obedience and trust in the

Father; is expressed through the Cross and resurrection; and reaches out to those who are members of Christ's body and to those who are not. When considering these expressions of God's love, it is well to reflect upon the truths as presented in Christ's teachings and in the actions of God the Father.

God's love is seen in the action it prompts or motivates. God's love is seen in the gift of His Son. The Apostle John expands upon this saying,

> *Beloved, let us love one another: for love is of God; and every one that loveth is born of God, and knoweth God. He that loveth not knoweth not God; for God is love.*
>
> *In this was manifested the love of God toward us, because that God sent his only begotten Son into the world, that we might live through him.*
>
> *Herein is love, not that we loved God, but that he loved us, and sent his Son to be the propitiation for our sins* [1 John 4:7–10].

This love is not generated or bestowed because of any merit, performance, or achievement on the part of those who receive it. Love has its perfect expression in the life and ministry of the Lord Jesus Christ.

Love in the members of the body of Christ is the result of His love and the fruit of His spirit operating among the members of His body. This particular love has God as its primary objective and exhibits itself in perfect obedience to His commands. We are to keep God's commands by doing as John succinctly yet forcefully states,

> *But whoso keepeth his word, in him verily is the love of God perfected: hereby know we that we are in him* [1 John 2:5].
>
> *By this we know that we love the children of God, when we love God, and keep his commandments* [1 John 5:2].

Hopefully, you understand that the primary injunction to *walk in love* contains more information and requests for action than originally anticipated or believed. It is not an impulse or a fleeting expression toward the brethren. It is not self-fulfilling or self-pleasing. It does not always originate with natural inclinations, nor is it only expressed toward those for whom there is some affinity.

Love seeks the well-being of everyone and the opportunity to do good to others, and in turn may they be a blessing to others. This is seen in *Love worketh no ill* (does no harm) *to his neighbour: therefore love is the fulfilling of the law* [Rom. 13:10]. Paul, under the influence of the

Holy Spirit, states that God wants to instruct us in the duty of love. Isn't that interesting? The duty of love! Yes, love has its duties. Christ's commands become our duties . When the Lord Jesus commands us to do something we have a duty to fulfill that command. Love is not excluded from the domain of obedience required by the Lord Jesus of each person professing Christ. Hear the words of the Lord Jesus and ponder them. Then ask yourself: do I believe, understand, and accept the teaching that love has its duties?

God wants us to attain love in every way. Calvin says the Apostle "was desirous to prove that the object of the whole law is to encourage us to cultivate love for one another."

The word *love* contains teachings in God's commandments. Those who understand them and are mature in true love do not think of harming their brethren or their neighbor if they *walk in love*. Scripture says, *but he that soweth to the Spirit shall of the Spirit reap life everlasting* [Gal. 6:8].

Therefore, we are to look to God for direction in our daily lives. We are to know the teachings of our Lord Jesus Christ and to obey His commandments, for they are not grievous once we know them. To state it very simply, we are to aspire to serve God as members of the body of Christ with a living faith.

Further, it says, *Let us not be weary in well doing* [Gal. 6:9]. This means "in showing kindness to others." Remember the injunction to become *kind, . . . tenderhearted,* (and) *forgiving one another, even as God for Christ's sake* (in Christ forgave) *hath forgiven you* [Eph. 4:32].

The injunction to *not be weary in well doing* is most appropriate because we have a tendency to become lazy in the duties of love. We allow stumbling blocks to get in the way. Yes, there are many hindrances encountered on our daily walk, but we are to show forth the love of God in Christ Jesus. Therefore, we are not to faint or grow weary, but we are to persist.

In addition, the Apostle says, *As we have therefore opportunity* [Gal. 6:10]. We are to make use of the opportunities given to us and not allow them to slip by through sheer negligence or a mindset that is focused on self. Therefore, as we have opportunity we are to *do good unto all men, especially unto them who are of the household of faith* [Gal. 6:10]. What does *good* mean in this verse? It means that which is pleasing to God. As members of Christ's body we are to conduct ourselves in a manner pleasing to God, as we *walk in love*.

This love expresses a deep, abiding, constant interest and concern toward worthy and unworthy objects. It produces and fosters a reverential love toward the Giver, God, and a practical love toward the other members of *the household of faith*.

The injunction to *walk in love* contains more than is seen at first glance or by skipping past the phrase. Isaac Watts described it succinctly in the hymn he wrote: "Love so amazing, so divine, Demands my soul, my life, my all." Yes, the first thing this verse contains is, *And walk in love, as* (or even as) *Christ also hath loved us*.

What is the second point? *And hath given himself for us.* A better translation is "hath given himself up for us." Note that the Lord did something. He was active, not passive. He gave himself up, not his possessions. *Who, being in the form of God, thought it not robbery to be equal with God* [Phil. 2:6].

What does this mean? "Christ did not regard it as a prize to be held onto, to be grasped and clutched. Nor did He hold to His prerogatives, His eternal deity, His possessions, His rights and everything that went with them. He deliberately laid them aside," as powerfully stated by Lloyd-Jones. Paul adds emphasis saying, *though he was rich, yet for your sakes he became poor, that ye through his poverty might be rich* [2 Cor. 8:9].

This is seen in the parable of the sheep and Jesus saying, *I am the good shepherd: the good shepherd giveth his life for the sheep* [John 10:11]. The Father loved Him, and He loved the Father. Yet He loved us so much and our salvation was so important to Him that He gave Himself up for us. In addition, God extends to us the same love He has for His only begotten Son.

The third point is *an offering and a sacrifice to God for a sweet-smelling savor* (aroma). Note that the Apostle uses two terms. The first is *an offering* to God, and the second is *a sacrifice* that is to be borne to God. However, "the word *offering* by itself is not sufficient to contain the meaning the Apostle intends," as expressed by Lloyd-Jones. Therefore, he added the word *sacrifice*. The meaning of that word comes out of the Old Testament. A *sacrifice* was offered upon the altar to God.

What was involved? The animal offered had to be perfect, without any blemish whatsoever. The high priest, representing all the people, put his hands on the head of the animal thereby transferring the sins of all the people to the animal. The animal was then slain.

Why? Because it was necessary to receive punishment for the sins of the people that had been transferred to it.

"Then the priest took the blood, which had been poured out, collected it in a bowl, and presented it to God in the innermost sanctuary of the temple. The high priest sprinkled the blood on the ark and before the ark. Then the slain animal was placed on the altar in the temple's outer court where it was burned. That is what is meant by the term *sacrifice*. That is what happened on Calvary's Hill when our Lord gave Himself up as an offering and a sacrifice," to quote and paraphrase Martyn Lloyd-Jones.

That leads us to the fourth point, *for a sweet-smelling savor* (aroma). The Old Testament and the New Testament go together. Noah built an altar after the flood and offered burnt offerings, which are described as follows: *And the Lord smelled a sweet savor* (soothing aroma); *and the Lord said in his heart, I will not again curse the ground any more for man's sake* [Gen. 8:21]. God's law made specific demands upon us that we could not fulfill. But Christ's offering and sacrifice constituted a *sweet-smelling savor* to God, and He was completely satisfied. It should be realized that the *sweet-smelling savor* was for us, only us.

When considering these truths and teachings remember our Lord was active, He was not passive. Any thought, teaching, or interpretation that He was or is passive is not scriptural. It is to be ignored or rejected.

Christ came in order to go to Calvary, to be *an offering and a sacrifice to God for a sweet-smelling savor* in our stead. No man took His life. He laid it down! He was the spotless lamb, and our sins were transferred to Him.

> *For he hath made him to be sin for us, who knew no sin; that we might be made the righteousness of God in him* [2 Cor. 5:21].

> *Who his own self bare our sins in his own body on the tree, that we, being dead to sins, should live unto righteousness: BY WHOSE STRIPES YE WERE HEALED* [1 Pet. 2:24].

These truths need to be taught, preached, and emphasized. Basic biblical doctrine is the offering, the sacrifice, the sweet-smelling savor, and the atoning death. It is in these things that we see clearly and pointedly God's love in the Cross. Perhaps at first we do not like to hear about the offering and sacrifice; but the better we understand it, the more knowledge we have, the more thankful we should be. Martyn Lloyd-Jones provides additional emphasis stating, "It is rather fitting that a person cannot really begin to understand the love of God and the love of the Lord Jesus Christ who does not believe the substitutionary and penal Doctrine of the Atonement."

Think about it. Where do you see God's love and Christ's love? Not simply in offering, sacrificing, and suffering, but in dealing with our sins, in bringing us into a right relationship to God. Here is where God's love is and where it is so evident. God did not spare anything. His Son did not spare anything. Why? Because of us and it for us.

The issue is not what men did to the Lord Jesus Christ but what God did to Him. That is the supreme issue. God gave His only begotten Son, and Christ gave Himself up.

Why? Because they both love us, and it was the only way to provide for our salvation and to bring us into a right relationship with God. Their love is tough, strong, resilient, elastic, obedient, self-denying, and forgiving. Further, their love fully and completely exemplifies the duties encompassed in it.

This little verse contains four great truths that we should dwell upon and not bypass. What are we to learn from them?

> *And walk in love, as* (or even as) *Christ also hath loved us,*
> *And hath given himself for us an offering and a sacrifice*
> *for a sweet-smelling savor (aroma), and*
> the atoning death.

Remember these things as you continue: walking with Jesus; encountering objectionable people; and experiencing attacks, persecution, falsehoods, envy, jealousy, spite, evil speaking, anger, lying, and many other abuses.

What are we to do when confronted by these things? We are to respond as Christ would have us to respond. This means we are to *walk in love* and pray for them. We are to obey God's commandments and understand what causes these actions, refrain from like conduct, and avoid or steer clear of objectionable people. We are to *bless them that curse thee*, stand fast in the love of God, and stand firm in the truth revealed by Jesus. Lastly, we are to be strong, not weak.

Again and again we are reminded it is relatively easy to accept Christ by faith. However, it is very difficult to *walk in love, as Christ also hath loved us.*

Remember, we are to exemplify the duties of love.

Amen!

3

Walking in the Light

> *But fornication, and all uncleanness, or covetousness, let it not be once named among you, as becometh saints;*
> *Neither filthiness, nor foolish talking, nor jesting* (coarse jesting), *which are not convenient* (fitting): *but rather giving of thanks.*
> *For this ye know, that no whoremonger, nor unclean person, nor covetous man, who is an idolater, hath any inheritance in the kingdom of Christ and of God* [Eph. 5:3–5].

Paul takes us on a *walk* with the Lord Jesus Christ. This *walk* enables us to discover certain truths as they are found in Him. They enable us not only to know Him better, but to know what is required as members of His body. Therefore, this *walk* already has considered *unity*, *holiness*, and *love*.

Now it is time to walk in the Light. Basically, Verses 3–14 of Chapter 5 provide light, and contrast the light to the darkness.

One characteristic of walking with Jesus is light. For He is the Light. When we walk with Him, there are certain things we are to do and not to do, and we are to know the difference. It continually amazes me that some people who say they are Christians or followers of Christ, really do not want to know what He taught, much less what He requires and even less obeying His commandments. It is like someone saying they want to become an engineer, lawyer, or doctor but say, do not bother me with all the demands and disciplines required to learn and to practice.

Some people prefer to live with their own ideas of what heaven will be like, or believe that an emotional experience or an idea is all that is needed or that if everybody loved everyone then the world would be a much better place. However, walking with Jesus is not like that. It has its demands, requirements, challenges, and wonderful moments. This is based on the realization that He is the Master, and we are the servants.

Recall the Transfiguration. Remember what happened: Jesus took Peter, James, and John up a high mountain apart from the others, Jesus was transfigured, and Moses and Elijah appeared. What did Peter want to do? He wanted to seize that moment, place, and time. He wanted to build three tabernacles. He wanted to stay right there. He did not want to come down from the mountain.

What happened? While Peter was speaking, while he was feeling good, while he was enjoying himself, while all these things were going on, God spoke and said two things. The first statement is one with which we are very familiar, *This is my beloved Son, in whom I am well pleased* [Matt. 17:5]. The second statement is oft times overlooked, bypassed, or ignored. God said, *hear ye him* [Matt. 17:5]. It is an admonition not only to hear Him, but to give ear to what He says, to hearken to what He says, and to do what He commands.

Yes, God is well-pleased with His Son, with the Son who went to the Cross. But God wants us to hear Him, to listen to Him, and to know what He says. Oh, how important this is! We are to hear what He says, not what we say to ourselves. There is an important difference between what we say and what God says.

After God made his two pronouncements, what happened? They came down from the mountain and encountered the scribes and the multitudes. They were back in the midst of everything. There was a controversy with the scribes. There were memories. There was a man bringing his son to be healed and a lack of faith by the disciples. Jesus healed the man's son. If this does not remind you of attending a worship service or Bible study and then returning to the affairs of the everyday world, then nothing will.

Jesus brings us into a deep, personal, joyful, and fulfilling relationship with Himself, a relationship in which we feel and believe there are only the two of us. Then, and this is really the beautiful part, He takes us, He goes with us, and He walks with us in the everyday secular world as members of His body. Not only does He walk with us, He uses His power in our behalf, if we let Him.

There is another important matter to consider. We are to examine, study, and learn *all* Scripture, not just the parts that we agree with, or appeal to our emotions and desires. We are to walk with Jesus wherever He leads us or takes us, regarding Scripture, which is the Word of God.

Being a member of Christ's body is a practical relationship. If we do not realize that, then we do not understand the teachings contained in Scripture.

There are certain things we are not to do as members of Christ's body. However, these items are not based upon a moral code or a code of ethics. They are based upon a living relationship with the Lord Jesus Christ. That is the reason for living as He would have us to live.

In these verses [Eph. 5:3–5], we are considering once again that the Apostle provides a negative as well as a positive injunction, plus a motivating reason. Oh, the mastery of Paul. He starts with the negative injunction. Note how he does it, saying *But fornication*. What member of the body of Christ can find fault with that injunction? Not one! Remember to whom he is writing, the followers in the Way, the converted ones, not the general populace.

Then Paul follows with the words *and all uncleanness*. That adds another dimension. That gets closer to home. Then he has the audacity to add *or covetousness*. This applies to everyone when you really think about it. It means a desire to have more, but usually in a negative sense.

Note what Paul does. He is all-inclusive. First, he includes the person who performs an act, who does something. Next, he includes the person who is in a certain condition or state. Finally, he includes the person who desires to have or do something, the person who thinks about it. He does not leave anyone out.

But he does not stop there. He continues, saying, *Neither filthiness*, . . . which is any obscenity that is contrary to purity. There ain't no half-way doings. My Latin teacher used to say, "Half-way doings ain't no account in this world or the next."

Then he adds *nor foolish talking*. By this he means foolish, dull, stupid talk, which is more than mere idle talk. This includes empty, frivolous, thoughtless, foul, revolting, or babbling talk.

And, to this he adds, *nor jesting* (coarse jesting). Paul does not mean that all conversations are to be grave and serious. However, he does mean the type of conversation that is much in evidence in civilized, intelligent societies. It is marked by no faith in God, no reverence for the teachings of Christ, and no sense of appreciation for the grandeur and value of life. Unfortunately, it is characterized by foul indecencies, ambiguous statements, and coarseness of conversation.

At the conclusion of this negative injunction, Paul says, *which are not convenient* (fitting). When reading these words, we need to know what the Greek definition means. In this instance, a much more accurate translation is: "Which are not 'becoming' or 'befitting.'" This is more accurate than *which are not convenient* (fitting).

So much for the negative injunctions. The positive commands are rather simple and straightforward. There are two. The first is *as becometh saints*. We are to conduct ourselves *as becometh saints*, members of Christ's body, His disciples, and hearers of His words and teachings. He has set us apart, and we are to act accordingly. However, if we do not realize this and do not learn from Him, then we cannot act *as becometh saints*.

The second one is *but rather giving of thanks*. The actual word used means "thanksgiving." A better translation is, "but rather, there is to be thanksgiving." We are to show our gratitude and thanksgiving. There is to be a joyful response.

The positive command is brief and to the point. We are to conduct ourselves in our daily lives *as becometh saints*, and while doing so we are to joyfully show forth thanksgiving. We are to thank God that He has blessed us and given us the power to put off the negatives.

Why does Paul present these negative and positive commands at this time? There are several thoughts to ponder.

A primary objective of the Christian faith is to make us holy and blameless in the presence of God. We are to remember, *And grieve not the holy Spirit of God* [Eph. 4:30]. We are to exhibit a living faith, and not to lose sight of the command *that we should be holy and without blame before Him in love* [Eph. 1:4]. Why is this so? Because, Christ *gave himself for us, that He might redeem us from all iniquity, and purify unto himself a peculiar* (his own special) *people, zealous of good works* [Titus 2:14]. We need to remind ourselves of this daily and remember that the truths we are studying are directed to those who have accepted Christ and are endeavoring to follow Him.

Paul wrote to us and to the Ephesians, who brought their own mindsets with them, professing belief in Christ. The Ephesians needed to be reminded of Christ's teachings and the requirements placed upon them.

They worked, they went to the market, they saw what other people were doing, they heard and repeated both gossip and stories, they had aspirations, they had desires, they faced temptations, and they were confronted with many of the dangers, toils, and snares which surround us.

In addition, they were guilty of uncleanness and impurity, of making indecencies and immoralities part and parcel of their conversations, and of laughing at coarse comments and ribald jests. Does all this sound familiar?

Unfortunately, it is as true today as it was then. It is true of congregations. Once, I attended a church meeting with some men who were officers of the church. We were to discuss church business. Neither of the ministers attended. The discussion was marked with coarse, ribald, and obscene comments. That has no place among those who are members of Christ's body, especially among so-called officers. The selection of church officers is most important. How can you conduct the affairs of the church if you do not have knowledgeable and committed people?

A second objective of the Christian faith should be to realize that there is a real danger in people contentedly enjoying the Christian faith in a theoretical manner or from a historical perspective or as classical literature, but they do not want to apply it or develop a personal relationship with the Lord Jesus Christ. They do not want to walk with Him. They do not want to study His teachings or know His demands and commands.

These people like the cozy comfort of the mindset that says do good works, give some money, be moral in a subjective sense, keep the "old man" since he is a good person, you will go to heaven because God loves everybody, and the last thing He would have is rules and discipline. Further, He would never reject anyone. Those are fanciful ideas, but they are not based upon Scripture.

In addition, there are those who believe their salvation is assured for various reasons. They make the following deduction: they are safe and they can do anything they wish, because if Jesus has gone to the Cross for us He will never let us go. They reveal that they are not acquainted with Scripture and Christ's teachings. A minister once said to me, "You cannot fall from grace, but you can jump from it."

A fourth objective should be that our faith in Christ and our positive relationship to Him is to show itself in every single detail of our daily living. This is very difficult, but we are to strive for it. It is not something to be enjoyed just on Sunday mornings or on the Mount of Transfiguration. It is to be applied every day, in every place, and in every way.

That is why Paul stresses acts, conditions, desires, and conversations. We are members of His body wherever we go and in whatever we do.

Finally, we are to fight the good fight! We are to *put on* the whole armor of God. Why? Because *we wrestle not against flesh and blood, but against principalities, against powers, against the rulers of the darkness of this world* (age), *against spiritual wickedness in high places* [Eph. 6:12]. Scripture makes it clear that we cannot regard the Christian life as one great experience or something that is in isolation from the rest of the world.

Life in Christ does not guarantee that problems or temptations will never occur after one great experience, or after making a profession of faith. That is not the case! We are engaged in a fight for the faith and of the faith. We need to watch and pray; we need to *put on* the whole armor of God. We need to realize what surrounds us and be prepared for every possibility.

We cannot stay on the Mount forever. We must go among the multitudes, the scribes, the Pharisees, the disciples, those seeking Jesus and those not seeking Him.

Why does Paul stress these negative and positive commands? Because of the motivating factor. The people who do those negative things regardless of what they profess *hath any* (no) *inheritance in the kingdom of Christ and of God* [Eph. 5:5]. Paul is concerned about us. He wants us to conduct ourselves *as becometh a saint* and to express thanksgiving. He wants us to live as members of the body of Christ.

Paul preaches and teaches, as Martyn Lloyd-Jones stated that, "The gospel as the power of God, as spiritual dynamite, can operate in men and change them." It is when men and women are changed by the Holy Spirit that conditions change.

Make no mistake about it, the devil is perfectly content when people are not changed by the power of the Gospel and the Holy Spirit. He is satisfied when church members hear moral essays or have the Gospel presented in a theoretical way, or appeals are made for people to be decent, law-abiding citizens. But he does not like the exhortation to *put off* the old and to *put on* the new.

We are to be concerned about our relationship to God and understanding the Gospel. Paul states this succinctly,

> *For I am not ashamed of the gospel of Christ: for it is the power of God unto salvation to every one that believeth; to the Jew first, and also to the Greek.*
> *For therein is the righteousness of God revealed from faith to faith: as it is written, THE JUST SHALL LIVE BY FAITH* [Rom. 1:16–17].

He is not ashamed of the Gospel. The Gospel is to be esteemed, valued, and respected. We are not to undervalue it; it is a special book containing the revealed Word of God. Why? Because it is the power of God unto salvation, unto a right relationship with God in Christ. Which do you prefer, the secular life or the Christcentered life?

We are to hear the Word, study it, and apply it. For the Gospel reveals God's righteousness by faith unto faith. We live in the presence of God only through His righteousness. Our righteousness depends upon faith, a living faith, an active faith, not a passive one. It depends upon walking in the light of the Gospel and in the light of the Lord Jesus Christ.

In conclusion, remember Christ's words to Nicodemus:

> *And this is the condemnation, that* (the) *light is come into the world, and men loved darkness rather than* (the) *light, because their deeds were evil.*
> *For every one that doeth (practices) evil hateth the light, neither cometh to the light, lest his deeds should be reproved (exposed).*
> *But he that doeth truth cometh to the light, that his deeds may be made manifest, that they are wrought in God* [John 3:19–21].

Jesus meets head-on the murmurs and complaints of people who want to censure what they regard as the demands of God, as expressed in Nicodemus' question, *How can these things be*? They feel it is harsh that those who do not believe in Christ should be given up to destruction.

Jesus shows that those who prefer darkness flee from the light. However, there are others who appear to be holy, but they reject Christ's teachings because they want to retain certain things from their past. They do not want to receive the whole Gospel or to walk in the full light.

Jesus said, *But he that doeth the truth cometh to the light, that his deeds may be made manifest, that they are wrought in God* [John 3:21]. Augustine expounds upon this by saying "That he that doeth the truth acknowledges how wretched we are and destitute of all well-doing." It is our sense of need that drives us to the light. Also, there is a sense of welcome and acceptance.

What does Christ want? "He wants us to desire nothing more than the light," according to the inestimable John Calvin.

Christ uses the term *truth* because when men are deceived by outward works of beauty, they do not think of what remains hidden within the heart and mind.

We are to go willingly into the presence of God, who is the only proper judge of our works. We are to walk in the light. We are to come down from the mount and go among the multitudes, scribes, Pharisees, and nonbelievers. But we are to walk with Him, even the Lord Jesus Christ.

Amen!

4

No Inheritance in God's Kingdom

> *For this ye know, that no whoremonger, nor unclean person, nor covetous man, who is an idolater, hath any inheritance in the kingdom of Christ and of God* [Eph. 5:5].

Have you ever been in a hurry to prepare a favorite dish or recipe, and then when it was finished cooking, you discovered that you had left out an important ingredient? Have you tried to assemble something at the last minute, like on Christmas Eve, and then had the experience that the gift would not function properly because you had omitted a key piece? Have you read something fairly important while you were anxious to get to the next project and then discover, to your chagrin, that you had overlooked a key word or statement?

The contents of this verse should remind us of the dangers of omission; rushing to the next project, overlooking important items, or key details; assembling ideas; and avoiding disappointment. We need to focus on this verse because it is one that could be omitted, rushed by, overlooked, not assembled in our minds, and result in disappointment.

It is one of those verses that at first glance seems to be a filler, or repetitious, or just tucked in there, but that is not Paul's practice. Yes, Paul was a great writer, but he was also a great, wise, and judicious editor.

When first looking at this verse we may think that it just repeats the third verse with a slightly different twist. When scrutinizing it, we realize the full impact and value of this gem. It is a prized possession as we walk with Jesus in the light.

This verse contains words used in Verse 3, but there is a difference. The third and fourth verses contain positive and negative injunctions, while the fifth verse hits us between the eyes with the motivation. It hits with impact! Grasp what it says, *For this ye know, that no whoremonger, nor unclean person, nor covetous man, who is an idolater, hath any inheritance in the kingdom of Christ and of God.*

What does this mean? When Paul says *For this ye know*, he is basing it upon his preaching and teaching, and the basic truths contained in the earlier passages of this letter. He has stated,

> *Till we all come in* (into) *the unity of the faith, and of the knowledge of the Son of God* [Eph. 4:13].
>
> *But ye have not so learned Christ* [Eph. 4:20].
>
> *Be renewed in the spirit of your mind* [Eph. 4:23].

The context in which he says *ye know* is that it is beyond doubt, beyond any disputation, it is self-evident. It is known, realized, and completely understood. Previously, these truths proclaimed by Paul (Eph. 5:5) had been discussed and accepted by the recipients of his letter as indicated by the phrase, *For this ye know* [Eph. 5:5].

Further amplification is provided on the fifth verse by Ruth Paxson in the following. "God has stated the destiny of those who prefer to remain in the kingdom of darkness and to practice the works of darkness, and further comment seems unnecessary. God's attitude towards sin remains inflexible. God and sin can never fellowship together. His love and grace ever go out toward the sinner; but He has only hatred and wrath toward sin.

"Wherever there is a departure from God there is a consequent deterioration in ethics and morals, and the breakdown in the latter is always gauged by the depth and degree of that in the former. The further one goes from God the nearer he comes to Satan. The old Adamic Nature remains unchanged . . . down through the centuries and left to itself it will wallow in the deepest mire of sin. If one needs proof of this he needs only to read the pages of modern literature, where the very sins mentioned in 5:3–5 are pictured with appalling frankness; and oftentimes the writer is advocating a personal liberty which is nothing less than free license to lust. Our Lord predicted in the days preceding His coming human society would have sunk to the very lowest level such as prevailed in the days of Noah, which brought upon mankind the judgment of the Flood."

Frequently in the New Testament the Greek word for *to know* indicates a positive relation between the person knowing and the object or person known. Further, what is known is of value to the one who knows. Paul says what is known is that *no whoremonger, nor unclean person, nor covetous man, who is an idolater, hath any inheritance in the kingdom of Christ and of God*. These truths are to be known, grasped, and understood. Some may ask, why do we speak of these things, why do we emphasize them? Because the apostles did and they were taught by the Lord Jesus! The Holy Spirit has preserved these truths for those who follow Christ and those who do not.

Note what is grouped together: *whoremonger*, morally *unclean*, *covetous* person, and *an idolater*, who turns from God and turns to things, or puts confidence in gold, silver, human beings, or his or her own gifts. The Gospel humbles us, and it builds us up.

Throughout Scripture, God makes it perfectly clear regarding the destiny of those who prefer to remain in the kingdom of darkness and to practice its works. His attitude toward sin remains inflexible, as Scripture makes abundantly clear. God and sin cannot have fellowship together.

Note, the fifth verse concludes by saying that the people guilty of these sins, who continue in them, do not have *any inheritance in the kingdom of Christ and of God*. Paul lists three categories of people in this verse and possibly a fourth. There are discussions by different scholars as to whether the idolater or one who worships is a separate category.

The first three categories denote an individual's sins against other people, which are also sins against God. The fourth one, being an idolater, is against God. The Apostle states it this way so we can relate to it. "An inheritance may mean the actual possession of a bequest or the title to receive it," as noted by Markus Barth. It is something that is bestowed. In this instance, it describes a status or the possession of something that has been given to the saints through special gifts or privileges.

What is being discussed is the retention of that which has been already granted. As we know, a codicil on a will can cancel a potential gift or bequest. The Apostle warns the saints not to disinherit themselves. They are not to jump from grace.

Have you noted that this verse concludes with the words *hath any inheritance in the kingdom of Christ and of God*? What is meant by the kingdom of Christ? Naturally, scholars have thoughts regarding this term.

Christ is the King and Lord of His church and over His church. This particular phrase is directed to His reign. He is the ruler and His subjects are to obey His commandments. Some say it should read "the kingdom of Christ and God" instead of *the kingdom of Christ and of God*.

It is the meaning and interpretation that are most important. By this, it is interpreted that the Lord Jesus Christ is God. He is the second person in the Godhead. The kingdom of Christ is that kingdom which He has opened to us and to which we belong. This term is unique.

If we are members of this kingdom, then we are subject to the rules, the commandments, and the discipline of the Supreme Ruler. We are citizens of the realm. Therefore, we are to conduct ourselves accordingly.

It is believed by some that being exposed to Christ and His rule means being confronted by God's own presence and dominion, and that the full power of God has been placed in the Messiah's hands.

Jesus refers to *my kingdom* as revealed in John's Gospel when He stated that, *My kingdom is not of this world: if my kingdom were of this world, then would my servants fight, that I should not be delivered to the Jews: but now is my kingdom not from hence* [John 18:36]. Jesus uses the term *my kingdom* three times in this verse. Pilate wanted to know if he was King of the Jews and if there were political over-tones. Jesus' response was such that there was no cause for a legal charge.

However, the term *my kingdom* indicates something in the present tense and also something that belonged to Him. Therefore, Paul's statement coincides one hundred percent with Christ's teachings. This is also seen in

> *Wherefore God also hath highly exalted him, and given him a name which is above every name:*
> *That at the name of Jesus every knee should bow, of things* (those) *in heaven, and things* (those) *in earth, and things* (those) *under the earth*
> *And that every tongue should confess that Jesus Christ is Lord, to the glory of God the Father* [Phil. 2:9–11].
>
> *Who hath delivered us from the power of darkness, and hath translated* (transferred) *us into the kingdom of his dear Son* (of the Son of his love) [Col. 1:13].
>
> *That ye would walk worthy of God, who hath called you unto his kingdom and glory* [1 Thess. 2:12].

Paul states, emphatically and firmly, that it is the kingdom of Christ. He wants us to understand, accept, and follow these central points: that it is Christ who reigns supreme; and that we are to be obedient members of His kingdom. Calvin clarifies the question regarding Paul's statement about *the kingdom of Christ and of God* saying, "He says the kingdom of Christ and of God because God gave it to His Son that we may obtain it through Him."

Those belonging to the kingdom of Christ are those renewed by God's spirit who are endeavoring to practice a life of holiness and righteousness according to the teachings and practices of our Lord Jesus Christ. Though we are members of His kingdom it must be acknowledged that this kingdom and its members are in this world.

Jesus, responding to the Pharisees demand to know when the kingdom of God will come, answered, *The kingdom of God cometh not with observation: . . . for, behold, the kingdom of God is within you* (in your midst) [Luke 17:20–21].

What do we learn from this portion of Scripture? The Apostle makes it clear that anyone whose habitual conduct is marked by the sins previously enumerated has no inheritance in the kingdom of Christ. He is not saying that anyone who has succumbed to temptations or has committed transgressions is excluded from the kingdom of Christ. However, those who continue to indulge in certain sins and do not seek to repent from them are excluded. Christ came to call the sinner, not the righteous one.

However, it does mean that if such conduct continues as a characteristic of a person, then they have no inheritance in the kingdom of Christ. We have been told to *put off the old man* and to *put on* the new. People do fall into sin; people do those things that they would not, but they are to strive with God's power to put them off and to follow Christ's commands. We are to know what is required of us. We are to become holy and righteous through God's power.

"If it seems harsh or inconsistent with God's goodness that all who have incurred the guilt of fornication or covetousness are excluded from the inheritance of the kingdom of heaven, the answer is easy. The apostle does not deny pardon to the fallen who have recovered, but pronounces sentence on the sins themselves . . . . Where there is repentance and therefore reconciliation with God, men cease to be what they were. But let all fornicators or unclean or covetous persons, so long as they are such, know that they have nothing in common with God, and are deprived of all hope of salvation.

"All covetous men must deny God, and put wealth in this place; such is the blindness of their wretched cupidity.... Why is covetousness denoted by the disgraceful name rather than ambition or vain self-confidence? I answer that this disease is widely spread, and infects the minds of many like a contagion, but it is not reckoned a disease, but rather praised in the common estimation. Paul attacks it more harshly in order to tear from our hearts the false opinion," as sagaciously proclaimed by the renowned theologian John Calvin.

God's teachings and His chastisements are provided for our benefit. They enable us to participate in His holiness. They may seem harsh, but they are provided to help us to become holy. The objective is not happiness. The objective is to become holy and joyful in the Lord.

When considering these teachings, remember we are to walk with Him. We are in His presence as members of His kingdom. Therefore, we are to abide by His commandments. The New Testament teaching is clear:

> *Know ye not that the unrighteous shall not inherit the kingdom of God? Be not deceived: neither fornicators* (the sexually immoral), *nor idolaters, nor adulterers, nor effeminate* (homosexuals), *nor abusers* (sodomites) *of themselves with mankind,*
> *Nor thieves, nor covetous, nor drunkards, nor revilers, nor extortioners, shall inherit the kingdom of God* [1 Cor. 6:9–10].

People continuing in those practices shall not inherit the kingdom of God. But note what follows: *And such were some of you: but ye are washed, but ye are sanctified* (set apart), *but ye are justified* (declared righteous) *in the name of the Lord Jesus, and by the Spirit of our God* [1 Cor. 6:11].

We are to put away the old and *put on* the new.

> *Be not deceived: evil communications* (companions) *corrupt good manners* (habits).
> *Awake to righteousness, and sin not; for some have not the knowledge of God: I speak this to your shame* [1 Cor. 15:33–34].

> *Be ye not unequally yoked together with unbelievers: for what fellowship* (in common) *hath righteousness with unrighteousness* (lawlessness)? *and what communion* (fellowship) *hath light with darkness?*

> And what concord hath Christ with Belial? or what part hath he that believeth with an infidel (unbeliever)?
>
> And what agreement hath the temple of God with idols? for ye are the temple of the living God; as God hath said, I WILL DWELL IN THEM AND WALK IN THEM; AND I WILL BE THEIR GOD, AND THEY SHALL BE MY PEOPLE.
>
> Wherefore COME OUT FROM AMONG THEM, AND BE YE SEPARATE, SAITH THE LORD, AND TOUCH NOT THE UNCLEAN THING; AND I WILL RECEIVE YOU [2 Cor. 6:14–17].

> If we say that we have fellowship with him, and walk in darkness, we lie, and do not (practice) the truth:
>
> But if we walk in the light, as he is in the light, we have fellowship one with another, and the blood of Jesus Christ his Son cleanseth us from all sin.
>
> If we say that we have no sin, we deceive ourselves, and the truth is not in us.
>
> If we confess our sins, he is faithful and just to forgive us our sins, and to cleanse us from all unrighteousness.
>
> If we say that we have not sinned, we make him a liar, and his word is not in us [1 John 1:6–10].

> Not every one that saith unto me, Lord, Lord, shall enter into the kingdom of heaven; but he that doeth the will of my Father which is in heaven [Matt. 7:21].

This is what the New Testament says. This is what we are to do and not to do. Christ came to bring us to God; to teach us, and to strengthen us; so that we might have life and have it more abundantly. Therefore, it is important to remember the words of Jesus, *Therefore whosoever heareth these sayings of mine, and doeth them, I will liken him unto a wise man, which built his house upon a* (the) *rock* [Matt. 7:24]. We have a choice: build upon the rock or build upon the sand.

There are times when we need to let Scripture speak to us. There are things we are to know, and they come from Scripture, not from the mind-set of the world. God justifies the ungodly, not the godly. Justification is by faith alone. But it is only one step in the process. There is regeneration, sanctification, and ultimately glorification. The scriptures are interrelated; they are tied together.

> *Whom he called, them he also justified: and whom he justified, them he also glorified* [Rom. 8:30].

> But of him are ye in Christ Jesus, who of God is made unto us (became for us) *wisdom, and righteousness, and sanctification, and redemption* [1 Cor. 1:30].

There is the whole process. If we are members of His kingdom then we will joyfully go through the entire process, though it may be arduous. There is to be evidence of this entire process in our daily lives. However, it is so much more than just token evidence. It is to be sought after, pursued, practiced, and enjoyed. Certainly, we do not want to hear these words that were spoken by the Lord Jesus, *I never knew you: depart from me, ye that work iniquity* (lawlessness) [Matt. 7:23].

How we respond to this verse and its teachings is very important. You will recall Jesus prayed, *Sanctify them* (set them apart) *through thy truth: thy word is truth* [John 17:17]. The teachings in this fifth verse and the other ones considered previously are for our edification, sanctification, and glorification.

We are not to omit, rush by, or overlook the truths available to us. We are to assemble them; consider the details, the fine print; grasp hold of them; and practice them. Also, we are to grasp hold of the Lord Jesus; we are to walk with Him. In so doing we are to avoid the great disappointment of not knowing Him and not being members of His kingdom.

In closing, grasp the truth as expressed by the Apostle John, *And every man that hath this hope in him purifieth himself, even as he is pure* [1 John 3:3]. The truth is in him, it purifies him, and he is to pursue it. It is neither on the lips nor does it occur occasionally.

The person who says, Lord, Lord and then is told to depart is someone who knows who the Lord Jesus is but does not have Him in his heart, nor does he have *any inheritance in the kingdom of Christ and of God.*

God forbid that we should be such a person!
Amen!

5

God's Wrath

> *Let no man deceive you with vain (empty) words: for because of these things cometh the wrath of God upon the children (sons) of disobedience* [Eph. 5:6].

The Apostle Paul effectively draws a contrast between light and darkness in these passages. Our relationship to Christ is to be in the light and His light is to be the beacon that attracts us and determines our conduct, character, and conversation (tenor of life).

So often our eyes are transfixed on the big picture, the big moment, or the big day. As a result we overlook the little lights that keep us from stumbling or falling. Paul was interested in the smallest details of daily living. He wanted the Ephesians to know the joy of a living faith and a vital relationship with the Lord Jesus Christ.

According to Paul and the other New Testament writers "our daily behavior is important for three great eternal reasons:

> first, our total conduct affects our relationship to God, not simply our relationship to others and to ourselves;
>
> second, our relationship to God has only two possibilities: either we are in Christ, or we are not. What happens to those who are deceived by *vain words* and remain outside Christ? The wrath of God cometh upon the children of disobedience: and
>
> third, our relationship to God is for eternity, not just for a week, a month, or a few years. Eternity is forever," as effectively expressed by Martyn Lloyd-Jones.

These three principles are important to everyone, whether they realize it or not.

When considering these principles we should focus on Jesus' high priestly prayer, *That they all may be one; as thou, Father, art in me, and I in thee, that they also may be one in us* [John 17:21]. Our happiness and joy depend upon our unity with Christ and with God, and having an *inheritance in the kingdom of Christ and of God.*

As we have seen in Paul's letter, we are to grow in Christ, *Endeavoring to keep the unity of the spirit in the bond of peace* [Eph. 4:3]. Christ is one with the Father, and His prayer is *That they all may be one; as thou, Father, art in me, and I in thee, that they also may be one in us: that the world may believe that thou hast sent me.* This is important.

Paul tells us to walk in unity and walk in the light. He has been describing the things that members of Christ's body are not to do. He knows they will encounter temptations as soon as they put down his letter, walk away from the study group, or leave the sanctuary.

So what does he say? *Let no man deceive you with vain* (empty) *words.* You cannot get more direct than that. Problems usually beset people when they listen to and follow vain or empty words. A person can be beguiled by them.

Of course, modern man believes that above everything else he has knowledge, learning, and understanding. Further, he believes that he has accomplished so much in the past one hundred years. Therefore, he or she asks, why do we need religion? A religion may not be needed, but a living faith is a necessity.

Yes, there is a dramatic difference between light and darkness. There is just as much difference between a religion and a living faith. Modern man rationalizes, he listens to himself, and he reasons that certain acts and conditions are not sinful; they are merely man expressing himself, man doing his own thing, man being free to do as he wants or was meant to do, man fulfilling himself, and man exercising his natural instincts and powers.

The people who adopt and espouse these ideas, whether they are members of the visible church or not, certainly are not walking in unity with God, walking in love with Christ, or walking in the light of *the kingdom of Christ and of God.* Walking in unity, love, and light requires discipline. Further, it requires obeying Christ's commandments and striving to be one with the Father.

We are all aware of the fact that discipline, ordering, governing, and obedience are frowned upon, rejected, and discouraged. The emphasis is upon psychology, or disease, or the environment. The idea of sin, an evil one, wrongdoing, or disobedience to God is pooh-poohed, or rejected, or whispered about in tones that say it does not apply to a modern, intellectual, understanding person.

It does not take much imagination to wonder what Paul, Peter, James, and John would have to say about the modern man expressing himself, about punishment, homosexuality, freedom, sins, impulses, and some of the General Assembly's pronouncements.

For the past one hundred or so years, the psychological attitude toward life has been increasing at the expense of the scriptural view. The emphasis has been upon glorifying man and setting aside the basic biblical truths that man: was created in the image of God; is responsible to God; is to obey God's commands; and is redeemed by the Lord Jesus Christ going to the Cross, shedding His blood, and bearing our sins."

What has this change of emphasis produced? More divorce, more crime, more juvenile delinquency, more transgressions against God's holy laws. No wonder the Apostle says, *Let no man deceive you with vain (empty) words.*

What does Scripture continue saying? Not what we would say. Certainly not what the so-called free, modern, intellectual man or woman would say. The Holy Spirit through Paul says, *For because of these things cometh the wrath of God upon the children* (sons) *of disobedience* [Eph. 5:6]. Remember, Paul is writing to *the called out*, to the members of Christ's body.

We know today that some members of the visible church do not like to hear about the wrath of God. Others say it is so typical of religion, trying to frighten and alarm people. As stated previously, we are not talking about, nor are we interested in, a religion. We are interested in a living faith, a personal relationship with the Lord Jesus, and becoming one with the Father. That is a big difference.

Unfortunately, there are people who want to ridicule or make light of *the wrath of God*. What does Scripture say? *The wrath of God* is evident throughout the Old and New Testaments. It was taught and preached by the patriarchs, kings, prophets, John the Baptist, the Lord Jesus Christ, and each of the apostles. If you do not believe in *the wrath of God*, then you do not believe Scripture and in the Lord Jesus Christ. You cannot accept the Bible and its teachings without accepting *the wrath of God*.

People prefer and desire their own bible, their own scripture, their own faith, their own religion, and their own god. But you cannot change God Almighty. And you cannot change Scripture, though some are trying.

That is why it is so important to study Scripture and to become knowledgeable. Then we can learn what Scripture is saying. We are not to ignore, eliminate, or discard the portions of Scripture that do not appeal to us. We are to understand them.

The wrath of God is not the same as the wrath of man. Man's wrath is directed toward a person. Usually, it is uncontrolled, violent, and marked by a temper fit. Of course, we are all familiar with the saying, "Hell hath no fury like a woman scorned."

How does God's wrath differ? It is controlled; it is directed toward evil and sin. In His wrath, God is just, merciful, and loving; and yet, He will punish sin and evil. God is holy, and we are to become holy.

God cannot abide with sin. He must punish it. That is why He sent His Son into the world and sent Him to the Cross. That is why Christ shed His blood, died, and rose again. Why? So that He might take all our sins on Himself and cleanse us so that we will be acceptable to God the Father. So that we may grow and walk in unity, love, and the light.

In many respects a religion is much easier than a living faith. The guidelines of a religion are man made. It is much easier to: offer sacrifices than to try to live as Christ did; fast or abstain from certain foods than to obey God's commandments; perform acts or do deeds than to deny yourself and serve the Lord; and abide by your own experiences and mindset than to apply the teachings of the Master.

"When does the wrath of God come? It comes in the present, and it comes in the future," according to Lloyd-Jones. However, it is not something that is put off forever or for a number of years. *Good understanding giveth favor: but the way of transgressors is hard* [Prov. 13:15].

When does a loving parent chasten a child? In the present.

> FOR WHOM THE LORD LOVETH HE CHASTENETH, AND SCOURGETH EVERY SON WHOM HE RECEIVETH.
> *If ye endure chastening, God dealeth with you as with sons; for what son is he whom the father chasteneth not?*
> *But if ye be without chastisement, whereof all are partakers, then are ye bastards* (illegitimate), *and not sons* [Heb. 12:6–8].

"However severe and wrathful a judge God shows Himself to be towards unbelievers (and believers) whenever He punishes them, His primary purpose is to provide counsel for their salvation and to have them come into a right relationship with Himself. This is one way by which He demonstrates His fatherly love," as John Calvin aptly described the wrath of God. It is amazing how up-to-date Scripture is and how it explains things clearly and concisely.

Certain verses in Romans 1:18–32 contain important truths to guide us as we continue walking with Jesus. They are to become our guideposts and a lamp unto our feet. They are for our edification, understanding, and strength. May we embrace each of these gold nuggets that God has provided:

> *For the wrath of God is revealed . . . against all ungodliness and unrighteousness of men, who hold* (suppress) *the truth in unrighteousness* [Rom. 1:18]. May we thank God for his kindnesses and making available true knowledge of Himself.
>
> *When they knew God, they glorified Him not as God* [Rom. 1:21]. May we glorify Him as God, our heavenly Father, for His eternity, power, wisdom, goodness, truth, mercy, love, grace, justice, and righteousness, and not ignore Him as the source of these attributes.
>
> *Professing themselves to be wise, they became fools* [Rom. 1:22]. May we remove self with its: rationalizations; bloated self-importance; adulation; and fallible mindset; and replace it by focusing on the Lord Jesus Christ, His truths, and His commandments. Every group has their conception of God based upon their experience, exposure, and mindset. They try to make God conform to their conception of Him and do not accept Scripture's revelation of our heavenly Father.
>
> *And changed the glory of the uncorruptible God into an image made like to corruptible* (perishable) *man, . . .* [Rom. 1:23].
>
> *Wherefore God also gave them up to uncleanness through the lusts of their own hearts, . . .* [Rom. 1:24].
>
> *God . . . gave them up* [Rom. 1:24]. May we realize that God is neither cruel nor vindictive, and that we are innocent of any wrongdoing. Paul exposes these wrongdoings because sin always resides in the sinner rather than in God, who has nothing to do with these transgressions except to forgive them and punish them.
>
> *O Israel, thou hast destroyed* (he destroyed you) *thyself; but in me is thine help* [Hos. 13:9]. May we realize our help is in the Lord, even if we are at our wits end.
>
> *Who changed* (exchanged) *the truth of God into a* (for the) *lie, and worshipped and served the creature more* (rather) *than the Creator* [Rom. 1:25]. May we remember that God is the Creator and that we are created in His image. Therefore, we are to serve Him and be obedient to His commands.

Where is this more evident than Darwin's "Origin of Species" and his theory of evolution where man is no longer considered a special creation of God? Where man is looked upon as evolving from an animal? Is it any wonder that modern man rebels against God? Is it any wonder that God gave them up? Remember, Paul was writing to the members of the visible church in Rome. He was stating what happens when we do not listen to His teachings; when we do not seek the truth as it is in Jesus; when we do not acquire knowledge of God; when we do not try to become kind, tenderhearted, and forgiving, *as God for Christ's sake hath forgiven* us; and when God withdraws Himself and will abandon us for a time, or forever.

How can a church or congregation operate according to the will of God if He withdraws Himself? Thank God He has told us, *But in me is thine help.* We are to walk in unity, love, and the light. We are not to worship and serve the creature rather than the Creator. What is bound to follow when God gives people up to uncleanness, and they change the truth of God into a lie? *And even as they did not like to retain God in their knowledge, God gave them over to a reprobate* (debased) *mind, to do those things which are not convenient* (fitting) [Rom. 1:28] or fitting to a member of Christ's body.

Since they refused to have God in their bank of knowledge, He *gave them over to a reprobate mind.* When Paul says this, he means that they were not pursuing knowledge of God with the intensity and determination they should exhibit, but were doing *those things which are not convenient* (fitting). Fitting, in this context, means that their conduct is contrary to what should be seen in the members of Christ's body. Further, *Being filled with all unrighteousness* [Rom. 1:29] means violating human justice as well as the will of God.

Paul continues by saying *haters of God* [Rom. 1:30] and lists several characteristics by which people exhibit their hatred of God's righteousness. What about the people who are whisperers, backbiters, boastful, proud, inventors of evil things, and deceitful? Think about what they do and how they transgress God's righteousness. Whispering destroys friendships and inflames passions. Backbiters do not spare the reputation of anyone; they revile both the innocent and the deserving. The boastful have a big case of inflated self-confidence along with massive egos. And the proud look down on others with contempt and scorn.

Individuals with these traits can be members of the visible church, but they are people filled with unrighteousness and are *without understanding, covenant breakers, without natural affection, implacable* (unforgiving), (and) *unmerciful* [Rom. 1:31]. Paul concludes this portion of Scripture saying, *Who knowing the* (righteous) *judgment of God, . . . not only do the same, but have pleasure in* (approve of) *them* [Rom. 1:32]. "When men abandon themselves to unrestrained license they remove all barriers between good and evil, pleasing and displeasing God, and righteousness and unrighteousness," as explicitly described by John Calvin.

The wrath of God is exhibited in ways that we have probably not considered. This portion of Scripture should increase our knowledge, improve our understanding, and help us to walk in the light.

The last half of the First Chapter in Romans points out what happens when God's wrath is visited upon the people in the present tense. Paul also describes what will occur in the future when Christ will come again, saying *Taking vengeance on them that know not God, and that obey not the gospel of our Lord Jesus Christ* [2 Thess. 1:8]. He will render vengeance, full vengeance, on two groups: those who do not know God when He has been revealed to them; and those who do not obey the Gospel of our Lord Jesus Christ.

Two things should be noted about this verse in Thessalonians. The vengeance spoken of in this instance is a vengeance that proceeds out of justice. First, it does not proceed from an injury, or hurt feelings, or indignation, or vindication. Second, it applies to those who do not obey, who do not put into practice the teachings of our Lord.

What then are we to do? We are to walk in the unity, love, and light of our Lord Jesus Christ, and in so doing, we are to increase in knowledge and understanding, realize our conduct affects our relationship with God, thank the Lord Jesus that he prayed that we may be one with the Father and Himself, and endeavor to practice a living faith.

May God strengthen us as we walk with Jesus.

Amen!

6

Children of Light

Be not ye therefore partakers with them.
For ye were sometimes (once) *darkness, but now are ye light in the Lord: walk as children of light* [Eph. 5:7–8]

The essence of studying, praying, and worshipping is to become like our Lord Jesus Christ. We are to dwell together in His presence as a member of His body, and to mature as He would have us to do. Reading, listening, and talking are the easy parts. They are important to acquiring knowledge and understanding, but the essential ingredients are doing and practicing. That is when things become difficult. That is the true nature of being tested.

I am continually amazed, yet grateful, as to how the Lord works, how He tests us, how He wants our undivided loyalty, and how He provides for us in times of need.

Recently, this message came home to me loud and clear. Certain developments occurred which upset me, which seemed contrary to the teachings we have been studying regarding walking in unity, love, and the light. Consequently, I became agitated and distressed. This, in turn, bothered me. During the middle of the night, while having a cup of tea, I said to my wife, "Why don't you straighten out my mind, get my thinking right?"

Finally, we went back to sleep. That morning after breakfast we were reading and meditating on Scripture as is our practice. The passage that morning was God's answer to my question. *If thou wilt take the left hand, then I will go to the right; or if thou depart to the right hand, then I will go to the left* [Gen. 13:9].

When did Abram say that? After God had called him and made a covenant with him. After Abram responded in faith by being obedient to God's command. Abram did not know where they were going, but he was going to be obedient.

Calvin says, "For it is certain that faith cannot stand, unless it is founded on the promises of God." God promises, blesses, and fulfills. God made the covenant with Abram and the children of God by and through faith. Abram becomes a child of light. God's covenant with Abram is firm and true in Christ, the seed of Abram.

What did Abram do after God made the covenant with him? He became a light, he exhibited a living faith, and he practiced as God commanded him.

When you are living a life of faith you will be tested. This fact should be remembered, remembered, and remembered. God will allow you to get into situations where your own welfare, ideas, and privileges may make a choice that seems to be the right and perfect thing to do, but it may not be the best thing to do. Therefore, we must progress to the state of maturity where we are willing to waive our own privileges, ideas, and welfare, or what seems to be right, and let God direct us.

This discipline transforms us into the spiritual realm which is governed by obeying the voice of God. We need to learn that whatever is right or good according to our standards may become our guiding lights yet darken or blind the spiritual insight that the Holy Spirit provides.

Oswald Chambers explained, "The great enemy of the life of faith in God is not sin, but the good which is not good enough. The good is always the enemy of the best." God wants the best! Too often we are willing to settle for what appears to be right or good.

At first glance it may seem the wise thing for Abram to choose. However, Abram had faith in God. He knew that God would bless him, and his people. Abram was growing in the spirit and was willing to rely upon God to choose. We, like Abram, must learn to walk in faith and obedience, with our eyes focused upon our Heavenly Father. May we be able to say with Abram, *If thou wilt take the left hand, then I will go to the right; or if thou depart to the right hand, then I will go to the left* [Gen. 13:9].

Some things are in God's hands, and we must recognize it. We are to walk as children of light, not as children of darkness. The light dwelled within Abram. The same light is to abide within us.

Character determines our conduct as the sons of light. We are to order our lives accordingly. We are not to walk as the sinners do. We are to exhibit a living faith.

The New Testament teaches that the importance of sanctification is not something you receive as an experience. Sanctification is not the result of one gift or occasion. It results from the truth of God working within us. Jesus said, *I am the way, the truth, and the life* [John 14:6]. That truth is to work within us if we are to progress in sanctification. When the truth works within us we are in the light and no longer in darkness.

"When we pray to be sanctified, are we prepared to face the standard of *And the very God of peace sanctify you wholly.* We take the term sanctification much too lightly. Are we prepared for what sanctification will cost . . . sanctification means intense concentration on God's point of view. It means every power of body, soul and spirit chained and kept for God's purpose only. Are we prepared for God to do in us all that He separated us for? And then after His work is done in us, are we prepared to separate ourselves to God even as Jesus did? For their sakes I sanctify myself." The reason some of us have not entered into the experience of sanctification is that we have not realized the meaning of sanctification from God's standpoint. Sanctification means being made one with Jesus so that the disposition that ruled Him will rule us. Are we prepared for what that will cost? It will cost everything that is not of God in us.

"Are we prepared to say—'Lord make me as holy as you can make a sinner saved by grace? Jesus has prayed that we might be one with Him as He is One with the Father. The one and only characteristic of the Holy Ghost in a man is a strong family likeness to Jesus Christ, and freedom from everything that is unlike Him. Are we prepared to set ourselves apart for the Holy Spirit's ministrations in us?" as beautifully and appropriately stated by Oswald Chambers.

There is a teaching that says the only thing necessary for sanctification is to look to God, state that there is no problem, and let Him do it for you. All you have to do is "Let go and let God." If that were true, why did the apostles ever write the last half of the different Epistles? Why do the apostles present argument after argument relating to personal conduct? Why?

The New Testament's way of presenting sanctification and holiness is to realize the truth and to apply it.

> Then Jesus said to those Jews which believed on Him, If ye continue (abide) in my word, then are ye my disciples indeed;
> And ye shall know the truth, and the truth shall make you free [John 8:31–32].

Jesus also prays, *Sanctify them* (set them apart) *through thy truth: thy word is truth* [John 17:17]. As stated previously, we neither know the truth nor become free if we fail to continue in His word and remain His disciples.

Jesus commends to us knowledge of the Gospel based on the fruit we receive from it and the effect it has upon us. Basically, it restores us to freedom. Jesus is the truth, and it is that truth that makes us free.

You will recall that recently we discussed the truth of God, the truth of Christ, and the truth of the Gospel. It is the truth and abiding in it that sanctifies us.

How does this happen? As the Word comes to us we are to grasp it, hold it, and understand it. We are not to pass it by or let it slip through our minds. Once we begin to understand it then we are to apply the truth. Look at Paul's process in the fourth and fifth chapters of Ephesians: unity of the faith; knowledge of the Son of God; new creature, new man; *put off, put on*; walk in love; and walk in the light.

Jesus said of Himself, *I am the light of the world: he that followeth me shall not walk in darkness, but shall have the light of life* [John 8:12]. He also said,

> Ye are the light of the world. A city that is set on a hill cannot be hid.
> Neither do men light a candle (lamp), and put it under a bushel (basket), but on a candlestick (lampstand); and it giveth light unto all that are in the house.
> Let your light so shine before men, that they may see your good works, and glorify your Father which is in heaven [Matt. 5:14–16].

Note how John begins his Gospel: *The light shineth in darkness; and the darkness comprehended* (understood) *it not* [John 1:5]. This is something to grasp and understand. This is how the New Testament presents the truth of Jesus and the truth in Him. This is the way we come to a living faith and do not merely participate in worship services.

The Apostle Paul tells the Ephesians, *For ye were sometimes* (once) *darkness, but now are ye light in the Lord: walk as children of light* [Eph. 5:8]. If we are to *walk as children of light* we are to behave as creatures of the light, be witnesses to the light, continuously learn God's will, put away the works of darkness, and be transformed by the light and its power (energy). The light is not only informative, but transformative. It transforms us from darkness to light. It exposes evil and overcomes it. The light creates a new person and saves him or her from darkness.

Scripture says we are to . . . *walk as children of light*. What are some of the benefits in so doing? "Character determines conduct; therefore live, speak, act as the sons of light. Order your lives as men native-born to the light. It is inconceivable that the walk of children of darkness and children of light should be the same in any particular. Everything in the walk of the Christian should be differentiated from that of the sinner. There is a walk that becometh sinners, but such a walk is unbefitting saints, even to its minutest details. Our conduct and our conversation betray us, for they reveal the kingdom in which we are citizens," according to Ruth Paxson.

What can be said of this light? It is real, it is a power that is outside and above a person. An individual lives because of the light and its blessings. However, it is not a condition brought about by human awareness. Yet it can be stated that awareness, knowledge, and insight are benefits received from the gift of light.

"When a person is exposed to the light or receives it as a gift, then he or she is exposed, to the creative, redemptive, life-giving God—not just with a better self," as Markus Barth noted. As a beneficiary of light, man in turn becomes a living proof of its power: *Now are ye light*.

When a person changes and becomes light it asserts the power of the light over a person's awareness and existence. When a person is in darkness it shows that the darkness is a power superior to the individual.

Light and darkness are terms to which we can relate. They describe conflicting ways of life. They are used to describe good or evil conduct. The child of light should be more than just a knowledgeable, moral, and ethical person. He or she should be joyful in the Lord and walk gladly in obedience to His commands and teachings.

What are the differences between light and darkness? First, there is a difference between the person who is in Christ and the one who is outside Christ. Recall Christ's encounter with Nicodemus. Jesus responds to Nicodemus saying, *Verily, verily*. This was done to catch his attention because He had something important to say.

We all know it is rather useless to plant seed in an unprepared field or garden. So it is with the Gospel. The hearer needs to be prepared. He needs to be in a condition where he is obedient and teachable.

Christ saw that Nicodemus's mind was a thicket clogged with thorns and weeds. Therefore, it had to be cleared out and prepared. That is a good way to start if we want to progress as followers of Christ. Clean things out so the light can come in.

The first step in the kingdom of God is to become a new man. The phrase *to see the Kingdom of God* is the same as saying, to enter the kingdom of God. *The Kingdom of God* does not mean heaven. It means entering into a positive relationship with God. Calvin says, "It is rather a spiritual life, which is begun by faith in this world and daily increases according to the continual progress of faith." What is the meaning of this? No one can be truly gathered into Christ's body and counted among the children of God until he has been renewed, reborn.

Some people do not want to be reborn; they do not want to become new creatures. A creation is bringing or making something out of nothing. It means creating a new life and casting off the old life. Paul says, *For ye were sometimes* (once) *darkness, but now are ye light in the Lord* [Eph. 5:8]. You are no longer in your former state. Ye are now in the light. *Now therefore ye are no more strangers and foreigners, but fellow citizens with the saints, and of the household of God* [Eph. 2:19].

You are to be different from what you were. You are to progress each and every week, month, and year. You are to be a light unto others, and your light is to grow brighter and brighter. Light is the name given to those that the Spirit of God enlightens. We are to be the children of light, and if that is true then we should walk in the light, which is Christ Himself.

However, as was true of Nicodemus, a person is not capable of receiving the Gospel until he begins to become a new creature, until the light comes into his life.

Second, Paul presents contrasts through darkness and light. Note how the apostles are in complete accord with each other and with their Master. John begins his Gospel with *In the beginning* and then proceeds to light and darkness.

Jesus says, *I am the light of the world*. Paul says to the Corinthians, *what communion hath light with darkness*. He wants the Ephesians to know that they are light, the light of the Lord Jesus Christ. Therefore, they are no longer what they were. The light may come in very dimly at first, it may be just a spark, but it is to grow stronger and stronger and burn evermore brightly.

As the Apostle says, we are either light or darkness. We are either in Christ or outside Christ. The light within will either grow brighter or it will fade away. How often have we seen those who glow brighter and brighter compared to the ones whose light becomes dimmer and dimmer until there is no light at all?

The New Testament explicitly says there is a difference between light and darkness and between the person in Christ and the one outside Christ. Yet today it appears that the distinction between the two has eroded, evaporated, or become extinct. This should not have happened, but responsible people within the church have allowed it to occur.

The Protestant Reformers stated what the church should be known for: unwaveringly proclaiming God's truths; administering the Sacraments; and applying discipline to the members of Christ's body.

What has happened? The teachings have become blurred, watered down, or compromised. Numbers have become more important than presenting the truth as it is in Jesus.

John Calvin persisted in the truth as it was revealed to him in Jesus. He started with a handful, but look how the light that was given to him went out into the world. It grew brighter and brighter as it spread throughout the world, with its ministers and teachers proclaiming the true teachings of our Lord Jesus Christ.

They were faithful to the Word and did not compromise the truth as it is in Jesus. They presented the full Gospel in all its majesty, power, and strength knowing that God the Father would bless them and produce much fruit.

We need to ask ourselves, are we in darkness or in light? How do we become light? By the Word and the Spirit. We need the light from outside ourselves and from within. The Spirit opens the Word unto us and opens the heart to receive it.

Do you remember the conversion of Lydia, whose heart the Lord opened? "True evangelism, is one that is utterly dependent upon the power of the Spirit to put light into man," proclaimed Martyn Lloyd-Jones. We need to be made light, and we need to be enlightened. We were sometimes darkness, and now we are light. In the beginning there was darkness,

> *... And the Spirit of God moved* (was hovering over) *upon the face of the waters.*
> *And God said, Let there be light: and there was light.*
> *And God saw the light, that it was good: and God divided the light from darkness* [Gen. 1:2–4].

Abram was called of God, and God made a covenant with Abram. Abram exercised faith and was obedient to God's commands. Abram went from darkness to light. The light was in Abram. Therefore, he was able to say to Lot, *If thou wilt take the left hand, then I will go to the right; or if thou depart to the right hand, then I will go to the left* [Gen. 13:9].

If there was ever anyone who went from darkness to light it was the Apostle Paul. There he was persecuting the church on the road to Damascus. Then there was a light brighter than the noonday sun. In addition to the light, there was a face, and there was a voice saying, *Saul, Saul, why persecutest thou me* [Acts 9:4]? Paul answered, *Who art thou, Lord? And the Lord said, I am Jesus whom thou persecutest* [Acts 9:5].

"Paul had seen the light of the knowledge of the glory of God in the face of Jesus," as beautifully expressed by Martyn Lloyd-Jones. He was born anew, he was a new creature, he had gone from darkness to light, he received the light and he was enlightened, he became a light in the Lord, he was joined to Christ, and he became a branch of the vine.

What about you and me? Have we seen the light? Are we new creatures? Have we grasped and taken hold of the light? Are we walking in the unity, love, and light of the Lord Jesus Christ? Are we being filled with the light?

Thank God that the light in Christ is not dim but bright and continues to grow brighter. May we be guided by it as we grow in the Lord. He is the light of the world, but he also said to His disciples, *Ye are the light of the world* [Matt. 5:14]. And may we so be.

Amen!

7

Knowing the Will of God

And have no fellowship with the unfruitful works of darkness, but rather reprove (expose) them [Eph. 5:11].

Recently, the comment was made that we need more sermons about love and more about loving one another. Probably, that is true. Certainly it should be considered within the context of the Lord Jesus Christ's teachings, His conduct, character, and conversation. Further, true love can only be seen in the selfless, caring, obedient, self-denying, disciplined, fruitful, and forgiving life of our Lord Jesus Christ and of His Father, who is our Father.

Maturing in this type of love requires more than hearing about love. It requires knowing the will of God and knowing the teachings of Scripture. In addition, it requires knowing the life of our Master, developing a personal relationship with Christ and applying the teachings, growing in a living faith, and knowing the difference between what is to be practiced and what is not to be applied during our daily living.

The material in the first half of Chapter 5 in Ephesians is directed toward recognizing God's will for us. When considering additional verses, remember the Apostle said, *And have no fellowship with the unfruitful works of darkness, but rather reprove (expose) them. For it is a shame even to speak of those things which are done of them in secret* [Eph. 5:12]. We must remind ourselves of the context into which it fits. The fifth chapter begins with the injunctions to *BE ye therefore followers of God,* and *And walk in love,* as (or even as) *Christ has also hath loved us* [Eph. 5:1–2]. Then it urges us to *let no man deceive you with vain* (empty) *words: (but) walk as children of light* [Eph. 5:6].

If we are to walk in the light then we are to know the difference between the darkness and the light. If we are to know the difference, then we must know God's will for us. In order to know God's will, there are certain events or developments with which we should be familiar: the mighty acts of God in Ephesians, Chapters 1 and 2, Christ died for the ungodly, the Gentiles were adopted as the children of God, we are members of Christ's body, and the Holy Spirit is available and dwells amongst us. Even though we have knowledge of them, we are to: continue experiencing the preaching and teaching of the Word; learning God's will; obeying His commandments; and walking with Jesus.

Therefore, we are to be exposed to all of Christ's teachings, not just some of them. We are to endeavor to understand them and exert the necessary effort to put them into practice.

Consequently, it is necessary to understand the teachings about darkness, just as we are to consume and digest the teachings on light. We are to know what to do and not to do.

The Apostle Paul, as well as the other New Testament writers, understood the Master's way of teaching, explaining God's law, putting things into practice, and growing in the Lord. Paul did not expect instant success or compliance, but he did expect the members of Christ's body to know, to understand, to gain knowledge, to try, to rely upon the power of the Holy Spirit, and to deny themselves.

Therefore, Paul describes what we are to do and what we are not to do. He says since we are new creatures in the Lord Jesus we are to walk as children of the light. And in the very next breath he forbids us to have any fellowship with the works of darkness. He tells us what we are not to do, and he is very direct about it. Is that any different from what the Lord Jesus taught?

More than fifty years ago there was an editorial in a publication called *The Sunday School Times*, which said, "Forbidding is as necessary as feeding. There are child psychologists and educators today who would tell us that we must never use 'negatives' with a child; tell the children what to do, but never tell them 'do not do this or that'; if we feed the child with positive truth, this is all that is necessary. God does not seem to agree with such worldly wisdom, for His word tells us many things we are not to do, as well as many that we are to do." That is just as true today as it was then.

We are not to have fellowship with the works of darkness. Therefore, once something is determined or revealed to be a work of darkness then we are to have nothing to do with it. We are to leave it and to abandon it. We are not only to say *no*, but we are to act *no*!

How are we to determine if something is darkness? We are to use the light that is in Christ. If Christ's light says *no*, then we should move in the opposite direction. The light that is in Christ, and should be in us, should prohibit any fellowship with darkness, no matter where it originates or from whence it is proclaimed. "It prohibits participation in open and gross sins, and questionable or foolish conduct as well," according to Ruth Paxson.

Since the works of darkness affect the conduct, character, and conversation (tenor of life) of the individual, one must not have fellowship with them. They affect the mind, intellect, and understanding. Consequently, the knowledge a person possesses and uses is impacted.

When we remain in darkness regarding a subject or a person, what can be said about us? We are ignorant. We lack knowledge. We do not have understanding.

"When a person says they do not like or appreciate Shakespeare or Beethoven, does it tell us anything about the author's or composer's works? No, it does not. It does tell something about that person," to quote and paraphrase Martyn Lloyd-Jones.

When a person is outside the body of Christ, then they are ignorant or in darkness about God, the Lord Jesus Christ, and Scripture. They may have their ideas and express them about these three important subjects. They may be members of the visible church, but they remain the victims of their own mindsets. Scripture says, *THE fool hath said in his heart, There is no God* [Ps. 14:1]. Does this mean there is no God? Of course not! Ecclesiastes says, *the fool walketh in darkness* [Eccl. 2:14].

There is ignorance about God, and people continue to live in darkness. This does not tell us anything about God, but it does tell us something about the people who live that way.

This is in stark contrast to the Jews of the Old Testament. They knew that God was so great, so mighty, and so holy that they never dared to use the word Jehovah. They would only speak about "The Name." This was how they conveyed their knowledge of the glory, majesty, power, and holiness of God.

Contrast this today with the people outside Christ's body. "They are not only in darkness, they are darkness; they do not know God, and the more they talk, the more they express their ignorance," as clearly stated by Martyn Lloyd-Jones. Not only are these people ignorant about God and His laws, they are ignorant of themselves, their values, and the relationship they should have with the Lord Jesus Christ. Further, they do not or have not considered the question, *What shall it profit a man, if he shall gain the whole world, and lose his own soul* [Mark 8:36]?

They do not realize the joy and riches available in Christ Jesus. They are ignorant about them and choose to remain in darkness. They are ignorant about their need for salvation; therefore, they are not interested in it.

Yes, darkness impacts the mind and the ability to understand. Also, it impacts the heart and the emotions. Some are ignorant of the truth. They are not responsive to the Gospel. They consider it dull, uninteresting, fatuous, or something not to be considered. Why is this their position? Jesus says, *And this is the condemnation, that* (the) *light is come into the world, and man loved darkness rather than* (the) *light, because their deeds were evil* [John 3:19]. Both the mind and heart love darkness rather than light.

We have heard the old adage, "A man is not what he thinks he is, but he is what he thinks." The actions of people correspond to what they think and believe and to what they know or are willing to accept. A point of view leads to one's behavior. *For as he thinketh in his heart, so is he* [Prov. 23:7]. The way to control behavior is to make sure that the person's thinking is correct. This is true of the child and the adult.

What impacts a person's behavior and attitude toward life? It is their thinking about themselves and God, plus their relationship one to another. Their thinking is based to a large extent upon their knowledge and their desire to know, especially to know God. Their thinking can be in darkness or in light, depending upon their relationship to God. As we grow in the light of the Lord Jesus Christ, first our thinking is affected, then our conduct and behavior. It is not the reverse.

The works of the flesh result from thinking. They result from one's attitude and are manifest in the conduct of a person. The Apostle tells us we are not to live according to the lusts of the flesh and he enumerates several things. Then he declares, *That they which do such things shall not inherit the kingdom of God* [Gal. 5:21].

Paul forbids certain things. Recall that the injunctions enumerated in Chapter 4 from Verses 25–32 were directed toward lying—truth; anger and wrath—sin not, stealing—laboring; corrupt communications—minister grace; bitterness, anger, wrath, evil speaking, malice; and kindness, tenderhearted, and forgiving. Conduct exhibiting any of these traits is affected by thinking and practicing. It is affected by light and darkness.

Chapter 23 of Matthew comes as a shock to some people. How in the world can Jesus talk that way to the ministers of His day? They had strayed from the basic truth of the Old Testament. And Jesus wanted to uphold the integrity of God's authority.

The people thought they could do whatever some of the scribes and Pharisees were doing or what other influential people were practicing. He did not want the people misapplying His teachings or practicing them erroneously. The Lord Jesus did not want the people to think that God's law or His commandments were heavy or burdensome.

Note how our Lord continued to expose the darkness of the Pharisees and the scribes. Jesus said in speaking to the multitude and His disciples,

> *All therefore whatsoever they bid you observe, that observe and do; but do not ye after* (according to) *their works: for they say, and do not.*
>
> *But woe unto you, scribes and Pharisees, hypocrites! for ye shut up the kingdom of heaven against men: for ye neither go in yourselves, neither suffer ye them that are entering to go in.*
>
> *Woe unto you, scribes and Pharisees, hypocrites! for ye devour widows' houses, and for a pretence make long prayer: therefore ye shall receive the greater damnation.*
>
> *Woe unto you, scribes and Pharisees, hypocrites! for ye compass* (travel) *sea and land to make one proselyte, and when he is made, ye make him twofold more the child of hell than yourselves* [Matt. 23:3, 13–15].
>
> *Woe unto you, scribes and Pharisees.* After saying that, he tells them why and gives them the following specific reason: *Ye . . . have omitted the weightier matters of the law, judgment* (justice), *mercy, and faith: . . .*
>
> *Ye blind guides, which strain at* (out) *a gnat, and swallow a camel.*
>
> *. . . ye make clean the outside of the cup and of the platter* (dish), *but within they are full of extortion and excess* (self-indulgence).

> . . . *ye are like unto whited sepulchers* (whitewashed tombs), *which indeed appear beautiful outward, but are within full of dead men's bones, and of all uncleanness.*
> . . . *ye also outwardly appear righteous unto men, but within ye are full of hypocrisy and iniquity* (lawlessness).
> . . . *ye build the tombs of the prophets, and garnish* (adorn) *the sepulchres of the righteous,*
> . . . *ye are the children* (sons) *of them which killed the prophets,*
> . . . *Ye serpents, ye generation* (offspring) *of vipers, how can ye escape the damnation of hell?* [Selections from Matt. 23:14, 23–31, 33]

Jesus was direct in telling the scribes and Pharisees what they had done as a result of living in darkness and not according to the will of God. Jesus concludes His rebuke of the scribes and Pharisees saying, *O Jerusalem, Jerusalem, thou that killest the prophets, and stonest them which are sent unto thee, how often would I have gathered thy children together, even as a hen gathereth her chickens under her wings, and ye would not* [Matt. 23:37]! These are stinging words. They reveal the Master's uncompromising, unrelenting opposition to darkness and the sins it begets. He rejects those who continue to live in darkness and do not repent.

These words of Jesus are as applicable today as they were two thousand years ago. They apply to today's scribes and Pharisees, as well as to those who are in Christ and those who are not. The Lord was direct with His comments.

Paul is also direct in writing to the Romans. He tells them,

> *For when ye were the servants of sin, ye were free from righteousness.*
> *What fruit had ye then in those things whereof ye are now ashamed? for the end of those things is death.*
> *But now being made free from sin, and become servants to God, ye have your fruit unto holiness, and the end everlasting life.*
> *For the wages of sin is death; but the gift of God is eternal life through* (in) *Jesus Christ our Lord.* [Rom. 6:20–23]

Paul boldly states significant truths to the Romans.

"Sin and righteousness are so opposed to one another that anyone who devotes himself to the one must leave the other," as succinctly stated John Calvin. The two are compared and balanced against one another. When a person is a servant of sin, he is cut off from righteousness.

Conversely, when he seeks after righteousness, then he will be delivered from sin.

Those *free from righteousness* are those who do not obey God's commands to be righteous. They serve the works of the flesh in darkness and are in bondage to evil.

Paul succinctly addresses a question to those who were servants of sin and darkness by asking, *What fruit had ye then in those things whereof ye are now ashamed?* "[Rom. 6:21] The answer to Paul's question is evident: there was no fruit.

What a difference it makes when we begin being enlightened by the Spirit of Christ and Scripture, and moving from darkness to light. The wonderful thing about it is that the more we move toward the light, the more light there is, and the more light there is, the more we want to move in that direction.

Righteousness produces the fruit of holiness and eternal life. The gift of God is our justification, and the fruit of the Spirit is our sanctification. Probably the best example of darkness and light, plus the works of the flesh and the fruit of the spirit, is seen in the parable of the prodigal son.

The life of sin and darkness took everything from the young man. Remember the words spoken by Jesus to the rich fool,

> *Thou hast much goods laid up for many years; take thine ease, eat, drink, and be merry.*
> *But, God said unto him, Thou fool, this night thy soul shall be required of thee: then whose shall those things be, which thou hast provided* [Luke 12:19–20]?

Paul states we are to *have no fellowship with the unfruitful works of darkness, but rather reprove* (expose) *them*. He does not stop by saying *have no fellowship* with them. This gets back to his earlier practice of giving a negative injunction and then a positive one, which is to reprove the unfruitful works. He continues by saying, *But rather reprove* (expose) *them*.

God calls and instructs every member of Christ's body to take a positive stand against the works of darkness. We are to expose them, both the popular and unpopular ones, both the acceptable and the unacceptable ones.

The believer is responsible for repudiating the unfruitful works of darkness. This does not mean that we become detectives, or spies, or judges. But we are to take a stand and to conduct ourselves according to the light in Christ.

Paul says that as long as the deeds remain hidden then the people doing them will continue in sin and darkness. Why is this so? Because they are ignorant of the things of God, the Lord Jesus Christ, and Scripture. But when their eyes are opened by God's Word, those who were in darkness begin to blush and to be ashamed. The warnings to the saints are blessed by God and enlighten nonbelievers.

Regardless of a person's condition, man was created in the image of God. This is true whether a person believes it or not.

A person at their lowest or vilest moment in darkness may have little sense of shame. If there is a flicker of light or a little spark, then by gradually eliminating the ignorance of God, the Lord Jesus Christ and the Holy Spirit may move that person from darkness to light.

Having *no fellowship with the unfruitful works of darkness* demands much of a person. It requires:

> knowing the will of God and His love;
> acquiring knowledge of God, the Lord Jesus Christ, and Scripture;
> exercising continuous effort;
> knowing the teachings of the Lord Jesus;
> knowing His commandments and being obedient to them;
> knowing the rebukings and the negatives, and accepting them;

and

> walking in the unity, love, and light of the Gospel as revealed in the Lord Jesus Christ.

May we fulfill these demands as we continue walking with Jesus
Amen!

8

What Is Acceptable

> *For ye were sometimes darkness, but now are ye light in the Lord: walk as children of light:*
> *(For the fruit of the Spirit is in all goodness and righteousness and truth;)*
> *But all things that are reproved are made manifest by the light: for whatsoever doth make manifest is light.*
> *Wherefore he saith, Awake thou that sleepest, and arise from the dead, and Christ shall give thee light* [Eph. 5:8–9, 13–14]

This Scripture illuminates the path we are to follow and provides light for our walk with the Master. It focuses on significant teachings of the Apostle, but more importantly on truths found in Jesus Christ. Paul admonishes and encourages us to certain types of action in living a life of faith. We are to walk as children of light, leave the darkness since we are members of Christ's body, and *have no fellowship with the unfruitful works of darkness, but rather reprove* (expose) *them* [Eph. 5:11].

Please note it says, *And have no fellowship with the unfruitful works of darkness, but rather reprove* (expose) *them*. It does not say have no fellowship with the workers or people in darkness but with the unfruitful works, and that is a significant difference. Further, Paul says, *But all things that are reproved* (exposed) *are made manifest by the light: for whatsoever doth make manifest is light.*

The word *manifest* means "to lay bare," "to make known," "to make visible." How are these unfruitful works made visible? By the light, and that light is Jesus Christ.

When He is proclaimed and presented, then His truth serves as a beacon, and people are drawn to it. Further, His light identifies the fruits of the Spirit and the unfruitful works of darkness. We are to walk in the light and show forth the fruit of the Spirit in all goodness, righteousness, and truth, *Proving what is acceptable unto the Lord* [Eph. 5:10]. Then Scripture says, *Christ shall give thee the light* [Eph. 5:14]. This is the context within which we are to examine these teachings.

How does the light manifest itself? *And this is life eternal, that they might know thee the only true God, and Jesus Christ, whom thou hast sent* [John 17:3]. Jesus prays that we might know the only true God. Therefore, the light is known in the mind. The truth found in Jesus is revealed to the mind, the intellect, and the understanding. It has nothing to do with vague feelings or some peculiar emotional experience. Rather, it is knowledge of God and His Son, not just knowing about them. God feeds the birds of the air. God enlightens those who have been called, the elect.

When God feeds the birds, he does not take the food and water to each nest and put it on a platter or in a bowl. The birds must seek and find; they must exert themselves. We also are to exert ourselves in obtaining Christ's nourishment.

The called out of God do not come to know God or the Lord Jesus by receiving information on a silver platter, by sitting back and ignoring the teachings of Scripture or by only going to worship services and acknowledging God and His Son. The elect are to exert their intellects and to grow in the knowledge of God and Christ.

Yes, God enlightens us. He enlightens us about life. When this happens we begin to understand, we begin to possess Him by faith, we grow in the faith, our lives are enriched, and we are transformed by the increasing knowledge of God. He becomes more important and real to us as we grow in a living, daily faith.

It is this election, knowledge, and transforming faith that incorporates us into the body of Christ and enables us to be changed. We become new creatures, heirs, and *joint-heirs*. The transforming power of the Lord Jesus Christ enables us to be changed and to do that which we could not do previously.

Jesus prays, *That they might know thee the only true God, and Jesus Christ, whom thou hast sent* [John 17:3]. Further understanding of this petition is necessary. Being called and being able to respond in faith to the Lord Jesus Christ enables a person to distinguish the God of Abram, the prophets, the apostles, and the disciples from empty or fanciful imaginations that do not have appropriate knowledge of God and faith in Him. As Calvin points out, this verse really means, "that they may know thee alone to be the true God."

How is He known? Through the Lord Jesus Christ and the power of the Holy Spirit. Who can know God? What does Scripture say?

> *But the natural man receiveth not the things of the Spirit of God: for they are foolishness unto him: neither can he know them, because they are spiritually discerned.*
> *But he that is spiritual judgeth all things, yet he himself is judged of no man.*
> FOR WHO HATH KNOWN THE MIND OF THE LORD, THAT HE MAY INSTRUCT HIM? *But we have the mind of Christ* [1 Cor. 2:14–16].

There is a definite distinction between the person endowed only with the powers of nature and the individual blessed with the power of the Spirit who has received spiritual discernment.

Paul explains to the Corinthians that there are those who reject the Gospel because they have not been enlightened and are still living in ignorance, because they have not received spiritual discernment.

Why have they not received the light? Because of their ignorance or spiritual blindness. Therefore, they disparage the Gospel and try to project their own ideas about God, or they parrot the statements of others who do not know the Father of our Lord Jesus Christ "to be the only true God." These teachings and truths are unknown because they are too profound to be grasped by the mind that has not received the light from Christ and responded in faith.

It is necessary to receive the power of the Spirit if a person is to acquire knowledge, understanding, and truth. This is different from having the intellectual capacity to understand music, poetry, history, physics, chemistry, and numerous other subjects. The ability to discern the truth of the Spirit is different.

What does belief in the Lord Jesus Christ and Scripture depend upon? Intellectual capacity? Brainpower? Studying? No, none of these! It depends upon the revelation of the Lord Jesus Christ and responding in faith. An excellent example is the Apostle Paul. Before He responded in faith, before He learned the truth, before He really knew the Father, he needed to receive the light and the light is the Lord Jesus Christ.

We need to move from darkness to light before we can really know the Father and His Son. When Paul moved from darkness to light, what happened? If that change affected Paul, what impact should it have on us?

First, Paul knew he had sinned against God. He became aware of the conflict raging within himself, the conflict between obeying God and satisfying self.

Second, Paul looked to the Lord Jesus Christ. He had known about Him and had heard about Him, but after his conversion he wanted to know Him. Once he had been enlightened, he wanted to know Him!

Third, he came to know the way of salvation, and he learned how to explain it to others. He could answer questions. Peter says, *But sanctify* (set apart) *the Lord God in your hearts: and be ready always to give an answer* (a defense) *to every man that asketh you a reason of the hope that is in you with meekness and fear* (reverential awe) [1 Pet. 3:15]. The person who knows these truths can understand the light that is contained in Scripture.

Fourth, he had the heart as well as the intellect to respond to the truth and light. Some people consider Scripture to be only literature, philosophy, poetry, or history. They are not moved or gripped by the message itself. Therefore, they do not respond to it. When a person responds with his or her heart and intellect, then he or she is moved to obey the commandments and realizes the commandments are not grievous.

It is then that one begins to desire holiness and to hunger and thirst after righteousness. Then the desire of the heart is to know God, to know the Lord Jesus Christ, to know Scripture, and to know the truth. Both the heart and intellect seek to know the things of God. We are to know the will of God. Therefore, the Apostle says,

> *For ye were sometimes* (once) *darkness, but now are ye light in the Lord: walk as children of light;*
> *(For the fruit of the Spirit is in all goodness, righteousness, and truth;)*
> *Proving what is acceptable unto the Lord* [Eph. 5:8–10].

What happens when we *walk as children of light*? There is fruit that is evident in goodness, righteousness, and truth. There are certain innate characteristics about fruit. It does not appear overnight. It is not stamped out, or fabricated, or ready-made.

What about fruit trees? Did you ever notice that at first they are barren, then they get buds and flowers, then the fruit is pollinated, it receives light? There are things within the fruit tree that develop or, I should say, respond to the light, then something makes them fertile, then the fruit begins to appear, and it grows, develops, and matures. It does not happen suddenly; it takes time, nutrients, care, pruning, spraying, and picking.

There is no such thing as instant fruit, nor are there instant Christians or immediate mature members of Christ's body. Some people think that such a thing is possible, but it is not. Why do I say that? Look at the apostles. Look at some of the great preachers, pastors, and teachers. They produced fruit, but it took growth, development, nourishment, and, above all, the light of Christ before they matured.

What are the characteristics of the fruit of light?

> There are no two that are exactly the same, no two apples, no two peaches, no two members of Christ's body. That is where we differ from other religions and the cults. They want everyone to be the same, to conform to certain standards. The fruit of Christ's body has variety.
>
> There is another peculiarity of fruit. If you look closely, you will note that it always comes from something within before it makes its outward appearance and is seen. It is like there is nothing, then a little something appears. To any but the trained eye, it may not seem to be an apple, or peach, or pear, but that is what it becomes.
>
> That is what we are to be like. We are to become fruit out of something that is within, out of our experiences, our life, our vitality, and out of the light that shines upon us.
>
> The fruit develops, the birds are fed, the members of Christ's body mature. However, the true Christian can mature only as he or she walks in the light, walks in the unity, and walks in the love of the Lord Jesus Christ.

The New Testament emphasizes one main point that is dramatically opposed to the way most church members think, and that is the New Testament does not emphasize what we do, but what we are and what we are to become. That bears repeating: the New Testament does not emphasize what we do, but what we are and what we are to become.

The light of Christ in our hearts and minds should have a positive impact upon our conduct, behavior, conversation, and character. How is this to be seen? *The fruit of the Spirit is in all goodness, righteousness and truth* [Eph. 5:9].

According to scholars, the original Greek in this verse should read "the fruit of the light." Christ is in all goodness, righteousness, and truth. The term *light* indicates the generation of fruit rather than mechanical production. It can be ascribed to the saints and to all that is good. It is used to describe good, righteous, and true men and women.

> *Wherewith shall I come before the LORD, and bow myself before the high God? Shall I come before him with burnt offerings, with calves of a year old?*
>
> *Will the LORD be pleased with thousands of rams, or with ten thousands of rivers of oil? Shall I give my first-born for my transgression, the fruit of my body* (my own child) *for the sin of my soul?*
>
> *He hath showed thee, O man, what is good; and what doth the LORD require of thee, but to do justly, and to love mercy* (loving kindness), *and to walk humbly with thy God* [Mic. 6:6–8]?

These verses show that obedience from the depths of the heart is much more important than sacrifices, cultic rights, and performing works.

The Apostle Paul uses the three terms *all goodness, righteousness, and truth* [Eph. 5:9]. Note the order.

Goodness describes the ideal character and moral quality of the regenerate person. It is a desire to be good and to do good. *Goodness* in this verse means "benevolence, doing for others." Goodness is not selfish, self-centered, or interested in self. Think of the goodness of God. It leads to repentance. He sends the rain upon the just and the unjust, and He makes the sun to shine upon the evil and the good, to quote and paraphrase Martyn Lloyd-Jones.

The second term is *righteousness*. The Greek word is *dikaiosunē*. It means "the quality of being right or just." Normally, it is used to describe an attribute of God. The righteousness of God means His faithfulness, His truthfulness, and that which is consistent with His own nature and promises.

> *Whom God hath set forth to be a propitiation* (mercy seat) *through faith in his blood, to declare* (demonstrate) *his righteousness for the remission* (passing over) *of sins that are past, through the forbearance of God;*

> *To declare, I say, at this time his righteousness: that he might be just, and the justifier of him which believeth in Jesus* [Rom. 3:25-26].

In this instance, it shows the righteousness of God in the death of Christ. It reveals that God is not indifferent to sin, therefore, His holiness must condemn sin.

The word *righteousness* is important. It is used by our Master in urging us to conform to the will of God.

> *Blessed are they which do hunger and thirst after righteousness: for they shall be filled* [Matt. 5:6].

> *For I say unto you, That except your righteousness shall exceed the righteousness of the scribes and Pharisees, ye shall in no case* (by no means) *enter into the kingdom of heaven* [Matt. 5:20].

> *Of righteousness, because I go to my Father, and ye see me no more* [John 16:10].

It is used to describe what has been appointed by God that is to be acknowledged and obeyed.

> *And Jesus answering said unto him, Suffer* (Allow) *it to be so now: for thus it becometh us* (is fitting for us) *to fulfill all righteousness* [Matt. 3:15].

> *For John came unto you in the way of righteousness, and ye believed him not: but the publicans and the harlots believed him: and ye, when ye had seen it, repented* (regretted) *not afterward, that ye might believe him* [Matt. 21:32].

It is also used to describe the sum total of God's requirements.

> *SIMON Peter, a servant and an apostle of Jesus Christ, to them that have obtained like* (the same kind of) *precious faith with us through the righteousness of* (our) *God and our Saviour Jesus Christ* [2 Pet. 1:1].

> *For every one that useth* (partakes of) *milk is unskillful in the word of righteousness: for he is a babe* [Heb. 5:13].

It identifies Scripture as containing the Gospel that declares the righteousness of God.

The meaning of the term is "right action." According to Scripture, it is that gracious gift of God whereby those who believe on the Lord Jesus

Christ are brought into a right relationship with God. This righteousness is obtained only by faith in Jesus Christ.

The person who trusts in Christ has the righteousness of God in Him, and he becomes righteous. Abraham accepted the Word of God and responded in faith through the mind and spirit. Therefore, God accepted Him. This word *righteousness* is powerful, and it is fruit of the light. There cannot be righteousness if there is a lack of godliness.

The third term in the phrase is *truth*. It means, as we have said before, all the truth as it is embodied, seen, revealed, and known in the Lord Jesus Christ.

We have these three significant terms, *goodness, righteousness,* and *truth*. They are preceded by *walk as children of light* and followed by *Proving what is acceptable unto the Lord* [Eph. 5:8, 10].

This latter statement is meaningful. The Greek word for *proving* is *dokimazō*. It is an interesting word and has a significant meaning. However, we need to realize that in this portion of Scripture, Paul is tying together doing God's will with the act of learning as knowledge is made available. The Greek word used for *proving* means "to test, to prove something with the expectation of approving it." In other words, it is to: arrange and execute a test and accept the results.

It implies more than a mere intellectual procedure. It describes a personal and critical relationship between the one who searches and decides regarding the person or object being scrutinized.

It reveals situations where God's will is recognized and affirmed. The ability to do this includes the total life and being of a person, including the intellect, the will, the emotions, and conduct.

Comprehending the will of God and conducting oneself as a "saint" or "wise man" requires a combination of learning and doing. We are to learn by experience, effort, and seeking to know the will of God. We are to learn the unique authority of the Bible, know the prophets and the teachers, heed God's will, and learn by doing.

This teaching is based upon the truth that God lives and makes His will known. God will not let His saints go. He grants the saints the knowledge and wisdom to comprehend His will and the courage plus the perseverance to do so.

What are we to do then? There may be several answers. However, it can be summed up by saying we are to do that which proves we are members of Christ's body. "It is that, over and above everything else, our ultimate, our final consideration is our desire to seek, to know, and to discover the will of the Lord in order that we may please Him. It is this personal relationship to this blessed Person," as beautifully stated by Martyn Lloyd-Jones.

As the Apostle says, *Whether therefore ye eat, or drink, or whatsoever ye do, do all to the glory of God* [1 Cor. 10:31]. The verse we are considering says, *Proving what is acceptable unto the Lord* [Eph. 5:10].

What is acceptable unto the Lord? It requires a living faith, a purpose-filled life according to the teachings of our Lord, understanding the nature of sin, searching for the spiritual food and water, and following in the footsteps of our Lord. It also means acquiring knowledge of the Cross, Christ's shed blood, God's forgiveness, and His will for us as we endeavor to live a life of faith. The emphasis is upon living. It is not upon performing certain acts or doing things at a specific time or on a special day. No, it is not. It is living life to the fullest each and everyday.

Our conduct, conversation, and character are to exhibit *what is acceptable unto the Lord*. This requires knowing, believing, and living.

As we reflect upon our actions or think about what we may do, the acid test:

> Is the thought, word, act, or deed acceptable to the Lord?
> Is it fitting for walking with the Master in unity, love, and light?
> Is it allowing us to glorify God and to enjoy Him?
> Is it producing fruit?
> Is it in the light of Christ?

If the answers to these questions are in the affirmative then we are walking on the right path and *Proving what is acceptable to the Lord* [Eph. 5:10].

Amen!

9

Not As Fools, But as Wise

> *See then that ye walk circumspectly* (carefully), *not as fools, but as wise,*
> *Redeeming the time, because the days are evil.*
> *Wherefore be ye not unwise, but understanding what the will of the Lord is* [Eph. 5:15–17].

The Apostle Paul proceeds systematically in presenting the truths of Christ to the Ephesians and in revealing how Christians are to walk in their relationship with Christ when he says,

> *See then that ye walk circumspectly* (carefully), *not as fools, but as wise,*
> *Redeeming the time, because the days are evil.*
> *Wherefore be ye not unwise, but understanding what the will of the Lord is* [Eph. 5:15–17].

The Apostle begins with the words *See then*. These two words should be translated "understand therefore" instead of *see then*. Paul is not saying, "Look how you walk." He is issuing a command to understand what we are to do and that we are to do it. He wants understanding and obedience. Paul says this is based upon walking in unity [Eph. 4:1–16], walking in holiness [Eph. 4:17–30], walking in love [Eph. 4:31–5:2], and walking in light [Eph. 5:3–14]. Now it is time to walk in wisdom.

"The fifth characteristic of a walk that glorifies the Lord is a walk in wisdom. . . . So let us take the larger view to be an exhortation to walk in wisdom.

"All through this section of Ephesians which deals with the Christians walk Paul has but one appeal, reiterated again and again, "Be what you are." The ground of his appeal is also invariably the same, that the walk of the saint must be in correspondence with his position in Christ. "Ye were sometimes—but now ye are," therefore walk "as becometh saints." The sinner walks "as fools," but the saint walks "as wise," as appropriately expressed by Ruth Paxson.

We are to understand the truth as it is in Christ Jesus. If we understand it and apply it, then we will walk with the Lord Jesus, and become what He wants us to become. Therefore, we are to walk in wisdom. This is to be characteristic of the members of Christ's body. The key points in these three verses are walk *circumspectly, not as fools, but as wise, Redeeming the time, . . . understanding what the will of the Lord is.* Paul does not waste words or thoughts. He says, "Okay, show us."

If we are members of Christ's body, then we should know there is one body, one Spirit, one hope, one Lord, one faith, one baptism, and one God and Father of all. When we know these things to be true, then there are other truths to be grasped which should become part of our relationship with Christ. These should signify that we are *not unwise, but understanding what the will of the Lord is* [Eph. 5:17].

Acknowledging and accepting these truths reveal if we are *in* (into) *the unity of the faith, and of the knowledge of the Son of God, unto a perfect* (mature) *man, unto the measure of the stature of the fullness of Christ* [Eph. 4:13]. They reveal if we *have not so learned Christ* [Eph. 4:20], if we *have put on the new man* [Eph. 4:24]. They also reveal if we *be kind one to another, tenderhearted, forgiving* [Eph. 4:32]. Finally, they reveal if we *walk in love, as Christ also hath loved us* [Eph. 5:2], if we *walk as children of light* [Eph. 5:8], and if we *have no fellowship with the unfruitful works of darkness* [Eph. 5:11]. We are not only to know, but obey Christ's commands and teachings, which enunciate and substantiate the foregoing truths.

When accepting and practicing these teachings and commands, we should understand that we are to *walk circumspectly* (carefully), *not as fools, but as wise*. Note the progression, note the tone, note the lack of choice.

What is meant by this exhortation? We are to *walk circumspectly*. This means accurately and carefully. If we do, then we will walk *not as fools, but as wise, understanding what the will of the Lord is*.

When considering these three verses (Eph. 5:15–17) remember that throughout Chapters 4, 5, and 6 Paul emphasizes again and again,

"Be what you are." You are to walk as a member of Christ's body, *For ye were sometimes* (once) *darkness, but now are ye light in the Lord* [Eph. 5:8]. The fool walks in the ways of the sinner, while the saint walks in the ways of the wise.

We are to take heed regarding how we walk and to concentrate on our walk. Why are we to do these things? First, because we profess to be members of Christ's body. Therefore, we should strive to have our conduct, character, and conversation conform to the truth as it is found in Him. He is the Head; we are the members.

Second, as professing members of Christ's body other people observe what we say and do. They scrutinize our conversation and conduct.

Ruth Paxson tells how "on one occasion when she was witnessing about God blessing their missionary efforts in China and describing the victories realized through the Holy Spirit, she noticed one person zealously listening to her every word and watching every gesture. Later, the person confessed that he had hoped to catch her in some word or act that would betray her stated commitment to the Lord Jesus Christ, but he could not."

The walk with Christ consists of thousands of steps. Each step is taken one at a time. Each one can have a positive or negative impact upon someone else. One wrong step may lead to a real mistake, or to backsliding, or to sorrow, or to suffering, or to a misdirected life. As Henry Mobley says, "It is only a matter of inches."

Disgrace and shame can be brought upon the church or the body of Christ because someone takes the wrong step by word or action, or does not take the right step. A balance must be maintained. Do not take the wrong step, but on the other hand, take the right step.

We need to be careful and accurate about every step we take as members of Christ's body. A vivid description of how we are to walk is contained in the following words of the esteemed Bishop Moule, "The appeal is again for a grave remembrance that a walk in the light is no mere promenade, smooth and easy, but a march, resolved and full of purpose, cautious against the enemy, watchful for opportunity for the King, and self controlled in every habit, and possible only in the power of the eternal Spirit."

Third, we were sometimes darkness, now we are light, and we are to walk as children of the light.

Next, the Apostle says we are to *walk . . . not as fools, but as wise* [Eph. 5:15]. What does this really mean? The words *fool* or *folly* appear a number of times in both the Old and New Testaments. At times, these words mean "emptiness, thick-headedness, thoughtlessness, or self-centeredness." However, the way in which it is used in this instance means the opposite of wisdom. Further, wisdom is considered a gift of divine revelation.

In the Old Testament, folly or being a fool was the person who disobeyed the law, or denied the reality and presence of God. In the New Testament folly or foolishness "leads to every kind of superstitious, idolatrous and immoral foolishness," as Alan Richardson points out.

"We walk as pilgrims in an unregenerate world. All around us is gross spiritual and moral darkness, the dazzling light of the . . . wisdom of man. We walk as Christians in the midst of an apostate Church, wherein the world, the flesh and the devil have been allowed great liberty in dictating its plans and in the control of its programs. In no period of church history was God's exhortation in (Eph. 5:15) more needed than to-day," according to Ruth Paxson. It applies as much today as it did in Ruth Paxson's day. May God enlighten those in accord with His Word, who proclaim God's commands, and Christ's teachings unabashedly.

In the biblical sense, to be a fool is a very serious matter. *Fool* means "apostate," "defective," "damned." Further, it is contrasted to wisdom from the Lord. Paul says to the Ephesians (and to us) that we are to be *not as fools, but as wise in understanding what the will of the Lord is.*

What are the characteristics of those who are foolish? Usually, they are *governed by feelings and emotions*, not by *reason*. It is a mark of the person who says they will vote for a person because they look nice, or they are cute, or have a quick wit.

Usually, these people do not want to use their brains. Further, they want happiness, enjoyment, no problems, and to travel on easy street. They say, forget the difficult or troublesome passages of Scripture, and let us have more singing, less studying, and less preaching.

"Second, this type of person is governed by desire. They must have what they like and what they want. Reasoning and understanding do not enter the picture," as noted by Martyn Lloyd-Jones.

Third, the unthinking person goes with the crowd, takes the route of least resistance, does it because everyone is doing it, does not consider the consequences, and ignores certain facts.

Fourth, they are governed by instincts and impulses. They take pride in them and believe it is the best way to function. Also, they do not know what they are going to do next. An idea will come, and they will act on impulse. They believe instinctive judgments or impulses are better than relying upon reasoning and understanding.

Fifth, the foolish person is governed by zeal. This can be beneficial up to a point. However, zeal and sincerity combined can be dangerous and can produce disastrous results. They assume since they are zealous, that they must be right. "Zeal needs to be governed and controlled by reasoning, understanding, and wisdom," as expressed by Lloyd-Jones.

In addition, the fool is usually mostly concerned with the moment. One of the more popular ideas in the 70s and 80s was existentialism, the immediate moment is all that really matters. This may be true in the case of someone accepting the Lord Jesus Christ as his or her Lord and Saviour. However, it is not true in a majority of the situations that occur. Some people evaluate the current moment to the point where it becomes the overriding element in their lives. They do not realize that for them and most people, there will be additional moments, and they should be concerned about them.

What about the wise person? For the Hebrew, true wisdom was perceived as having the right attitude toward God.

> *The fear of the Lord is the beginning of wisdom: and the knowledge of the Holy* (One) *is understanding* [Prov. 9:10].

> *The fear of* (An awe filled reverence toward) *the Lord is the instruction of wisdom* [Prov. 15:33].

> *The fear of the Lord is the beginning of wisdom: a good understanding have all they that do his commandments* [Ps. 111:10].

In the New Testament, wisdom is understood to be the gift of God.

> *That the God of our Lord Jesus Christ, the Father of glory, may give unto you the spirit of wisdom and revelation in the knowledge of him* [Eph. 1:17].

> *If any of you lack wisdom, let him ask of God, . . .* [Jas. 1:5].

> *But the wisdom that is from above is first pure, then peaceable, gentle, and easy to be entreated* (willing to yield), *full of mercy and good fruits, without partiality and without hypocrisy* [Jas. 3:17].

Wisdom is basically seen in its relationship to God. It is evident in certain passages of Scripture. It is seen in what Christ was and in what He did.

> *Who is the image of the invisible God, the first-born* (first in rank) *of* (over) *every creature:*
> *For by him were all things created, that are in heaven, and that are in* (on) *earth, visible and invisible, whether they be thrones, or dominions, or principalities* (rulers)*, or powers* (authorities)*: all things were created by* (in) *him, and for him:*
> *And he is before all things, and by him all things consist.*
> *And he is the head of the body, the church: who is the beginning, the first-born from the dead; that in all things he might have the pre-eminence* [Col. 1:15–18].
>
> *And when the sabbath day was come, he began to teach in the synagogue: and many hearing him were astonished, saying, From whence hath this man these things? and what wisdom is this which is given unto him, that even such mighty works are wrought* (performed) *by his hands* [Mark 6:2]?

This is seen not only in Colossians and in Mark, but also in the first chapter of John's Gospel which says, *No man hath seen God at any time; the only begotten Son, which is in the bosom of the Father, he hath declared him* [John 1:18].

One fact to remember is that the Redeemer is also the Creator of the universe. What is the meaning of *wise* in the verse being considered? It means the believers who are endowed with spiritual and practical wisdom.

What are the characteristics of the wise person? He or she is always thinking and does not act on impulse or instinct. He or she examines every proposition and every possibility. He or she considers all the facts, the evidence available from all sides. The wise person is a good listener. He or she wants to have all available information and evaluate it before making a decision. This applies to the members of Christ's body, who not only have knowledge of doctrine, but strive to apply the teachings of the Lord Jesus Christ. The wise person has a definite goal or purpose. He or she wants every step to take him or her nearer to the ultimate goal of being in a right relationship with God and becoming like Him in their conduct, conversation, and character.

A final characteristic of the wise person is that he or she is objective, not subjective. He has the ability to remove himself from the situation and to consider the facts in an objective manner.

It is easy to accept the Lord Jesus Christ by faith. It is difficult to walk as a wise member of Christ's body. But it is very difficult to put into practice His teachings.

How does one walk as a wise person? People encounter or are exposed to difficult, perplexing problems as they endeavor to perform their daily tasks. They have difficulties with family, friends, business, country, and church.

How can they handle the situation? How can a person walk according to the teachings of the Lord Jesus Christ? How does a person develop his or her ideas with respect to dishonesty, corruption, and communion with the people denying the deity of Christ? How do people maintain their allegiance to the Lord Jesus Christ? How are these questions and similar ones resolved?

The place to begin is with Scripture, its guidance and wisdom. Scripture advises that there are two types of wisdom, the wisdom of the world or men and the wisdom of God. The wisdom of the world is seen in the following verses:

> *For the preaching* (message) *of the cross is to them that perish foolishness; but unto us which are saved it is the power of God* [1 Cor. 1:18].
>
> *Where is the wise? where is the scribe? where is the disputer* (debater) *of this world? hath not God made foolish the wisdom of this world?*
> *For after that in the wisdom of God the world by wisdom knew not God, it pleased God by the foolishness of preaching* (the message preached) *to save them that believe* [1 Cor. 1:20–21].
>
> *But we preach Christ crucified, unto the Jews a stumbling block, and unto the Greeks foolishness* [1 Cor. 1:23].
>
> *Howbeit we speak wisdom among them that are perfect* (mature): *yet not the wisdom of this world, nor of the princes* (rulers) *of this world, that come to nought* (nothing) [1 Cor. 2:6].

Unfortunately, too often in today's world the control of the church at various levels is in the hands of those who are wise in the ways of the world and strangers to the purposes of God as revealed in Christ Jesus.

The ways of the world are adopted and espoused, while the ways of the Lord are ignored or relegated to a secondary position.

On the other hand, there is the wisdom of God as revealed in Christ. Paul enlightens the Corinthians regarding God's wisdom when he says,

> *The foolishness of God is wiser than men; and the weakness of God is stronger than men.*
>
> *For ye see* (consider), . . . *brethren, how that not many wise men after the flesh, not many mighty, not many noble, are called.*
>
> *But God hath chosen the foolish things of the world to confound* (put to shame) *the wise . . . and the weak things to confound* (put to shame) *the things which are mighty* [1 Cor. 1:25–27].
>
> *But . . . in Christ Jesus, who of God is made unto* (became for) *us wisdom, and righteousness, and sanctification, and redemption* [1 Cor. 1:30].

Paul adds to this saying,

> *But God hath revealed them unto us by his Spirit: for the Spirit searcheth all things, yea, the deep things of God* [1 Cor. 2:10].
>
> *Which things also we speak, not in the words which man's wisdom teacheth, but which the Holy Ghost teacheth; . . .*
>
> *But the natural man receiveth not the things of the Spirit of God: for they are foolishness unto him: neither can he know them, because they are spiritually discerned.* [1 Cor. 2:13–14].

The wisdom described in these verses is the wisdom we are to seek and to receive. This wisdom was bestowed upon the followers of Christ in the first century and in the great periods of revival since then. These people knew the purposes of God, they depended upon the guidance of the Holy Spirit, and they walked in the light of Christ. They were not only inspired and guided by this divine wisdom, they were willing to take a courageous stand for the truth as it is in Jesus; the standards revealed in Scripture regarding individual conduct; and the manner in which the affairs of the Lord's church, or the called out, are handled. May we do less?

May God's wisdom as revealed in Christ through the Holy Spirit be our guiding light and the standard for our conduct, conversation, and character.

Amen!

10

Walking Circumspectly

See then that ye walk circumspectly (carefully), *not as fools, but as wise,* . . . [Eph. 5:15].

What is wisdom? It is not merely knowledge, light, ability, intelligence, or genius. It is the power, capacity, and capability to apply all those things and to bring them into a positive relationship with the ordinary, daily requirements and demands of living.

As members of Christ's body, we are to possess wisdom and manifest it. The Apostle's method of presenting Christ's teachings is to use contrasts. He states a negative injunction and a positive one, then he presents the motivating reason for applying the teaching. He says, *walk circumspectly* (carefully), *not as fools, but as wise,* . . . *but understanding what the will of the Lord is* [Eph. 5:15, 17].

We are to act as a light in our personal conduct, character, and conversation and to have a positive impact upon others. The wise person understands the teachings of Christ and applies them to the best of his or her ability. As members of Christ's body our eyes are opened to the wisdom revealed in the Lord Jesus Christ.

What is true of the person who is a member of Christ's body? His or her eyes have been opened to the truth and the wisdom as it is in Christ Jesus. It allows a person to think and act differently with respect to life and to living a life of faith. The individual enlightened spiritually approaches life from a distinct perspective with new thoughts and increased understanding. It enables them to show the light of Christ and acquire the wisdom and knowledge available from Him.

Members of Christ's body have a new principle guiding their activities. Their method of operating day by day is according to the teachings of the Master and is seen in the life, power, and principles He exhibited. They have the desire to please God, to obey His commandments, and to learn more about Him and His Son. This enables one to act as a wise person and to ignore or reject the foolish things of the world.

The Holy Spirit reveals Christ's commandments and teachings to the members of the community of believers. The Holy Spirit provides the power and the illumination. Paul writes to Timothy saying, *For God hath not given us the spirit of fear; but of power, and of love, and of a sound mind* [2 Tim. 1:7].

Discipline and wisdom have been given to us, along with the power to respond positively and to follow in His steps. We are to walk in unity, holiness, love, light, and wisdom, remembering that the Holy Spirit provides us with a sound mind, discipline, orderliness, and wisdom.

The Apostle Paul, under the influence of the Holy Spirit, weaves together a web of three distinct qualities in Chapter 5 Verses 15–17. He wants to trap us. He wants to wrap us with these ingredients and he wants them to become part and parcel of our make-up.

What are these three qualities? To walk as the wise, to redeem the time available to us, and to understand the will of the Lord. He contrasts these attributes by saying do not walk as fools, realize the days and times are evil, and be not unwise.

Ruth Paxson provides insight for today regarding walking as the wise, not as fools saying, "[a]ll about us are the devil's snares and pitfalls. We walk in danger constantly then watch your step and know where the next step will lead you. We need to be scrupulously careful about every detail of our conduct, for nothing is trivial or unimportant. Our manner o f speech, fashion in clothes, companions in pleasure, use of time, choice of magazines and books, expenditure of money, are all indicative of the degree of supremacy of light over darkness in our lives. Strictest consistency in common things is obligatory, for we are taught to avoid every appearance of evil. We are to refrain from doing both that which could give rise to scandal and evil-speaking, and that which belies the sanctity of our life in Christ."

Paul says, understand that you are to *walk circumspectly* (accurately and carefully) as a wise person, *Redeeming the time, because the days are evil* [Eph. 5:16].

What does he mean by *redeeming the time*? He does not mean that you take a stamp or coupon and present it to someone who will provide you with a special allocation of time. The casual reader or the person reading it as part of Scripture may race by it and not give it a second glance. Someone else may say it is a peculiar thought to introduce at this point, or that it does not have any connection between walking accurately and carefully as a wise person and *understanding what the will of the Lord is*. However, it is an important connecting link.

First, we are to seize and make available the time to *walk circumspectly* and to *understand what the will of the Lord is*. People in Christ do this. Their platform for living will change, and they will allocate their time differently.

We are to remember Paul's admonition, *Only let your conversation* (tenor of life) *be as it becometh the gospel of Christ* [Phil. 1:27]. The word *conversation* in this verse is interpreted "Act as a citizen." Therefore, it should read, "Only let your actions be as it becometh the gospel of Christ."

Peter advises us as to how we are to use our time saying, *That he no longer should live the rest of his time in the flesh to the lusts of men, but to the will of God* [1 Pet. 4:2]. Then Peter compares life in the times past and says, *Who shall give account to him that is ready to judge the quick* (living) *and the dead* [1 Pet. 4:5].

Peter stresses that we are to become Christlike. It is by His Spirit that we become conformable to Him. We are to subdue the flesh and to live in the Spirit. Peter says we are to arm ourselves in order to effectively combat the forces of evil and do as Scripture says, *Redeeming the time, because the days are evil* [Eph. 5:16].

Peter reveals that right living depends upon knowing the will of God and living according to it, not by responding to the desires of the flesh. The Apostle urges us to become obedient to God and to no longer live according to the flesh. He reminds us that it would be foolish if we did not alter our lifestyle after being enlightened by Christ. Peter, as is also true of Paul, makes a definite distinction between the old person in the flesh and the new creature in Christ.

He lets us know that we have been redeemed and that we are to walk in the way of the Lord serving and obeying Him. We are to be strangers to the ways of the flesh, but followers of Christ in the spirit.

Paul makes it clear that walking circumspectly, as a wise person, is not happenstance or the luck of the draw. It requires study, prayer, meditation, consideration, and "above all an intimate knowledge with practical understanding of the Word of God," as declared by Ruth Paxson.

We are to have not only an *understanding of what the will of the Lord is* in general terms, but in the practical realities of daily living as we endeavor to walk as wise disciples of Christ. "Perhaps one of the greatest difficulties of the earnest Christian to-day is how to "walk as wise." He faces baffling and perplexing problems relating to his family, his business, his country, and his church. How is he to walk before some member of his family who willfully rejects the Lord, and because of this hates him and will have nothing to do with him? What is he to do if he has become a partner in business with one who professed to be sound in his Christian faith and yet practices dishonesty in business? . . . What is to be his attitude toward those in his church who have filled the house of prayer with tables of money-changers? How can he take the holy communion from the hands of a man who denies the deity of Christ and does [so] despite . . . the precious blood of which the wine he offers is the symbol? . . . How are Christian parents to keep the confidence of and fellowship with their children, and yet uphold the divine standard of separation from the world and of chastity of life when even so much in the teaching received in school and college cuts across home training? What is to be the answer of every truly Christian woman to the wholly unscriptural propaganda for birth control? . . . These are but a few of the innumerable problems earnest Christians face in present-day life. How are they to be solved? . . . Does God give us no light on these problems and no clue to their solution? He surely does, . . . and gives us a working basis for a walk in wisdom," as practically expressed by Ruth Paxson.

Why are we to redeem the time? First, for our own sake, and second, for others. Time is an important commodity. It is a precious thing in God's sight. Scripture tells us to use it, seize it, avail ourselves of it, and not to waste it.

We are to use the time to advantage, because the days are evil and there is evil all about us. Therefore, we are to leave the darkness and walk in the light. An excellent example of redeeming the time is the First Psalm. It contains spiritual as well as practical advice and instruction. It tells us what we are not to do and what will happen if we do them. The psalmist says we are to

> *... walketh not in the counsel of the ungodly* (wicked), *nor standeth in the way of the sinners, nor sitteth in the seat of the scornful.*
> *... the ungodly shall not stand in the judgment, nor sinners in the congregation of the righteous.*
> *... the way of the ungodly shall perish* [Ps. 1:1, 5–6].

But we are to delight in the law of the Lord and meditate on it day and night because the Lord knoweth the ways of the righteous. This is also seen in Peter's first letter:

> *Dearly beloved, I beseech you as strangers and pilgrims, abstain from fleshly lusts, which war against the soul;*
> *Having your conversation* (conduct) *honest* (honorable) *among the Gentiles: that, whereas they speak against you as evildoers, they may by your good works, which they shall behold, glorify God in the day of visitation* [1 Pet. 2:11–12].

We are not to waste our time with unworthy functions or harmful literature and associations. We are to provide the time for reading and studying the Bible and for praying. We are not to fritter time away.

We are to consider the words of our Master in the Sermon on the Mount,

> *Lay not up for yourselves treasures upon earth, where moth and rust doth corrupt* (ruin), *and where thieves break through and steal:*
> *But lay up for yourselves treasures in heaven, where neither moth nor rust doth corrupt, and where thieves do not break through nor steal:*
> *For where your treasure is, there will your heart be also* [Matt. 6:19–21].

We are not to have an insatiable desire for possessions or to satisfy lusts. We are to lay up treasures in heaven. We are to concern ourselves with the will of the Lord and the teachings of Christ. If we are persuaded that our happiness and joy are in our relationship to God then we will pursue those things and seek to attain them.

Paul expressed the same thoughts. He sought to lift up the followers of Christ and wanted them to have a zeal for the life in Him. Paul wants us to be in a right relationship with Christ, now, not sometime in the future. He adds emphasis by describing forthrightly what we are to do and not to do in the following statement:

> *. . . that now it is high time to awake out of sleep: for now is our salvation nearer than when we (first) believed.*
>
> *The night is far spent, the day is at hand: let us therefore cast off the works of darkness, and let us put on the armor of light.*
>
> *Let us walk honestly (properly), as in the day; not in rioting (revelry) and drunkenness, not in chambering (licentiousness) and wantonness (lewdness), not in strife and envying.*
>
> *But put ye on the Lord Jesus Christ, and make not provision for the flesh, to fulfill the lust thereof* [Rom. 13:11–14].

Paul concludes this portion of his letter to the Romans by issuing a command, a strong command to *put ye on the Lord Jesus Christ*.

In grasping the meaning of these verses and applying them, we are to understand them. Therefore, we are to: be alive and alert; be accurate and careful in what we do; honor the Lord Jesus Christ in all our actions and words; do not dishonor Him in any way; shake off the darkness of night which means ignorance of God; be in a right relationship to Christ, not alienated from Him; and receive the light, which is the divine truth. This means the light, knowledge, and revelation that reach the mind. When it is absent, man is incapable of receiving spiritual light, since he lacks the capability to receive spiritual things. Something is required to receive the light.

Believers are called the "sons of light" because they not only have received a revelation; but they have the capacity to understand it and apply it to their lives.

The Apostle says, *the day is at hand*. By this he means that we should begin to see the "Blessed splendour of the heavenly life," or as Calvin says, "life in a right relationship to God." What we see is the beginning of it. We should rejoice in it as we would in anticipation of a day filled with potential excitement, good times, and good fellowship.

When God calls us, we are to respond by focusing attention on Christ, His teachings, His life, and His person. We are to realize that the light of faith is at hand and respond in a positive manner.

Paul says, *put ye on the Lord Jesus Christ* [Rom. 13:14]. We are to become fit to discharge the "duties of holiness" as Calvin called them. Therefore, we are to be renewed, we are to *put on*, we are to become new creatures, and we are to act accordingly.

This is difficult, but we must place our confidence in the Lord. We are to provide for the needs of the flesh, but we are not to indulge in the lusts of the flesh. We must prepare for the future and recognize that one day we shall appear before the judgment seat of Christ.

How will we answer if the question is asked, "How did you spend your time?" We must realize what we are and who we are. John's words in his first letter are revealing and demanding. They are not to be taken lightly, as is evident when he says,

> BEHOLD, what manner of love the Father hath bestowed upon us, that we should be called the sons (children) of God: therefore the world knoweth us not, because it knew him not.
> Beloved, now are we the sons (children) of God, and it doth not yet appear what we shall be: but we know that, when he shall appear, we shall be like him; for we shall see him as he is.
> And every man that hath this hope in him purifieth himself, even as he is pure [1 John 3:1–3].

John stresses the fact that we will be transformed into the likeness of Christ at some time. In the meantime, we are to be diligent in pursuing the truth in Christ and in endeavoring to exhibit Christlike conduct and becoming holy. We are to act as children of light, not as children of darkness.

When the Apostle John says we will be like Him it does not mean that we will conform to Him as He is, because He is the Head and we are parts of the body. However, the Apostle wants the believers to know that the ultimate aim of our adoption as members of Christ's body is to conform to Him. What has first occurred in Christ shall be completed in us. We are to conform to the standards He has established and to which He commands obedience.

The second reason for redeeming the time is the impact it has on others. Have you ever heard comments made in a derogatory manner about church members who did something contrary to the teachings of Christ? Of course you have. The people of the world look for the professing Christian to stumble and fall.

They enjoy it when someone who used to be active in the church commits a crime or a significant misdeed. Then they can cast critical comments at the church, the Bible, God, and the Lord Jesus Christ. Since they do not know Scripture or the Lord Jesus Christ, they make judgments based upon what they see. This is a primary reason why we must be so careful, why we must walk circumspectly. This places a tremendous responsibility upon anyone who is a member of Christ's body, the church. We must live in such a way as to silence or eliminate criticism and in such a manner that we attract people and make them feel they are missing something.

This does not mean that we are to be the "Hail fellow, well met" sort, but it does mean that we are to exhibit certain traits, not only in our daily living but also over an extended period of time. We are to live an orderly and disciplined life. We are not to be erratic or inconsistent. "The Christian is a man who sees life steadily and he sees it whole, and therefore he is not erratic," as aptly stated by Matthew Arnold.

We are not to exhibit negative characteristics such as temper, anger, or lack of control. A person exhibiting these characteristics certainly does not recommend the life in Christ to others.

The real test is in what we are, how we act, and what we say. This is true in the tough, difficult times as well as in the good, easy days. The psalmist says, *He shall not be afraid of evil tidings: his heart is fixed* (steadfast), *trusting in the Lord* [Ps. 112:7]. No matter what the situation may be our heart is to be *fixed, trusting in the Lord*, and our foundation is to be on this rock.

Redeeming the time is a significant phrase. We are to use time carefully, judiciously, and in so doing recognize that time is a precious resource not to be squandered. It is also the link connecting us to *understanding what the will of the Lord is* [Eph. 5:17].

What does this mean? It does not mean we are to seek special guidance about everything we are going to say or do. However, we are to know what Scripture says. God provides the food, water, and directions for us to walk in wisdom and light. It is available if we will only open our hearts and minds to receive it. God makes the provisions available for our journey. Paul says to the Romans, *And be not conformed to this world: but be ye transformed by the renewing of your mind, that ye may prove what is that good, and acceptable, and perfect, will of God* [Rom. 12:2].

To know and understand the will of God requires seeking more and more knowledge about God and His Son in Scripture, in the exposition of Scripture, and in a close personal relationship with the Lord Jesus Christ. You cannot learn to swim without getting into the water. You cannot learn to cook without going into the kitchen.

God's will is revealed in His Word. Therefore, walking in the will of God requires walking in the whole of God's truth, not just in selected parts. His whole Word provides the principles and precepts for both our daily living and our journey through life. It contains examples, warnings, exhortations, commands, and motivating reasons. However, "understanding God's will requires the systematic, prayerful study of God's Word under the tutelage of the Holy Spirit, . . . to open the eyes of our understanding and to enlighten us," as clearly stated by Ruth Paxson.

We need to ask ourselves:

> Are we studying Scripture?
> Are we walking with Him?
> Are we walking circumspectly?
> Are we *redeeming the time*?
> Are we *understanding what the will of the Lord is*?

Remember, we are to be imitators of God, to *walk as children of light, according to the wisdom of God, not man.*

Amen!

11

The Reality of the Spirit

> *And be not drunk with wine, wherein is excess* (dissipation), *but be filled with the Spirit;*
> *Speaking to yourselves in psalms and hymns and spiritual songs, singing and making melody in your heart to the Lord;*
> *Giving thanks always for all things unto God and the Father in the name of our Lord Jesus Christ;*
> *Submitting yourselves one to another in the fear of God* [Eph. 5:18–21].

During his three years in Ephesus, the Apostle Paul visited the members in their homes. Probably, when doing this he was accompanied by some of his followers. This would give them the opportunity to discuss the things closest to their hearts and minds, namely the Gospel of our Lord Jesus Christ. They would have dialogue as they walked or visited in different homes. Therefore, it is natural for Paul to say, *I THEREFORE, . . . beseech you that ye walk worthy of the vocation* (calling) *wherewith ye are called* [Eph. 4:1].

So far this walk has examined five very important areas: unity, holiness, love, light, and wisdom. These are to be the characteristics of our walk with the Lord Jesus. Now we come to the sixth point, to walk in praise. We are to be filled with the Spirit so that we will continually praise God.

Paul was a most remarkable person after his conversion. He undertook a demanding, extensive period of studying the ministry and teachings of the Lord Jesus Christ. Then he began his ministry. He was an evangelist and a preacher who founded churches. He was a theologian and teacher who visited the members of the churches. He was kind, tenderhearted, and forgiving, and he loved his relationship with the Lord Jesus Christ. He applied Christ's teachings to his daily living in proclaiming the Gospel. Paul did what he said we are to do.

One of Paul's traits was that he never approached different situations in Christian living without first considering Christ's teachings. Therefore, Paul begins this section (Eph. 5:18–Eph 6:9) by saying, *be filled with the Spirit*. He reminds the followers in Ephesus that they are to live "a life in the spirit."

Paul begins this section with a vivid contrast. After exhorting us to be wise, to walk circumspectly, to redeem the time, and to understand the will of the Lord, he says, *And be not drunk with wine, wherein is excess* (dissipation); *but be filled with the Spirit*. Note, how the sentence continues,

> *Speaking to yourselves in psalms and hymns and spiritual songs, singing and making melody in your heart to the Lord;*
> *Giving thanks always for all things unto God and the Father in the name of our Lord Jesus Christ;*
> *Submitting yourselves one to another in the fear of God.*

That is the whole sentence. That is the transition from unity, holiness, love, light, and wisdom to praising God. That is the foundation for talking to us about marriage, home, and work.

Remember, we are new creatures in Christ, and Paul is writing to the members of Christ's body. You cannot take the second step until you take the first one; you cannot take the 100th step until you take the 99th one.

This admonition, *be not drunk with wine, wherein is excess* (dissipation), is not the basis for a temperance sermon. It is not the Apostle's sole intention to denounce drinking or offensive public displays, though that is part of the statement. Paul describes the positive aspects of the life in Christ. He emphasizes not only the proper conduct but the resulting joy from being filled with the Spirit.

When examining this verse, be aware of the hidden meanings, those beneath the surface. It is true that people of the ancient world, as well as the modern one, were guilty of excessive drinking to the point of drunkenness and debauchery. Now that they are members of Christ's body, they are no longer to be filled with wine, or indulge in riotous or wasted living. At Pentecost people thought some of the followers were drunk with wine. But Luke says, *And they were all filled with the Holy Ghost* [Acts 2:4].

The Greek word for *filled* in Acts 2:4 and in Ephesians 5:18 is exactly the same. It is *plethō* and it means "to be filled," "to be made full," "to be filled up." The Greek word for being drunk is *methuskō*. It means to begin "to soften." It is the process of becoming intoxicated. The Apostle says, do not become softened, weakened, or intoxicated with wine, but be filled with the Spirit.

What is the contrast? The person who becomes drunk usually exhibits one or more of the following traits: "loss of self-control; stimulated by a false and temporary excitement; a nature marked by false pleasure; a personality marked by Jekyll & Hyde traits; affecting negatively the strength of the mind and the will to function properly; and often times leads to "moral, mental and physical disorders," as expressed by Ruth Paxson. Paul opposed conduct seeking a temporary thrill or a fleeting "good time," resulting in leaving the mind and body in a disheveled state or desperate straits.

On the contrary, Paul wants us filled with the Holy Spirit. He wants the best for the Ephesians. He is not asking them to abstain from alcohol, to straighten up and fly right. He wants the best for them; he wants them to know the truth; and he wants them to live on the highest plain. It is the Holy Spirit that makes this possible.

We are to be filled with the Spirit. Paul prays for the Ephesians *to know the love of Christ, which passesth knowledge, that ye might be filled with all the fullness of God* [Eph. 3:19]. Further, he tells them, *Till we all come in* (into) *the unity of the faith, and of the knowledge of the Son of God, unto a perfect* (mature) *man, unto the measure of the stature of the fullness of Christ* [Eph. 4:13]. Why does Paul place so much emphasis upon being filled with the Spirit, *being filled with all the fullness of God*, and being filled with *the fullness of Christ*? Because he is speaking about a fullness that acts positively and provides Christ's followers with self-control, a joyful heart, and a faithful relationship with God.

There is a contrast between being drunk with wine in excess and being filled with the Holy Spirit. The person who is drunk is incapable of performing even the basic functions required, while the person filled with the Spirit is able to perform in a fruitful and productive manner.

The person being softened or intoxicated with wine is someone who will give himself or herself over to the influence of a negative factor, whereas the Spirit-filled person is someone who has self-control because he or she has voluntarily succumbed to the Holy Spirit.

The person who is drunk cannot disguise or hide his or her condition to very many people. To be drunk or under the influence of alcohol implies a craving that can be satisfied by only one more glass. However, to be filled with the Spirit means thirsting for the "living waters."

There is one contrast that drives home this point with considerable clarity. The drunkard keeps craving wine or alcohol, while the member of Christ's body keeps craving the living water. That is a significant difference. Paul says, *And be not drunk with wine, wherein is excess* (dissipation). The Greek word for *excess* in this verse is *asōtia*, and it means "recklessness," "prodigality," and "riotous living."

Recall the parable of the prodigal son. Jesus says, *and there wasted his substance* (possessions) *in riotous living* [Luke 15:13] in referring to the younger son. Guess what? The same Greek word used for "riotous" by Luke is used for "excess" in Ephesians 5:18. Isn't that interesting?

What about the person filled with the Spirit? What traits does he or she exhibit? First, they live a controlled, orderly life. Paul, writing to Timothy, says, *For God hath not given us the spirit of fear; but of power, and of love, and of a sound mind* [2 Tim. 1:7]. The person who is a member of Christ's body should realize the power that is available, the love that is available, and the sound mind (self-control) that is available.

Second, the person filled with the Spirit leads a productive life. "He is the exact opposite of the Prodigal Son," as noted by Martyn Lloyd-Jones. He does not squander his time, money, or talent. He uses them to serve the Lord Jesus Christ.

Third, the person who is in Christ conserves what is available. He or she builds up and adds to their own resources. This makes one aware of the *unsearchable riches of Christ*. It preserves what is best in an individual and allows him or her to produce beneficial results.

This person is a good and just steward. He is able to take care of the items entrusted to his care. He recognizes his responsibilities and seeks to discharge them. "He is a steward, not only of his money but of everything else," as stated by Martyn Lloyd-Jones.

The person filled with the Spirit does not become exhausted. While in contrast, the person who drinks to excess becomes exhausted. He or she is not able to function effectively, let alone to capacity.

The Holy Spirit infuses us with power and strength. There are times when my strength has ebbed away, but not from excess wine. On those occasions the Holy Spirit strengthened me. It was not my doing.

Therefore, we can say with confidence that while excess drink exhausts a person, the spirit energizes him or her.

There is a point in our lives when we should acknowledge, accept, and express in our daily living, that life in the Spirit is a positive, productive life filled with joy and gladness. Too often people get hung up on the negatives when studying the teachings contained in the New Testament and overlook the positives. The Apostle Paul uses contrasts and always states the positives.

He wants us to know and to do the positives because they are beneficial and reflect Christ's teachings. The knowledgeable person will say, "No, do not do it that way; do it this way." That is true of cooking, working, athletics, dancing, or whatever you may be doing. The life in the Spirit is not a list of prohibitions, but a list of positive injunctions producing beneficial results.

Before proceeding, please note that the life in Christ is not one of morality, or ethics, or standards. The preaching and teaching of these items as being Christian is a contradiction of the New Testament. Matthew Arnold sums it up accurately and succinctly, stating, "It has been the preaching of the good life, of being a good little gentleman, and of viewing religion as morality touched by emotion that has been the curse." Such men shed and, in many respects, shred the truths contained in Christ's teachings. They dislike the idea of man's sinful nature, the atonement, the virgin birth, becoming and being new creatures, the shed blood on the Cross, and Christ's death and resurrection.

What other characteristics of the life filled with the Spirit are contrasts to the life soaked with excess wine? The life filled with the Spirit is stimulating and exhilarating, not depressing. Alcohol and wine serve as depressants. The Holy Spirit stimulates the mind and intellect as well as the heart and will. On the contrary, excess wine depresses the mind and intellect. Further, it does not move the heart in a positive manner, and it paralyzes the will.

There is more to discover, more to learn, more to apply, and more ways to improve. The walk becomes increasingly joyful; there is less of self and more of Christ, and there is more about which to be thankful. The life filled with the Spirit is joyful.

Think, can you name anyone who is not interested in being happy or living a joyful life? That is why you see so many people turning to activities, to excess wine. They are searching for something. Unfortunately, they do not turn in the direction they should or search in the places where they will find joy.

Probably one of the best descriptions is found in Philippians. We have considered it before, but it is worth re-visiting.

> *Rejoice in the Lord always: and again I say, Rejoice.*
> *Let your moderation be known unto all men. The Lord is at hand.*
> *Be careful* (anxious) *for nothing; but in every thing by prayer and supplication with thanksgiving let your requests be made known unto God.*
> *And the peace of God, which passeth all understanding, shall keep* (guard) *your hearts and minds through Christ Jesus* [Phil. 4:4–7].

Paul wrote to people having a difficult, tough time. They had experienced defeats, losses, and suffering. He was aware of their circumstances and concerns, but he did not commiserate with them. He exhorted them. He showed them that spiritual joy will mitigate and even overcome bitterness and sorrow. Calvin says it may seem, "somewhat inconsistent that the faithful at the same time exult joy and are sorrowful."

However, those filled with the Spirit know that these traits coexist. "People do not exist or stand around, as a potted plant," as Ollie North's attorney said. They have feelings, they are affected by sorrow, dangers, persecutions, castigations, poverty, and assorted evils. Yet being filled with the Spirit mitigates the impact and enables them to rejoice.

Although joy overcomes these things, it does not eliminate them. It enables people to focus upon and to recognize God's blessings, especially when they realize how He has blessed them, strengthened them, and enabled them to walk with the Lord Jesus Christ.

Peter stated it so beautifully, *Whom having not seen, ye love; in whom, though now ye see him not, yet believing, ye rejoice with joy unspeakable and full of glory* [1 Pet. 1:8]. Jesus said near the close of His ministry, *but I will see you again, and your heart shall rejoice, and your joy no man taketh from you* [John 16:22b].

The Scripture being considered contains two commands, spoken with equal authority and persistence. No one is exempt. The one is negative, the other is positive. *And be not drunk with wine, wherein is excess* (dissipation); *but be filled with the Spirit.* It is not a one-time command, but a continuing one. It is not optional whether we obey or not. It is obligatory.

One thing needs to be made clear: being filled with the Spirit is not an experience marked by emotion. It is a joyous experience that proceeds step by step. It produces the fruit of the Spirit. "It makes for a sound mind, a radiant heart and a poised spirit," as declared by Ruth Paxson. It strengthens us, controls us, energizes us, stimulates us, makes us joyful, and allows us to praise Him as we continue our daily walk forward and upward.

Amen!

12

Being Filled With the Spirit

And be not drunk with wine, wherein is excess (dissipation); *but be filled with the Spirit* [Eph. 5:18].

There are certain things to bear in mind as we continue walking through Ephesians: when Paul first arrived in Ephesus, he asked, *Have ye received* (did you receive) *the Holy Ghost since* (when) *ye believed* [Acts 19:2]? He talked about the Holy Ghost; he spent nearly three years in Ephesus; and during his last meeting with the Ephesian elders at Miletus, he exhorted them to *Take heed therefore unto yourselves, and to all the flock, over which the Holy Ghost hath made you overseers, to feed* (shepherd) *the church of God, which he hath purchased with his own blood* [Acts 20:28].

Paul instructs them to keep watch over the affairs of the church. He stresses that they were not ordained by men, but by God through men. Further, the care of the church has been committed to them. They are *to feed* (shepherd) *the church of God,* but they are to feed it in a special way, with the teachings of Christ.

Calvin eloquently describes this special way saying, "God is cheated" of His glory if we think that the Gospel is given to us either by chance, or by the will or activity of men." Paul knew that the Gospel is provided through the Holy Spirit by God. He knew that men could and would stray. Therefore, he urged them to be diligent, to beware of the grievous wolves that would attack.

There are those who seek to work and influence the life of the church, but they ignore Scripture. They are more comfortable with the ways of the world and their secular experiences, so that is what they proclaim and seek to impose. When recognizing this, it is easier to understand Paul saying *be filled with the spirit*. He wants us under the power and control of the Holy Spirit.

Recall what precedes and follows our Scripture:

> *Put off the old man, Put on the new man;*
> *Renewed in the spirit of your mind;*
> *Walk in love;*
> *Let no man deceive you with vain (empty) words;*
> *Proving what is acceptable unto the Lord;*
> *Christ shall give thee light;*
> *Walk circumspectly (carefully), as wise, redeeming the time; and*
> *Understanding what the will of the Lord is.*
> [Selections from Chapters 4 and 5 of Ephesians]

We are called to a living faith in Christ, not to a religion. We are not involved in a religion. We are involved in a personal relationship with the Son of God.

Oswald Chambers writes with pinpoint accuracy and understanding, "The essential thing is my personal relationship to Jesus Christ—that I may know him. To fulfill God's design means complete abandonment to Him. Whenever I want things for myself, the relationship is distorted. It will be a big humiliation to realize that I have not been concerned about realizing Jesus Christ, but only about realizing what He has done for me."

Paul says the way to deal with the conditions or situations encountered in daily living is to *be filled with the Spirit*. He says that as members of Christ's body they are to address things differently, they are to act and react in a different manner. May we reach the point of maturity where we say, "My goal is God Himself, not joy nor peace, Nor even blessing, but Himself, my God," as beautifully and meaningfully stated by an unknown author. Therefore, we need to give further consideration to being *filled with the Spirit*. We are no longer what we once were. We are not to conduct ourselves as we once did. "Them things do not belong to a Christian."

Paul does not say, act as a Christian; he does not say, adopt a moral code or the ethics of a so-called Christian. No, no, no! He says *be filled with the Spirit*—that is the way to deal with the situations encountered in our daily living and the difficulties or problems that come our way. He tells us that once we are members of Christ's body, new creatures, we are to address things differently and respond differently to whatever comes our way, day in and day out.

What does the New Testament espouse? A social gospel? Applying ethics? Establishing standards? Being involved in activities or politics? How to get rid of armaments? None of the above! That is neither the theology of the New Testament, nor is it according to the practice of the early church.

Have you noticed any such proclamations in the first nine chapters of Acts or in the letters of Paul, John, and Peter? No, you have not, and you will not. What is emphasized in the first nine chapters of Acts? The emphasis is on conversions; the Holy Ghost; receiving power; obedience; continuing steadfastly in the apostles' doctrine, in fellowship, in breaking bread, and in prayers; being filled with the Holy Ghost; preaching the Gospel; and repentance. It includes this beautiful, meaningful verse: *Repent ye therefore, and be converted, that your sins may be blotted out, when the times of refreshing shall come from the presence of the Lord* [Acts 3:19].

We are to be refreshed when in the presence of the Lord. We are to recognize and be aware of the fact that we are in His presence. The early church emphasized being in the presence of the Lord Jesus Christ and having complete faith in Him.

The New Testament emphasizes preaching the pure Gospel. Why? Because when the Gospel and only the Gospel is preached, then people are converted. And when people are converted they act differently and they think differently. Preaching against wars and armaments and numerous other things does not convert anyone, but preaching and teaching the Gospel of the Lord Jesus Christ does.

What has this to do with the power of the Spirit? There is a great deal of talk in the modern world about Christian ethics, codes, morals, and standards. Further, that they are needed and people should adopt them. However, one important point needs to be considered. To whom did Christ present His teachings, to whom were the apostles writing? The followers, the members of Christ's body, not the people on the outside, not to those who had not or have not accepted the Lord Jesus Christ. A person who does not have a personal relationship with the Lord Jesus Christ cannot conduct himself or herself according to the teachings and commands of the Master.

Martyn Lloyd-Jones proclaimed, "You cannot live the life of the Kingdom of God until you have entered the Kingdom of God. You cannot share the life of the kingdom of God without being a citizen of that Kingdom. So it is wrong to talk to men who are outside the Kingdom (about) living the life of the Kingdom; it is a contradiction of the whole of the New Testament teachings. There is no greater denial of the Christian faith than just that."

What does Scripture say about the person outside the kingdom of God? The person outside the kingdom is dead in sins and trespasses, governed according to lusts and desires, selfish and self-centered, unjust and unrighteous. We need to understand this and to have knowledge of the type of person outside the body of Christ. Further, we need to understand what we are like when we are not members of the kingdom and when we do not conduct ourselves as having a personal relationship with the Lord Jesus.

We need to understand that man is not fundamentally all right by himself or through his own efforts. Further, his troubles are not due to the fact that he or she is a victim of circumstances or an environment. When people realize their real need is a right relationship with God, then they will accept the need not only to be filled with the Holy Spirit but to be continually filled with it. Man cannot accomplish things on his own. That is why the Spirit is necessary.

It is not a case of Christian ethics, moral codes, or standards. But it is a case of being a new creature, putting on the new man, and being in the right relationship to God and the Lord Jesus. That is why it is necessary to *be filled with the Spirit* and to have that power available.

If man could accomplish things on his own, then undoubtedly for the last two thousand years many more people would have adopted and followed the teachings contained in the Sermon on the Mount. Why have people not accepted and implemented the teachings contained in the Sermon on the Mount? They cannot because of sin. To implement those teachings requires being a member of the Kingdom of God plus the presence and power of the Holy Ghost.

What does the New Testament have to say about the Holy Ghost? That we need Him, that God through Christ makes Him available, that God realized our real, definite need for the Holy Ghost in our daily living; and that He provided Him, the Comforter.

The Holy Spirit is sent to regenerate people, to give them a new nature. We are to be filled with the Spirit so we can properly live our lives in marriage, the home, and workplace by being in a right relationship to God. Without the Spirit it is impossible.

There is only one way for a person to be a member of Christ's body, to be a Christian. He must be filled with the Spirit and have its power functioning in his or her daily life. Man, meaning you and me, needs to be changed. There is only one way for that to happen, by the intervention of the Holy Spirit.

What is the difference between being baptized with the Spirit and being filled with the Spirit? The Apostle says, *in whom also after that ye believed, ye were sealed with that holy Spirit of promise* [Eph. 1:13]. Later he says, *whereby ye are sealed unto the day of redemption* [Eph. 4:30]. Paul says they were sealed with the Holy Spirit. It was a specific act, and it occurred one time. We should know that we have been sealed.

Take heed of what the Lord Jesus says, *But ye shall receive power, after that* (when) *the Holy Ghost is come upon you: and ye shall be witnesses unto me both in Jerusalem, and in all Judea, and in Samaria, and unto the uttermost part of the earth* [Acts 1:8]. Note he says, *ye shall receive power . . . and ye shall be witnesses unto me* [Acts 1:8]. Some will ask since it says they were filled with the Holy Ghost, why are we exhorted by Paul to *be filled with the Spirit*? Scripture says they were filled with the Holy Ghost, received power from Him, and witnessed unto the Lord Jesus Christ.

The Reformed tradition accepts and believes in the Sacrament of Baptism, and in God's blessing of being sealed with the Spirit. They are two separate and distinct acts. In addition, there is the continuous, repetitive process of being filled with the Spirit as members of Christ's body.

Consider what happened to the Apostle Paul after his encounter with the Lord Jesus on the way to Damascus and then going into Damascus. The Lord Jesus appeared unto Ananias and told him to go to Saul of Tarsus. Ananias objected, but the Lord Jesus said,

> Go thy way: for he is a chosen vessel unto me, to bear my name before the Gentiles, and kings, and the children of Israel:
> And Ananias went his way, and entered into the house . . . and said, Brother Saul, the Lord, even Jesus, that appeared unto thee in the way as thou camest, hath sent me, that thou mightest receive thy sight, and be filled with the Holy Ghost

> ... *and he* (Paul) *received sight forthwith, and arose, and was baptized.*
> *And when he had received meat* (food), *he was strengthened* [Selections from Acts 9:15, 17–19].

Paul was filled with the Holy Ghost, received his sight, was baptized and strengthened. It was Ananias who laid his hands upon Paul.

After Paul was filled with the Spirit, he received his sight. He learned, "that the true light must not be sought anywhere else but from Christ, and is not conferred in any other way but by His favor," according to John Calvin.

Paul's desire to learn is emphasized by his action. He did not eat any food until he had been baptized. He wanted his soul to be invigorated before he began restoring his body. Oh, that we could be like that! Later it says, *Then Saul* (who also *is called* Paul) *filled with the Holy Ghost, set his eyes on* (looked intently at) *him* [Acts 13:9].

Paul was filled with the Spirit in order that he might rebuke "*Elymas the sorcerer . . . child of the devil*" [Acts 13:8, 10]. Paul was aware of the fact that the Spirit had come upon him and that he could speak with authority, because he had power and control. Being filled with the Spirit is a state or condition. It is best seen in the life of Christ.

> *AND Jesus being full of the Holy Ghost* (Spirit) *returned from Jordan, and was led by the Spirit into the wilderness.* [Luke 4:1]

> *For he whom God hath sent speaketh the words of God: for God giveth not the Spirit by measure unto Him* [John 3:34].

Jesus was always filled with the Spirit in all its fullness. There are other instances in the New Testament of being full of the Holy Ghost and being filled with the Spirit. It was true of individuals like Stephen, Barnabas, Peter, and Paul. It was also true of the disciples: *The disciples were filled with joy, and with the Holy Ghost* [Acts 13:52]. Therefore, we too should believe and boldly claim that we can be full of the Holy Ghost and that we can be filled for a special task or purpose.

When talking about being full of the Holy Ghost or being filled with the Spirit we must carefully think of it in the context of the New Testament. The Holy Spirit is a person. It is not a substance or a liquid, nor is it like electricity. The Holy Spirit is the Third Person of the Holy Trinity. Therefore, being filled with the Holy Spirit is being under His influence.

According to Thayer's Greek Lexicon, "to be full" is a condition in which what "Wholly takes possession of the mind is said to fill it," according to Lloyd-Jones. You have known people so engrossed in a subject or hobby that it occupied most of their time and conversation. Therefore, you said they were full of that topic or hobby.

Paul states we are to be under the influence of the Holy Spirit and that our heart, mind, and will are to be controlled by Him, the Holy Ghost. How is this accomplished? First, Scripture states, *What? know ye not that your body is the temple of the Holy Ghost which is in you, which ye have of God, and ye are not your own* [1 Cor. 6:19]? Do not forget this!

Second, remember that Jesus said, *I will not leave you comfortless* (orphans)*: I will come to you* [John 14:18]. Jesus is not going to leave us. He is going to be with us, day in and day out. The way to be controlled by the Holy Spirit is to remember that He is there. He is ever present. He will be a gracious and willing guest as long as we remember Him and welcome Him. We must do this actively and deliberately.

Next, we must have fellowship and communion with Him. Remember Paul's benediction to the Corinthians: *The grace of the Lord Jesus Christ, and the love of God, and the communion* (fellowship) *of the Holy Ghost, be with you all* [2 Cor. 13:14]. We are to remind ourselves constantly of this communion and to actively seek it. We are to have fellowship and communion with Him.

We are to obey Him, be girded by Him, respond positively to His directions, listen to His counsel, heed His exhortations, and have a personal relationship with Him. There is no shortcut in doing these things. It requires work, effort, time, listening, meditating, doing, and struggling. But it is worth all this and then some!

The Holy Spirit provides the Word. He is pleased when we come to know it and when we put it into practice. He wants the teachings of Christ to govern our actions, behavior, conduct, decisions, and the whole of our life. However, if we do not know Him, if we are not full of Him, this cannot happen.

> *Choose you this day whom ye will serve, . . . but as for me and my house, we will serve the Lord* [Josh. 24:15].

Amen!

13

Giving Thanks Always

Speaking to yourselves in psalms and hymns and spiritual songs, singing and making melody in your heart to the Lord;
Giving thanks always for all things unto God and the Father in the name of our Lord Jesus Christ [Eph. 5:19–20].

Language is most interesting. It comes in numerous varieties. It is formal and informal. There is spoken language, the written word, and body language. It can mean one thing to one person, and something entirely different to someone else. There is intent and interpretation.

I could travel to Europe and spend time on the continent, but I might not know what people are saying. I could listen attentively, but if the people were speaking to me in German, French, or Italian, I would not understand what they were saying. It is important to know the language. Also, it is important to know what certain people mean by the words or expressions they use.

Webster's definition is revealing. It says language is "the words, their pronunciation and the methods of combining them as used and understood by a considerable community." Also, language is "a systematic means of communicating ideas or feelings."

What does this have to do with the nineteenth and twentieth verses of the fifth chapter of Ephesians? First, we need to know how Paul was communicating with the Ephesians. Second, we need to know the hidden meanings contained in the words he used.

The Apostle starts the sentence beginning with the eighteenth verse saying, *And be not drunk with wine, wherein is excess* (dissipation); *but be filled with the Spirit* [Eph. 5:18].

Then he continues the sentence saying,

> *Speaking to yourselves in psalms and hymns and spiritual songs, singing and making melody in your heart to the Lord;*
> *Giving thanks always for all things unto God and the Father in the name of our Lord Jesus Christ.*

Note, he said *be filled with the Spirit*, before he said, *Speaking . . . singing and making melody . . .* (and) *Giving thanks always for all things unto God and the Father in the name of our Lord Jesus Christ.*

What is so complicated about that language? What possibly could be hidden in those words? It tells us how we are to speak amongst ourselves, that we are to have a melody in our hearts, and that we are to give thanks for all things, always.

Since the Apostle has said these things, some would now say, let's proceed to hear what else he is going to say. Wait a minute. Let's pause and see what the Holy Spirit has to say. Probably you remember the advertising phrase, "Coke, the pause that refreshes."

A friend of mine, Cook Freeman, would say, "When reading Scripture, pause and let it speak to you, let the Holy Spirit work within your mind and reveal the truths contained in the written word." What sage advice!

There are times when Scripture jumps out at you. There are other times when it slowly builds up a head of steam like the old railroad locomotives, and there are other times when we need to ask, why is it there? What is it saying? Where is the writer coming from? How can I learn from this? For the Holy Spirit to illuminate our minds, we must be willing to open them, to know what was true of the early followers and what happened during the first century.

First, go back and recall Luke's account of the events at the end of Chapter 2 in Acts. The people had heard Peter preaching the Gospel and their hearts *were pricked*. Do you know what that means? It means a lot more than a little prick on a finger or toe that evaporates in a few seconds or minutes. Their hearts were stabbed; they were pierced through. They were stunned by the message. Their minds were motivated positively. It was to have a lasting impact on them. And they reacted by saying, *What shall we do* [Acts 2:37]?

What were they told to do? They were told to repent; to be baptized in the name of Jesus Christ for the remission of sins; and to save themselves from this untoward, crooked, perverse generation. It should be noted that though *they were pricked* (stabbed) *in their hearts*, they responded in obedience. A humble and contrite heart is an acceptable sacrifice to God.

Peter told them they would *receive the gift of the Holy Spirit* from Christ because the promise of God is unto them and their children. "We must always pay attention to this, that the will of God is made known to us in no other manner than by His Word," as clearly stated by John Calvin. Therefore, we are to know the Word not only in a general sense but in detail, how it applies to us as individuals and what is required. We are to understand that salvation is ours, because the promise it offers applies to us.

What did these people do after they repented, were baptized, and received the Holy Spirit? They continued steadfastly in the apostles' doctrine and fellowship, in the breaking of bread, and in prayers.

Note that Luke puts the apostles' doctrine and fellowship first. He is showing those actions by which the early church was known and how it witnessed to the community at large. They had become members of Christ's body; therefore, they learned doctrine, Christ's teachings, and they had fellowship with each other. Also, there was the breaking of bread. This means celebrating the Lord's Supper because of its language, because the events were visible to other people, and because of Christ's command. However, Luke begins with doctrine because that is the heart and soul of the community of believers. The apostles' doctrine is that body of truth, which was given to the apostles by the Lord Jesus Christ.

There is a significant observation to make about the church throughout the past two thousand years. Where the Gospel is proclaimed as it was in the first century and where people apply themselves to hearing it, that is where the living Christ is present and where the true church will be found. It takes these two things: proclaiming the Word; and applying the Word.

There is another significant reason the early followers continued in the breaking of bread. They believed and knew that in so doing the living Christ was present with them. Third, they continued steadfastly in prayers.

Probably you have questions regarding the verse, *And all that believed were together, and had all things common* [Acts 2:44]. When considering this verse you must do so in its context and in the context of the New Testament. It says, *All that believed were together.* They were in agreement about the doctrine, the breaking of bread, and the prayers. *And the multitude of them that believed were of one heart and of one soul* [Acts 4:32]. The fruit of their commitment was that they helped one another, they helped the poor, and they helped those in need. They were united, and they gave of themselves.

They did not hold their children in common, nor did they hold their husbands or wives in common. What they held in common was the apostles' doctrine and fellowship, the breaking of the bread, the presence of the Lord Jesus Christ, and their prayers.

Recall Luke's words,

> *And they, continuing daily with one accord* (mind) *in the temple, and breaking bread from house to house, did eat their meat* (food) *with gladness and singleness* (simplicity) *of heart,*
> *Praising God, and having favor with all the people. And the Lord added to the church daily such as should be* (were being) *saved* [Acts 2:46–47].

They were learning doctrine. They were growing in their relationship to the Lord Jesus Christ. They continued in the breaking of bread at home. When families were by themselves or were with others, they were aware of the presence of the Lord Jesus Christ. They were glad and joyful. They realized that dangers may present themselves, but they praised God for their blessings, for His Son, and for His Holy Spirit.

What happened to the early church? *The Lord added daily to the church such as should be* (were being) *saved* [Acts 2:47]. There is nothing magical about adding to the church rolls. It is by doing what the early church did: proclaim the Gospel; prick (stab) their hearts; teach doctrine; repent and be baptized; continue in breaking the bread; realize the presence of the living God; receive the gift of the Holy Spirit; and praise God for all His blessings and gifts.

What kind of programs do we need? The first century commitment and programs. What is known about the first century Christians with respect to psalms, hymns, and spiritual songs? By spiritual songs Paul meant those songs that were revealed by the Spirit, which contained wisdom and understanding about God and His Son.

The early congregations were known for their singing and joyful worship. Yes, they sang the Psalms and hymns, but also they composed new spiritual songs. Their singing supported one another in their worship services. It had a special place in the service, and it enhanced their faith, love, joy, and obedience. It was an expression of witnessing to one another, not just for each individual's enjoyment and satisfaction. They were joyful believers.

I shall never forget the impact during the noon service on Tuesdays at the First Presbyterian Church in Pittsburgh, when 1,400 to 1,500 men would sing together and witness to each other. It was awesome! It was compelling! It was uplifting!

Thomas Aquinas taught that singing in the worship service addressed itself to three persons: to God, to one's neighbor, and to one's self. John Calvin taught that we are not just to sing unto ourselves, but our singing is to praise God and in so doing to edify one another. Pliny the Younger confirms the accounts in Acts and the book of The Revelation about the early congregations singing Psalms and hymns "to Christ as to God." This confirms the fact that they wrote new songs to Christ and about Christ.

D.M. Stanley notes that there are three types of hymns in the New Testament: enthronement hymns, servant hymns praising Christ's suffering and glorification, and son of man hymns. Certainly, psalms, hymns, and spiritual songs had a positive impact upon the worship service and daily living of Christ's early followers, as noted in the following Scripture:

> *Let the word of Christ dwell in you richly in all wisdom; teaching and admonishing one another in psalms and hymns and spiritual songs, singing with grace in your hearts to the Lord.*
> *And whatsoever ye do in word or deed, do all in the name of the Lord Jesus, giving thanks to God and the Father by him* [Col. 3:16–17].

It is important to remind ourselves frequently as to how Christ's Word is to dwell within each of us.

> *Let the word of Christ dwell in you richly in all wisdom; teaching and admonishing one another in psalms and hymns and spiritual songs, singing with grace in your hearts to the Lord* [Col. 3:16].

The teaching of the Gospel is to be as familiar to the members of the church as it was to the early followers. These teachings are to be profitable and useful for instruction.

Paul, writing to the Colossians, specifies psalms, hymns, and spiritual songs or odes. In the early church, a psalm was usually sung to the accompaniment of a musical instrument, a hymn was a song of praise, and a spiritual song or ode contained praises and exhortations. The Apostle in Colossians appeals to our intellects, wills, and total beings. We are to sing with our hearts, minds, and souls to God and to praise His name. When we do we will witness to each other.

Return once again to the verse which says, *Giving thanks always for all things unto God and the Father in the name of our Lord Jesus Christ.* This is a direct command, not a request. We are not to think about it, we are to do it. There are things for which I find it difficult to give thanks. But I am supposed to do so and to do it in all things. That is difficult.

The renowned theologian, John Calvin, expounds upon the phrase, *Giving thanks always* saying, "He (Paul) means that this is a pleasure which ought never to bore us by custom; an exercise of which we ought never to weary. The innumerable benefits which we receive from God yield fresh cause of joy and thanksgiving. At the same time, he warns believers, that it will be ungodly and disgraceful laziness, if they shall not all through their life study and practise the praises of God."

The New Testament often enjoins believers to give thanks and to express thankfulness to God. We see it in this twentieth verse as well as in other parts of the New Testament:

> *Be careful* (anxious) *for nothing; but in every thing by prayer and supplication with thanksgiving let your requests be made known unto God* [Phil. 4:6].

> *Rooted and built up in him, and established in the faith, as ye have been taught, abounding therein with thanksgiving* [Col. 2:7].

> *In every thing give thanks: for this is the will of God in Christ Jesus concerning you* [1 Thess. 5:18].

We are to rejoice in all things and to continuously give thanks to God for His blessings, gifts, and watchful care as we proceed through life walking with Jesus.

Also, you are aware of the fact that Paul often begins his letters by giving thanks. The giving of thanks is not meant to be merely words, or a perfunctory" thank you," or "Gee, thanks." It is to be seen in one's daily living; it is to be the main spring in providing service and the right motive behind it.

How are we to express our thanks to God? By presenting our lives to Him and being obedient unto His commands. Obedience to the will of God does not earn our salvation. However, it should be an expression of our gratitude to Him. It can be only a token of our thanks, since our obedience can never equal our indebtedness. Thankfulness should be a real motive for our acts, our thoughts, and our words.

"Every real Christian gives thanks sometimes, but who gives thanks always, for all things? Every true Christian gives thanks for some things, but who could give thanks for all things, including, as it may, sickness, financial loss, sorrow and troubles of various kinds? It seems an impossible standard. But, if we know of even one life in which there is perpetual thanksgiving in the midst of unceasing suffering then that proves the possibility. Last night I read a page in the August Moody Monthly which told the story and showed the picture of the radiant face of Lloyd Jensen of Sunshine corner." I quote from the story hoping it will interpret to you, as it did to me, the meaning of the word "always." Dr. Lockyer writes:

"I was shown into a room of indescribable physical anguish, which I have elected to name 'Sunshine Corner.' And I shall never cease to praise God for what that visit meant to my soul. Lloyd Jensen, one of God's heroes has discovered the art of turning a bed of pain into one of the brightest spots on earth. Healthy and active the first twelve years of his life, at the age of thirteen, a mysterious illness overtook him. The trouble was ultimately diagnosed as the worst form of arthritis which has since developed into Still disease, a fearful malady resulting in the hardening of the members.

"For eleven years now, Lloyd has lain in one position on his back. During the last six years this hero has been perfectly helpless and cannot move any part of his emaciated frame. All his joints are set. His hands, corrupt and distorted rest upon a pillow of cotton wool. Exposed, these rock-like, ugly lumps have been fixed upon his chest for almost six years. His legs and feet are gruesome. The mouth cannot open beyond the width of a cracker, and yet it is in this way that his patient mother feeds with small pieces of food.

"When he first took sick, Lloyd was not a Christian. His young heart was somewhat rebellious at being kept in bed when others of his age could walk and play. The prayers of a godly mother prevailed, however, and through the influence of a radio program, Lloyd became a born-again soul. Two years ago, a very severe heart attack almost sent Lloyd home to heaven. Rallying, he determined to read the Bible through. He felt that shame would be his if he met the Lord without having meditated upon His Word from cover to cover. His Bible rests upon a small music stand and with head half turned, its only position day and night for years, he reads the open pages, then Mother comes in and turns the leaves.

"Of his suffering Lloyd has nothing to say. If visitors take him sympathy, they soon have to pocket it or expend it upon themselves for having grumbled over little troubles. To all who come Lloyd smilingly testifies of a Saviour's love."

"Lloyd Jensen lives on "Giving-thanks-always-for-all-things" Avenue. Where do you make your home? If you have been living in the slums of murmuring, complaint and discontent, won't you move to-day at least into "Praise" Alley? And soon you will be living way uptown on "Joy" street or "Thanksgiving" Boulevard, in the precious fellowship of the spirit-filled Christians of the earth," as joyfully and meaningfully presented by Ruth Paxson.

According to Jewish practice in the Old Testament, it was God, not the food, that was blessed. Jesus set the proper example when He blessed the food for the five thousand men and, as Luke tells us, *He took the five loaves and the two fishes, and looking up to heaven, he blessed them, and brake, and gave to the disciples to set before the multitude* [Luke 9:16]. Consider your thoughts during the serving of the Lord's Supper. Are they concentrated on the elements and the Lord Jesus Christ rather than on the action as a whole?

One is to focus on the bread as Christ's broken body and the wine as His shed blood for us, individually and personally. For this we are to give thanks again, again, and again forever.

The custom in Jewish homes or assemblies was for the host to say the *berakah* or thanksgiving. Then he would break the bread, eat a fragment, and distribute it to others. After the meal there was a final *berakah* at which time the host or chief guest would say, "Let us give thanks," then take the cup, take a sip, and hand it to the others who were present. There would be a long thanksgiving during the final *berakah*.

After the Lord's Supper on the night He was betrayed, the followers took those parts of the supper to which Jesus had given a new meaning and separated them from the customary Jewish practice. These parts were called the Eucharist. All those assembled gave thanks when breaking the bread and drinking the wine.

What was the meaning Jesus intended? Remember, the Jewish custom of bread breaking and wine drinking were separated by the entire meal. They were independent of each other. Probably Jesus was thinking of the body and the blood as the two elements that make up a person.

Jesus knew that it was going to be the last time He would have a meal with His disciples. So what did He do? He gave them a pledge, a promise of His real presence with them during the days and years of their separation. The broken bread was to have one meaning only: the real personal presence of the Lord Jesus Christ, though He remains unseen.

What about the cup of blessing? It is the new covenant God made with His people through the Cross. The cup is for the disciples, then and now, the tangible promise by God in Christ of their inclusion in the new covenant.

The bread is the promise He will be there. The cup is the promise that He is the Saviour who initiated the new covenant by His death. Jesus put new meaning into the bread and cup.

What developments occurred? The bread and the cup were brought together. The two elements were given new meaning.

The early disciples and followers realized that the Supper is an expression of fellowship between those who partake of it in spirit and in truth, and the Lord Jesus Christ. What should be our attitude when fully realizing that the Lord Jesus is present while partaking of the bread and wine? There is the command to do this *in remembrance of me.*

This remembrance is not to be confused with religious rites, nor is it to be interpreted as a memorial service nor a mere ceremony. It is God in Christ intervening in behalf of His people in the present and not just in the past.

Therefore, no wonder the early followers sang Psalms, hymns, and spiritual songs; assemblies were joyful; and they witnessed to each other, gave thanks, and were thankful in word, action, and deed.

What else should be noted about the Lord's Supper? It is not a sacrificial meal. There is no trace in the New Testament that the bread or wine is offered as a sacrifice. What is offered to God is our thanks and praise. There is no memorial ritual. Christ is alive, He is not dead. For this we are to rejoice and be thankful.

The New Testament gives no support to any mechanical or magical ideas about the elements. Christ promised His personal presence in the new covenant. That is all that is needed. There is nothing in the New Testament to intimate that the Supper is merely a symbol.

What is the Lord's Supper? It is to be understood and accepted graciously as a divine moment; the real presence of our risen, glorified Lord; a meeting place appointed and promised by Christ for His own followers, the members of His body; and a thanksgiving for our redemption! In addition, it proclaims the Cross of Christ, His broken body, and His shed blood; and it points to the final consummation and reunion with Christ. Therefore, how can we do anything but give thanks always for all things unto God the Father, in the name of our Lord Jesus Christ?

Amen!

14

Walking in Harmony

Submitting (subjecting) *yourselves one to another in the fear of God* [Eph. 5:21].

We come now to that very important phrase which concludes the sentence beginning with the eighteenth verse. In many respects it is a watershed statement: it is the result of what the Apostle has been saying since the beginning of the fourth chapter. And it is the basis of what he will be saying through the ninth verse of the sixth chapter.

In considering this verse, it is appropriate to ask, what do you really desire in life as you walk day by day along life's pathway? If we listed several items such as love, money, recognition, health, happiness, friends, harmony and a few others, I am rather confident you would put harmony near the top of the list—harmony in family life and marriage, harmony in the home and workplace, and harmony in the church.

God, through the Holy Spirit, wants us to live in harmony with Him, with others, and with ourselves. Achieving a state of harmony requires knowledge, understanding, willingness, and effort, lots of effort. Yes, effort.

There have been six characteristics of our walk with the Lord Jesus Christ since the first verse of Chapter 4 in Ephesians. They are:

> walk in unity [Eph. 4:1–16];
> walk in holiness [Eph. 4:17–30];
> walk in love [Eph. 4:31–5:2];
> walk in light [Eph. 5:3–14];
> walk in wisdom [Eph. 5:15–17]; and
> walk in praise [Eph. 5:18–20].

Now we are entering the seventh phase, which may be called "walking in harmony." The question is how to achieve a harmonious walk in all the various facets and functions of life, in which it is our privilege to participate and to share. That is what God, through the Holy Spirit, is leading Paul to discuss.

However, before presenting the requirements for a harmonious life Paul presented doctrine and offered a prayer. Then he described eloquently what we must do as members of Christ's body to *walk worthy of the vocation* (calling) *wherewith ye are called,* [Eph. 4:1]; show we are *filled with the Spirit* [Eph. 5:18]; and *Submitting* (subjecting) *yourselves one to another in the fear of God* (Christ) [Eph. 5:21]. Again, what are we to do to walk harmoniously and to show that we are *filled with the Spirit* [Eph. 5:18]? Paul stated it very simply, *Submitting* (subjecting) *yourselves one to another in the fear of God* (Christ) [Eph. 5:21].

Calvin and other authorities believe it should read "in the fear of Christ." This gives additional emphasis to what the Apostle is saying. He is telling us to continue being filled with the Spirit, and to submit ourselves *one to another in the fear of God* (Christ) [Eph. 5:21].

Fear as it is used in this verse does not mean being terrified regarding God and afraid that He will punish us with or without reason. However, it does mean having "a wholesome dread of displeasing Him," (Vines Expository Dictionary of New Testament Words). Certainly that is different from what we hear today with the familiar intonations from the secular world.

What are we to do when encountering statements like this in Scripture? Understand the context in which it is presented, open our minds, accept Christ's teachings, and apply the truths to our conduct and tenor of life.

In the matter of hearing and applying the Word, the first century Christians, early reformers, the Covenanters, and the Puritans had a significant advantage. Why? Because they realized and accepted the fact that they were coming from a different lifestyle to a new life in Christ. They believed that they needed to repent, to accept Christ, and to continue steadfastly in the apostles' doctrine and fellowship.

We come from a different background, culture, and understanding. We have been told by the secular world that we are okay, basically good, able to improve ourselves, and self-sufficient. We have been taught that man has progressed and can continue to do so all by himself. These impediments are formidable obstacles to realizing the impact of sin, recognizing our deficiencies, and having the right "Christ relationship."

Therefore, we must look at ourselves as the Bible teaches and grow in a close relationship to Christ.

What does the Apostle mean by *Submitting* (subjecting) *yourselves one to another in the fear of Christ* [Eph. 5:21]? *Subjecting yourselves* appears to be a hard saying, and it is one from which we shy away. However, we must face it. It comes from the Lord, and it affects us individually and collectively. Subjecting one's self is a continuous process and governs everything we do. It is not an off again, on again situation.

"Let us face it (subjecting yourselves) courageously is a direct word of the Lord to us personally, and gladly, as one of the first-fruits of a Spirit-filled life. Therefore we know that what seems to us bitter is in reality sweet. "*Subjecting*"—a present participle, indicating a continuous process, an attitude governing every act. "*Yourselves*"—voluntary self-negation rather than to assert one's rights; true humility which esteems others better than one's self, and looks not upon his own things but upon the things of others," as explicitly expressed by Ruth Paxson.

When the Apostle adds *one to another*, it does not mean that the person in Christ becomes a milquetoast or prey for domineering, selfish individuals. It means that a person exhibits selfless attitudes and seeks to show forth Christlike qualities and attributes.

"One human will does not yield to another human will, but both wills are mutually yielded to the will of God in every matter relating to both persons. Mutual subjection is a voluntary meeting on the common ground of mutual desire to do the will of God, in the love of Christ, through the guidance of the Holy Spirit," according to the wisdom and faith of Ruth Paxson. That is a beautiful, meaningful description of subjecting oneself: mutual subjection, voluntary meeting, common ground, mutual desire, will of God, love of Christ, and guidance of the Holy Spirit. There it is, God the Father, Christ the Son, and the Holy Spirit.

The Apostle closes this phrase by saying *in the fear of Christ*, which means a reverential fear, not a fear of His awesome power and God's ability to exact righteous retaliation. It is a fear based upon the absolute dread of disappointing or displeasing God; and it guides people, who wish above everything else, to please God.

In submitting ourselves one to another *in the fear of Christ*, remember that the Apostle says we are to be *filled with the Spirit; Speaking in psalms and hymns and spiritual songs; Giving thanks always for all things unto God; Submitting* (subjecting) *yourselves one to another* [Eph. 5:18,

19–21], and behaving as followers of Christ in all our activities day in and day out. This should result in exhibiting the Christlike attributes that we will now examine.

Be thoughtful. Think, then act. Think how much grief, how many troubles, are caused by people not thinking. They act impetuously, they say something cutting or piercing in trying to be funny, or they try to put some one down in order to elevate themselves.

Be neither selfish nor self-centered. That type of person does not think except about his or her own desires and objectives.

Be filled with the Spirit. Realize you are an individual in the sight of God, but you are never to be individualistic. Once you are individualistic, you are thinking and acting in the wrong manner.

Be not self-assertive. Self is the basic cause of all our troubles individually and collectively. Self-assertion has plagued people ever since the Garden of Eden.

> *The serpent was more subtil* (cunning) *than any beast of the field . . . And he said unto the woman, Yea, hath God said, Ye shall not eat of every tree of the garden* [Gen. 3:1]?

What happened to Eve? She succumbed to self-assertion as is revealed in Scripture,

> *And when the woman saw that the tree was good for food, and that it was pleasant* (desirable) *to the eyes, and a tree to be desired to make one wise, she took of the fruit thereof, and did eat, and gave also unto her husband with her: and he did eat* [Gen. 3:6].

Once again, self-assertion has happened billions, even trillions of times since then.

Be knowledgeable according to the facts and commands of God: be not self-conscious and proud; know what you believe; obtain an understanding of discipleship; and pursue the truth as it is found in the Lord Jesus.

Be not opinionated. It leads to being dictatorial, wanting to have one's own way, and lording it over others. Peter points out three vices commonly found among elders and pastors: sloth, desire for gain, and a lust for power. Sound familiar? What about today? Against those three vices Peter exhorts them to

> *Feed* (shepherd) *the flock of God which is among you,*
> *Neither as being lords over God's heritage* (those entrusted to you) [1 Pet. 5:2–3].
>
> *Likewise, ye younger, submit yourselves unto the elder. Yea, all of you be subject one to another and be clothed with humility;*
> *Humble yourselves . . . under the mighty hand of God;*
> *Casting all your care upon him* (Christ) *for he careth for you.*
> *Be sober, be vigilant, because your adversary the devil . . . walketh about, seeking whom he may devour* [Selections from 1 Pet. 5:5–8].

Calvin says to exhibit "moderation and meekness" in discharging your responsibilities.

Peter tells the elders and pastors that they are to exercise great care over God's flock. Recall what Jesus said regarding the scribes and Pharisees,

> *All therefore whatsoever they bid you observe, that observe and do; but do not ye after* (according to) *their works: for they say and do not.*
> *For they bind heavy burdens* (hard to bear) *and grievous to be borne, and lay them on men's shoulders; but they themselves will not move them with one of their fingers.*
> *But all their works they do for to be seen of men* [Matt. 23:3–5a].

Peter exhorts the elders and pastors to tend to the flock of God. But the flock is to be fed only one way, with pure doctrine! With the pure teachings of Christ! With the spiritual food contained in the Scriptures!

Unfortunately, other ways are tried by elders and pastors today as they were in the first century. That is one compelling reason why the laity must be informed. There is to be expository, as well as topical, preaching and teaching. It is more difficult, but it is more edifying, energizing, enriching, penetrating, and scrutinizing in developing a close relationship with Christ.

Be self-seeking never. The self-seeking person usually does not want suggestions from other people or from Scripture. He or she usually resents criticism and is impatient with the viewpoints of others. When Robert E. Lee was head of the Army of Northern Virginia, he would not only solicit advice and suggestions, but he would not let someone be turned away, if he knew about it, who sincerely wished to provide additional information or ideas.

When Paul says, *Submitting* (subjecting) *yourselves one to another in the fear of* (Christ) [Eph. 5:21] he is writing to members of the body of Christ, those filled with the Spirit, those who have had the eyes of their understanding enlightened, and those who are walking with Christ. When submitting yourself, there is a condition and a command. You are to do so according to the teachings of Christ; based upon doctrine; not by forsaking, or ignoring Scripture; and in the fear of displeasing Christ.

Could you ever imagine Paul submitting himself to those people or groups who denied the deity of Christ, or who compromised the Master's teachings, or who said peace at any price or what difference do certain principles or standards make? No! Paul would not do that, neither would Peter or John, or the other writers of the New Testament and the Old Testament, or the saints through the ages.

The Apostle Paul does not say we are to be pliable or accommodating, or that we are to compromise doctrine. No, he does not even suggest that. His statement is addressed to those agreeing about doctrine, the teachings of Christ, and the commandments of God. He is not talking to people who disagree about these things. He is basing it

> *... upon the foundation of the apostles and prophets, Jesus Christ himself being the chief corner stone;*
> *In whom all the building fitly framed* (being joined) *together groweth unto an holy temple in the Lord:*
> *In whom ye also are builded* (being built) *together for a habitation* (dwelling place) *of God through the Spirit* [Eph. 2:20–22].

In the early church, the heretics were expelled. Scripture tells us to contend for the faith. Recall the position of Paul and Peter on circumcision. Paul withstood Peter to his face. Paul, the Johnny-come-lately, took issue with Peter.

John writes,

> *If there come any unto you, and bring not this doctrine, receive him not into your house, neither bid him* (give him a greeting) *God speed:*
> *For he that biddeth* (greets) *him God speed is partaker of* (shares in) *his evil deeds* [2 John 1:10–11].

Those are strong words. There is nothing namby-pamby about them.

There is tough talk in Scripture. It is direct, not ambiguous. We are to have knowledge and understanding, but we are not to submit to false teachings or doctrine. Look at Luther, Calvin, and Knox. They did not submit themselves to false teaching. But they submitted themselves *one to another in the fear of Christ*. God forbid that we should: misinterpret this verse; ignore it; or fail to practice it.

Yes, we are to be filled with the Spirit. We are to show forth the . . . *fruit of the Spirit: love, joy, peace, long-suffering, gentleness* (kindness), *goodness, faith* (faithfulness), *meekness,* (and) *temperance* (self-control) [Gal. 5:22–23]. In addition, we are to give thanks always in all things unto God, and to submit ourselves *one to another in the fear of Christ* [Eph. 4:21].

Amen!

15

A Relationship as That of Christ to the Church

> *Wives, submit yourselves unto your own husbands, as unto the Lord.*
> *For the husband is the head of the wife, even as Christ is the head of the church: and he is the saviour of the body* [Eph. 5:22–23].

The relationship of a man and woman in marriage is probably one of the most important institutions ever conceived and established. To say the least, it is unique.

An individual's thoughts about marriage not only affect the relationship between two people, it affects their relationships with other people and, in turn, with more people. The influence is almost endless. It is like casting a stone in a pond or a lake—the ripple effect goes in all directions and is noticed by both the inhabitants of the water and upon the shore as the water ebbs and flows.

Paul does not begin to discuss marriage until he has prepared the members of Christ's body, and they are ready, or should be ready, to receive it. He wants them to have the right attitude and proper information before he shines additional light into their hearts and minds.

A friend of mine has the knack of saying that everyone needs, from time to time, an AA, an "Attitudinal Adjustment." Therefore, when considering these passages [Eph. 5:22–23] bear in mind five things.

The first thing we are to bear in mind is Paul's admonition that we are to conduct ourselves according to the following commands:

> *... be not drunk with wine ... but be filled with the Spirit;*
> *Speaking to yourselves in psalms and hymns and spiritual songs, singing and making melody in your heart to the Lord;*

> *Giving thanks unto all things unto God and the Father in the name of our Lord Jesus Christ;*
> *Submitting yourselves one to another in the fear* (reverence) *of God* [Eph. 5:18–21].

This is Paul, the Apostle, providing us with commands in the name of the Lord Jesus that will enhance our lives and bring joy to our hearts.

Second, we are to remember as members of Christ's body that He is the Head, He is a Person, and He is the Son of the living God. We are to believe in Him. Our salvation is through Him. Our conduct, character, and conversation are to be like His. He is to be the Lord of our lives.

This gets into the sticky-wicket area. If we are to obey His commands and do as He did, it often times means we are at odds with Him because we do not do as He did. Also, what we want is not exactly what He wants. Further, we do not particularly like the idea of being subject to Him seven days a week.

Third, sanctification is a process we may not fully understand. However, our daily lives are to reflect the living Christ. We are to bear witness to Him, even though those to whom we may be bearing witness do not understand what we are saying or doing.

Sanctification is what Oswald Chambers says is "Christ in you." He further states that "sanctification means" imparting "the Holy qualities of Jesus Christ." Note the term used is *imparting*, which means "giving or granting from one's abundance and transmitting it to another." It is entirely different from either acquiring or imitating.

Sanctification is a process by which we yield ourselves to His will, and He imparts to us "His patience, His purity, and His Godliness," notes Oswald Chambers. When these qualities are imparted to us and we receive them willingly, then our character, conduct, and conversation reflect His qualities.

Fourth, we are to continually seek knowledge and understanding about Scripture. We are to be on our inquisitive high when we read, hear, and study Scripture. We are to be like the little child who continually asks why, and what does that mean?

We are to understand the context in which these passages of Scripture were written, why they were written, what they meant in the first century, and how they are applicable today. We must realize that although conditions change, man remains basically the same when he is outside the body of Christ.

Finally, Paul is writing to those people identified as Christians, members of the body of Christ, or followers of the Lord Jesus Christ. It is important to remember to whom this letter was written. It was not addressed to the general populace at Ephesus, the non-followers. Therefore, we are obligated to know the context of these verses.

What has preceded them? The first three chapters of this letter were devoted to the basic teachings of the Lord Jesus Christ, showing the church as the body of Christ, presenting Christ as the Son of God, and fulfilling the promises of God.

Then we examined the different phases in the walk with Christ: unity, holiness, love, light, wisdom, and praise. Those phases of the walk are something we should desire to achieve. We are to put our efforts toward achieving unity; becoming holy; experiencing the love of Christ, or having apple pie, motherhood, Christmas, and the Fourth of July every day and in everything; shedding more light on our relationship with Christ, others, and ourselves; and increasing in wisdom.

Certainly, we want to be more intelligent, and we want more wisdom, but are we willing to pay the price? Are we willing to deny ourselves, to suffer, and to obey in order to grow in wisdom? Those questions need to be answered, and answered affirmatively. Look to the apostles, the giants of the Christian faith, those unknown followers who walk with Christ, and what do we find? They were willing to pay the price, to deny themselves, to suffer, and to obey the commands of God and Christ. What happened to them? The road may have been arduous, but God blessed them with overflowing waters of wisdom. What was their response to the ordeals they encountered as they strived to please God and walk with Jesus despite burdens, doubts, opposition, and temptations? They praised God and Christ continuously and forevermore for their blessings and for their wisdom.

The Holy Spirit is almost unbelievable. He is almost unreal. He works through Paul presenting these truths and getting our agreement, then He wants to zap it to us and hit us right between the eyes. It reminds me of that oft-quoted statement about the minister and his sermon, when the person says the preacher has gone from preaching to meddling.

How much more meddling can you do than to focus on marriage: the relationship of husband and wife, the home, parents and children, the workplace, master and servants, supervisor and subordinate? All of

A Relationship as That of Christ to the Church

us fit into one or more of these categories. Paul and the Holy Spirit are now starting to meddle, and you know what? They are going to do it through the remainder of this wonderful letter. Is that not interesting?

Approximately 20 percent of this Epistle involves meddling in our affairs. Note the overview. Note the statements. Note how the Apostle combines doctrine with practical applications. Note the continuous thread of Christ in describing the relationship between husband and wife:

> *Wives . . . unto your own husbands, as unto the Lord.*
> *Christ is the head of the Church: and Savior of the body.*
> *Husbands love your wives, as Christ also loved the Church, and gave himself for it;*
> *. . . sanctify* (set it apart) *and cleanse it . . . by the word,*
> *That he might present to himself a glorious church, . . . holy and without blemish.*
> *So ought men to love their* (own) *wives as their own bodies.*
> *For no man ever yet hated his own flesh; but nourisheth and cherisheth it,*
> FOR THIS CAUSE SHALL A MAN LEAVE HIS FATHER AND MOTHER, AND SHALL BE JOINED UNTO HIS WIFE, AND THEY TWO SHALL BE ONE FLESH.
> *This is a great mystery: . . . concerning Christ and the Church.*
> *Nevertheless, let every one in particular so love his wife even as himself; and the wife see that she reverence* (respects) *her husband*
> [Selections from Eph. 5:22–33].

These truths are contained within twelve verses. It is our responsibility not only to be aware of them, but to understand them and to apply them. The teachings presented by Paul face a crucial test. The exhortations contained in these verses are supported by one motivating factor: Christ Himself.

Please consider: first, Paul presents the wife's subjection to her own husband on the same basis as being subject to Christ, the head of the church. When considering this we should remember that Christ willingly and completely obeyed His Father.

Second, the husband's love for his wife and the basis of his relationship to her is the same as the Master's relationship to His church. The Messiah's love, attitude, and actions toward His church are the basis for comparing a husband's relationship with his wife. How can those outside Christ know this? They cannot.

It is evident that Paul's teachings about the husband-wife relationship rests on the foundation of Jesus Christ Himself being the chief cornerstone. Paul does not say anything to the husband and wife unless it has its roots in Christ's teachings as revealed in Scripture. It is a characteristic of Paul's to present Christ's teachings, not his own ideas or thoughts.

In these verses, Paul does five significant things: he uses what is termed a Christ hymn in Verses 25–27, he quotes from the Old Testament in Verse 31, he uses fragments of Jewish sayings in order to relate to the people, he wants them to understand, and he wants them to relate to his teachings.

What is Paul doing in these verses? He intends to develop and establish a definite link between what he is teaching and a follower's faith in Christ, as well as his understanding of Scripture and the events that transpire in daily living. These factors relate to and support the Apostle's teachings. They provide the members of Christ's body with additional knowledge about Christ, and allow each one to praise God accordingly.

Paul wants these members to understand that the relationship between a husband and wife is relevant to the relationship between the Lord Jesus Christ and His church. It is evident that Christ has a dominant role in the relationship between Himself and His church. When the church seeks to assert herself or to ignore His teachings or to adopt the ways of the world, she encounters difficulties. Therefore, Paul provides a distinct example as to how Christ functions, how the husband is to act based upon the example given by the Master Himself; and the divine command: *Nevertheless let every one of you in particular so love his wife even as himself; and the wife see that she reverence* (respects) *her husband* [Eph. 5:33]. Paul focuses attention on what is normally considered a secular matter and transforms it into a situation where the Gospel is preached and Christ is presented as the Son of the living God.

It may help our understanding when applying this Scripture to keep in mind the manner in which Christ and His church submit themselves to each other, which is the prime example for the husband and wife. Ruth Paxson beautifully described it this way, "Christ submitted Himself in a self-denying, self-sacrificing love, even, unto death, for His bride, whom he cherishes and cares for in the most tender manner. The church, the Bride, responds with the submission of absolute loyalty in yieldedness and obedience. It is the mutual submission of a pure love for a perfect lover." This is the pattern we are to know and to apply. It is the basis, as Paxson continues to say, for the "divinely appointed relationship between husband and wife with" the resulting responsibility for both parties to obey God's commands.

Paul's commitment to Christ and his dependence upon Him are such that he proclaims the Gospel and applies it to those institutions that are considered secular. "Paul praises Christ in such a way that neither sin, nor death, nor former divisions, nor institutions, nor structures, and certainly not marriage, can escape the power and riches of grace," as properly stated by Markus Barth.

Let us turn now to the twenty-second verse, which reads *Wives, submit yourselves unto your own husbands, as unto the Lord*. Actually this verse in the original Greek does not read that way. It merely says, *Wives, . . . unto your own husbands, as unto the Lord*. Why are the words "submit yourselves" omitted? Most authorities agree that Verse 22 is a continuation of Verse 21. Therefore, the Apostle did not repeat himself.

There is another important point to consider. In this instance, Paul places the wives first and the husbands second. "This is not an accident or a case of being polite. The Bible does not do that," as noted by Martyn Lloyd-Jones. Usually the husband or man precedes the wife or woman in the Bible. However, it should be noted that the Apostle in these verses deals with both the husband and wife, though in this instance the wife comes first.

Also, the Apostle in verse twenty-two says, *unto your own husband*. Why does he say this? You will recall the previous verse states a general truth, *Submitting yourselves one to another in the fear* (reverence) *of Christ* [Eph. 5:21]. We need to realize that the twenty-first verse contains a significant truth, and that it is a controlling principle in presenting the teachings contained in verses twenty-two and twenty-three.

When considering marriage it may be well to ask certain questions: What method is the Apostle employing? Why is he placing such emphasis upon marriage? What does he want the hearers to do?

It should be clear that Paul is addressing his message to those who have accepted Christ. He begins his letter by saying, *to the saints which are at Ephesus, and to the faithful in Christ Jesus* [Eph. 1:1]. This does not mean that they do not need instruction in the ways of Christ, or that they automatically think and do the right things. They need to grow and mature. They need an AA, an "Attitudinal Adjustment," from time to time.

Unfortunately, there are some evangelists and preachers who say that all you have to do is to accept Christ and all your troubles will go away, and you will live happily ever after. Many young people believe if you marry Prince Charming or Lady Beautiful that everything will be sunshine and roses.

If those ideas were correct and the only thing you had to do was make a decision, then guess what? All Jesus would have had to do was call different individuals to be his disciples and followers. There never would have been the need to write any of the New Testament letters. The fact that we have become members of Christ's body does not mean we will be automatically 110 percent correct in our conduct, character, and conversation (tenor of life).

The fact that we are followers of Christ and increasing in knowledge and dependence upon Him raises new questions and new problems. New information and new knowledge change our thinking and our perspective. This means there are new challenges, new ways to act, and new practices to apply according to the teachings of Christ, and they are to replace the secular teachings that often have taken precedence. It is not easy. It requires strength and patience. It requires imparting the qualities of Christ to the believer (you and me), having them accepted and diligently practiced.

Christ's teachings have something to say about our total lives and how they are to impact our total being. The person in Christ should realize that he or she is a total human being, not a series or accumulation of parts. An individual may perform different functions, but it is the same person doing them. We are not to say that one thing applies to my living faith, while something else applies to my business life, and something different to my social life. The living faith in Christ applies to all aspects of our lives, to all the functions, to all the relationships, and to everything we do.

The teachings of Christ directly and through the New Testament writers "never contradicts or undoes fundamental biblical teachings with respect to life and living," according to Martyn Lloyd-Jones. The New Testament and the Old Testament do not contradict one another. Some people do not want to be governed by the Old Testament or the New Testament. They want to pick and choose. However, the Apostle's teaching is based upon Christ's example and teachings. The Old Testament says, *Therefore shall a man leave his father and his mother, and shall cleave* (be joined) *unto his wife: and they shall be one flesh* [Gen. 2:24]. Paul does this to show that the original teachings come from God. Therefore, they are to be understood, observed, and applied.

The New Testament does not give us a list of rules or a set of commands to follow: one, two, three, and four. What does the New Testament do? It gives reasons. It gives explanations. It gives commands. It does not impose rules and regulations in an arbitrary manner. It explains why we are to act in a certain manner. Why we should behave as we are called to do.

The teachings of God revealed in Scripture pay us a wonderful compliment. They do not treat us as children, or as "nincompoops." They reason with us, and they appeal to our understanding, if we will keep an open mind and not let self get in the way. The teachings are reasoned out. This is the process for imparting holiness and sanctification, and we should be thankful for it.

Have you noticed in these verses something we should have mentioned before? How Scripture intertwines the teachings of Christ and God with the practical application of the teaching. The doctrine and practice go together. Especially in this case where the Apostle is talking about marriage and the relationship of the wife and husband. Here we are in the middle of what many consider to be a practical everyday situation—marriage—and what does the Holy Spirit lead Paul to discuss—doctrine, the relationship of the Lord Jesus Christ to His Church. "You find that the Apostle in dealing with the most practical matter suddenly introduces us to the most exalted doctrine," as Martyn Lloyd-Jones amplified upon an important truth.

When reading and studying this Epistle we must be ready for some surprises. However, one thing we should grasp is that doctrine and practice go together. They cannot be separated.

Note how the Apostle treats this subject of marriage. He does not list rights or duties. He does not try to prove one way is right and another wrong. No, he does not do any of those things. He elevates marriage. He brings it up to the Lord Jesus Christ. He reminds the hearers, the wives and husbands, that they are to submit themselves *One to another in the fear* (reverence) *of Christ* [Eph. 5:21]. He goes from the general to the specific. He focuses our attention where it should be when discussing this most important institution of marriage. He focuses our attention on the Lord Jesus Christ.

What is the Christian view of marriage? It is governed entirely and solely by Scripture. The Christian submits to the teachings of Scripture. He or she does not pick and choose.

Marriage was instituted by God. It is His ordinance. God has appointed it, ordained it, and established it for men and women, not for men and men, nor for women and women. The terms of the relationship are stated clearly and unequivocally.

We can only really understand marriage when we understand the teachings of Scripture pertaining to our Lord Jesus Christ and His church. When we do not have a clear understanding about the relationship between Christ and His Bride, then we have difficulty understanding marriage.

In closing, let us be clear about one thing: accepting Christ and following Him is more than dealing with your soul and salvation. It touches the whole of your life. It meddles in all your affairs. It applies to your marriage, to your home, and to the workplace. It makes a positive difference in all these relationships. Thank God it does!

Amen!

16

Wives... Unto Your Own Husbands

Wives, submit yourselves unto your own husbands, as unto the Lord [Eph. 5:22].

The teachings of our Lord Jesus Christ impact our whole living arena. They are directed toward the entire scope of living joyful, meaningful lives while being in a right relationship with God.

These teachings are expounded upon by the Apostle Paul as he instructs us or, as some say, he meddles in our private lives and family relationships. They are intended to mold, shape, direct, and influence our thoughts and our actions. They are to be applied in basic everyday relationships. Why? So that we may live in harmony with one another. So that we may be witnesses to the community of believers.

To do this, we must understand God's plan and the teachings of Scripture. Further, we are to be obedient to God's commands and to know all the teachings contained in Scripture, not just a few of them. When considering the relationship of a husband and wife, bear in mind the relationship between Christ and His church.

The Lord Jesus Christ obeyed God's commands. He did the will of His Father. He subjected Himself to the Father in denying Himself and in going to the Cross. The church, the called out, is to respond willingly by submitting itself in faith and obedience to the Lord Jesus Christ.

Why does the Lord Jesus submit Himself to the Father, and why does the church submit herself to the Lord Jesus Christ? Because the Father and the Lord Jesus only want the best for the called out, for the members of Christ's body. They do not do anything from a selfish motive to hurt or to injure one another. There is nothing to fear by subjecting ourselves to God and to Christ or, as Scripture says, *Submitting* (subjecting) *yourselves one to another in the fear* (reverence) *of Christ* [Eph. 5:21].

How do we submit ourselves to God? By knowing how He acted, knowing what He wants us to do, knowing His teachings, and being aware of His presence. When we begin to know and realize these things, we can respond in faith.

We begin our walk at first with faltering steps and then with measured ones. Then we open our hearts and minds a little wider so we can receive more from Him. Then we can walk up hills and down into valleys, because we know He is with us. Further, we can walk through the storms of life as well as the bright noonday sun. Finally, we get to know Him better and better, and we depend upon Him more and more.

When walking with Jesus and subjecting ourselves to Him, how much more meaningful the Twenty-third Psalm becomes.

> THE Lord is my shepherd; I shall not want (lack).
> He maketh me to lie down in green pastures (pastures of tender green grasses): he leadeth me beside still waters (of rest).
> He restoreth my soul: he leadeth me in the paths of righteousness for his name's sake.
> Yea, though I walk through the valley of the shadow of death, I will fear no evil: for thou art with me; thy rod and thy staff they comfort me.
> Thou preparest a table before me in the presence of mine enemies: thou anointest my head with oil; my cup runneth over.
> Surely goodness and mercy (loving-kindness) shall follow me all the days of my life: and I will dwell in the house of the Lord forever [Ps. 23:1–6].

Our relationship in marriage is to be that of the sheep to the Shepherd and the Shepherd to the sheep.

We are to subject ourselves one to another out of reverence for Christ. *Wives, submit yourselves unto your own husbands, as unto the Lord.* Before proceeding to examine further this portion of Scripture, it is important to ponder practically every word and understand the context in which this teaching is presented. It is for our benefit. Therefore, we are to examine it and then apply it.

The Apostle has carefully prepared us for this teaching, not only with Verses 18–21 of Chapter 5, but also with the truths contained from the beginning of Chapter 4 through Verse 17 of Chapter 5. He exhorts the wives, who have accepted Christ, to submit unto their own husbands, as unto the Lord. The Greek word for submit or subject is *hupotassō*. It means "to subject oneself," "to obey," and "to be subject to."

When considering the meaning of this passage we should bear in mind that both the husband and wife are bond-slaves of the Lord Jesus Christ. However, the wife is not the bond-slave of the husband, neither is she exhorted to be nor is she expected to be. What is the wife exhorted to do and what reasons are given? Whenever the Lord exhorts us to do something He also gives reasons.

First, the wives are exhorted to submit themselves unto their own husbands, *as unto the Lord*. In submitting themselves to their husbands they are showing their obedience to the Lord Jesus Himself. When they subject themselves gladly because of their relationship to Christ, they are in reality being obedient unto Christ's teachings and commands. She is only to submit herself *as unto the Lord*, not to anything the husband does, desires, or expresses that is contrary to Christ's commands, teachings and words. Her obedience is to be only *as unto the Lord*. Husbands, take note!

The submission of the wife to the husband in the marriage relationship is not done for the sake, or satisfaction of her husband. That is not the reason or the motive for so doing. It is done for Christ's sake and because it is well pleasing to Him. Remember, Scripture says, *Whether therefore ye eat, or drink, or whatsoever ye do, do all to the glory of God* [1 Cor. 10:31]. All our conduct, no matter what it is, should be as Calvin says, "related to the glory of God." This is particularly true of the marriage relationship.

Another reason is the exhortation says, *For the husband is the head of the wife, even as Christ is head of the church* [Eph. 5:23]. In addition, Scripture says *Therefore as the church is subject unto Christ, so let the wives be to their own husbands in every thing* [Eph. 5:24]. The position of the husband according to Scripture is by "divine appointment." When you think about this, you must keep in mind the relationship between God and Christ.

The position of the husband as being head of the wife in the marriage is similar to Christ being the head of the church. The reasons given for the wives to subject themselves unto the Lord were:

> *For the husband is the head of the wife, even as Christ is the head of the church: and he is the saviour of the body.*
> *Therefore as the church is subject unto Christ, so let the wives be to their own husbands in every thing.*

> *Husbands, love your wives, even as Christ also loved the church, and gave himself for it* [Eph. 5:23–25].

Husbands are to know and exercise their responsibilities in this relationship. Husbands are to understand and act according to the following commands:

> *Love your wives, even as Christ also loved the church, and gave himself for it;*
> *That he might sanctify* (set it apart) *and cleanse it with the washing of water by the word.*
> *That he might present it to himself a glorious church, not having spot, or wrinkle, or any such thing; but that it should be holy and without blemish.*
> *So ought men to love their* (own) *wives as their own bodies* [Eph. 5:25–28].

The reasons given to the wives and the husbands following this exhortation are powerful and compelling. Think of our Lord's ministry on earth. What did He do? He wanted to know the Father's will, and He wanted to do it.

Again and again we have the same situation. Know the teaching, apply the teaching. Certainly, there was nothing at all that was the least bit degrading in learning and doing the Father's will and in being subject to the Father. There is nothing demeaning or degrading in being subject to the Lord Jesus Christ. Therefore, there should be nothing at all negative in a wife being subject to her husband *as unto the Lord*. It should be to the glory of God.

What should be the nature and extent of the wife's subjection to the husband in their marriage as it pertains to the home and the family? "It is not a slavish obedience to every whim and fancy of unreasonableness and selfishness on the part of the husband, but the loving and joyous subjection of loyalty to love. For the one to whom she is united as 'one flesh' she will have only respect and reverence," as beautifully expressed Ruth Paxson. Yes, wives are to be subject unto their own husbands, and *the husband is the head of the wife, even as Christ is the head of the church* [Eph. 5:23].

These truths are to be applied according to the teachings of Scripture. They are not to be applied according to the secular world and its practices outside the body of Christ. When these truths are first read they appear to be unfair, or to present a bias in favor of the husband.

However, an examination of Scripture reveals that that is not the case. It is not true.

What becomes evident when studying Scripture? First, it is by divine appointment that the husband is the head of the marriage and the family. There has to be a plan for the family, and this is the one designed and implemented by God. Second, the relationship of Christ to the church is to serve as the model for both the husband and wife as they journey through their married life.

The husband is to be to the wife what Christ was and is to the church in thought, act, and deed, or as we have stated earlier, in conduct, character, and conversation (tenor of life). Certainly, the husband has not the slightest reason or motivation to be selfish or self-centered. He does not have a license to do as he would according to the ways of the world. The husband has responsibilities, and he must discharge them according to Scripture. He is to act and speak as the Lord Jesus would. Scripture says, *Therefore shall a man leave his father and his mother, and shall cleave* (be joined) *unto his wife: and they shall be one flesh* [Gen. 2:24]. But before that, what happened?

> *The Lord God formed man of the dust of the ground, and breathed into his nostrils the breath of life; and man became a living soul* [Gen. 2:7].

> *And the Lord God said, It is not good that the man should be alone; I will make a help meet* (helper comparable to him) *for him* [Gen. 2:18].

What do we notice from the teachings in Genesis? Man was created first, woman was made out of the man, the woman was to be a help meet for the man, and nothing else could supply or provide for man's need. Note, nothing else! A husband should realize this and be thankful for it. The woman is to complement the man. She is to help him perform the various, wonderful, glorious, and important tasks assigned to man. The man, or the husband, is responsible for his wife, whereas the wife is to help the man perform his tasks. This was the situation before the woman ate of the fruit and gave it to her husband as noted in Genesis 3:6. This was before they disobeyed.

Note, *Unto the woman he* (God) *said, I will greatly multiply thy sorrow* (pain) *and thy conception; in sorrow* (pain) *thou shalt bring forth children; and thy desire shall be to* (toward) *thy husband, and he shall rule over thee* [Gen. 3:16]. This is the same as saying that the wife will not be free to do as she would, but is to be dependent upon her husband and subject to his authority. The wife had exceeded her authority prior to the Fall in eating the fruit and offering it to her husband. Now, after the Fall, she is informed that she is to be subject to her husband.

Paul's letter to Timothy casts additional light on this matter, saying,

> *For Adam was first formed, then Eve.*
> *And Adam was not deceived, but the woman being deceived was in the transgression.*
> *Notwithstanding she shall be saved in childbearing, if they continue in faith and charity* (love) *and holiness with sobriety* (self-control) [1 Tim. 2:13–15].

These verses support the teaching from the Old Testament. However, they are not to be misconstrued. The Apostle states he is not merely dealing with having children, but he is addressing the problems that wives have in bearing children and raising them.

God is pleased with those who believe that this condition of being a wife is actually a calling from God and her actions display that attitude. The importance of the phrase *if they continue in faith and love and holiness with sobriety* cannot be overemphasized. These traits contribute abundantly to the development, growth, and strength of a marriage, a family, and the children with whom they are blessed. It is a task of great magnitude requiring the might, power, and strength of God along with His wisdom. The Greek word for *sobriety* means "sound judgment." It is inner self-government with a constant rein on all the passions and desires, which keep temptations from arising.

What happened in the book of Genesis, Chapter 3? Eve *took of the fruit thereof, and did eat, and gave also unto her husband with her: and he did eat* [Gen. 3:6]. Eve made the initial decision herself instead of asking Adam and discussing it with him. The result of her dealing with the situation is the Fall. She assumed authority without discussing it.

Of course, that teaching brings a reaction and certainly some objections. For example, people object by saying, "that it is only the teaching of Paul who was against women" or "those were the conditions in the first century when women were held in low esteem." Let us be clear about this: do not mistake some general conditions as being in accord with the teachings and practices of the Apostle and the Master.

Acts, Chapter 16, reveals Paul teaching Lydia and the Lord opening her heart. *Neither is the man without* (independent of) *the woman, neither the woman without* (independent of) *the man, in the Lord* [1 Cor. 11:11]. The two are bound together as one. The one cannot get along properly without the other. When they do not function together there is disharmony. However, when each one supports and serves the other as seen in Christ and His church, then there is harmony.

The Apostle says, *There is neither Jew nor Greek, there is neither bond* (slave) *nor free, there is neither male nor female: for ye are all one in Christ Jesus* [Gal. 3:28]. It must be remembered that the Apostle deals with the duties of both the husband and the wife. He addresses both sides.

The Apostle Paul does three things in writing his letters: he knows and quotes the Old Testament, he knows the teachings of the Lord Jesus, and he writes as an inspired apostle under the influence of the Holy Ghost. There were those in his day who took issue with Paul, but consider what Peter said,

> *Wherefore, beloved, seeing that ye look for such things, be diligent that ye may be found of him in peace, without spot, and blameless.*
>
> *And account* (consider) *that the long-suffering of our Lord is salvation; even as our beloved brother Paul also according to the wisdom given unto him hath written unto you;*
>
> *As also in all his epistles, speaking in them of these things; in which are some things hard to be understood, which they that are unlearned* (untaught) *and unstable wrest* (twist), *as they do also the other scriptures, unto their own destruction.*
>
> *Ye therefore, beloved, seeing ye know these things before* (beforehand), *beware lest ye also, being led away with the error of the wicked, fall from your own steadfastness.*
>
> *But grow in grace, and in the knowledge of our Lord and Saviour Jesus Christ. To him be glory both now and for ever. Amen* [2 Pet. 3:14–18].

Even in the first century people wanted to pick and choose. They wanted to trifle with Scripture.

Peter wanted them to know that Scripture was from God and that those who follow the Holy Spirit will have a light to guide them on their walk. However, those who do not follow the Holy Spirit will have difficulty and will stumble even in the bright sunshine.

Therefore, we can acknowledge that people have disputed portions of Scripture for centuries when it does not agree with their opinions based upon their experiences in the secular world. What is needed is a desire to probe Scripture and to understand what was originally intended and stated, such as *Wives . . . unto your own husbands, as unto the Lord.*

We have considered certain teachings of Scripture. However, we should recognize from a practical standpoint that whenever there are two or more people involved in a project that someone must be in a position of authority. This is true in the church as we know it, in the Army, in business, in politics, and in all types of organizations. It also applies to the family.

It does not always mean the most gifted person is the one in charge. But it does mean that the people involved will discharge their responsibilities to the best of their ability. If they do not, then there will be disharmony.

The husband and wife are not separate. They each have difficult functions to perform, different purposes, and special duties. They are to do these things as members of Christ's body. In doing them, they should remember that they are each part of the whole and that performing their assigned duties and responsibilities in a unified manner produces harmony. If they realize they are members of Christ's body and that He is the Head of both, then they should willingly and joyfully serve and support one another.

When the wife is exhorted to submit unto her own husband, it does not mean certain things: she is not to be passive; and she is not inferior to her husband. Her position is one of honor, respect, and equality. A woman in submitting to her husband wishes to please him, but also to help him, aid him, support him, and enable him. She provides proactive as well as reactive support.

It does not mean: that the wife should do or will do anything against her Christian conscience or the teachings of Scripture; or that the husband can dictate what the wife will do or can do.

The wife cannot and must not submit to the husband if it interferes "with her relationship to God and the Lord Jesus Christ," as explicitly stated by Martyn Lloyd-Jones.

If the husband is guilty of adultery then the wife is no longer bound by the exhortation *Wives, submit yourselves unto your own husbands, as unto the Lord.* Why? Because the unity has been broken and disharmony created. Hopefully, you see the context in which Scripture says, *Wives, . . . unto your own husbands, as unto the Lord.*

Both the wife and husband have responsibilities. Both need to understand Scripture and to apply it. And may they so do!

Amen!

17

Husbands, Love Your Wives

> *Husbands, love your wives, even as Christ also loved the church, and gave himself for it;*
> *That he might sanctify* (set it apart) *and cleanse it with the washing of water by the word* [Eph. 5:25-26].

Paul's teaching about marriage, the husband-and-wife relationship, is intertwined with the doctrine of the relationship between the Lord Jesus Christ and His Bride, the church. Think on that!

Paul, under the influence of the Holy Spirit, raises marriage, that formal, mysterious relationship between a particular man and a particular woman, to the highest possible level. He is comparing their relationship to that of the Lord Jesus Christ Himself to the church.

Paul's teaching was directed to those who had accepted Christ and were members of His body. It was not and is not directed to the world in general. It is for the true members of Christ's body. To fully understand it, one must have accepted the Lord Jesus Christ as Saviour and have a certain knowledge of Scripture, the Father, Son, and Holy Ghost.

Conditions existing in the first century were similar to those existing at the beginning of the twenty-first century. Divorce was widespread, if not rampant. Adultery was practiced. The Jews had a low opinion of women. A Jewish man would thank God in his prayers that he was not "a Gentile, a slave or a woman." According to Jewish law the wife had no right to divorce, except if her husband became a leper, an apostate, or practiced some unacceptable trade.

The conditions existing in the Greek world were worse. Demosthenes stated it rather coarsely or directly, "We have courtesans for the sake of pleasure; we have concubines for the sake of daily cohabitation; we have wives for the purpose of having children legitimately and of having a faithful guardian for all our household affairs."

The Greek wife lived a secluded existence. She did not participate in public life, go out alone, or appear at social functions. She was almost a nonentity. Marcus Aurelius was confronted by his wife for associating with other women. His response was that "the title of wife was one of dignity, but not of pleasure." Further, there was no legal procedure in Greece for obtaining a divorce. The only security that a Greek wife had was that her dowry must be returned.

In Rome, the conditions, if possible, were even worse. "The marriage bond (in Rome) was on the way to a complete breakdown," noted the renowned pastor and preacher William Barclay.

What about conditions today? Divorce, adultery, individual rights, self-centeredness, lack of scriptural knowledge, and attitudes of men and women plus teenage boys and girls toward each other result in desire, everything for the moment, and existentialism. Not too much difference over two thousand years with respect to the world in general. Of course, women have some rights today that they did not have then. However, the conditions and attitudes remain similar to what they were.

Paul writes to the saints at Ephesus (and to us) knowing what people see, hear, and observe in their daily lives and knowing that they are confronted with temptations. He knows that they must be strengthened, become new creatures in Christ, and witness to others by setting Christlike examples. He knows they must submit themselves to Christ and be filled with the Spirit; they must not be self-centered or assert their so-called rights. And in doing these things, they will have new relationships and new standards because of the Lord Jesus Christ. This is quite a challenge today. It was quite a challenge to Paul. How can it be understood and applied unless it is taught, unless it is preached?

It needs to be addressed and stressed! Is there anything more vital to society and the world in which we live than to understand and apply Scripture regarding marriage, the relationship of a husband and wife, and Christ and His church? The only thing more important is having a personal relationship with the Lord Jesus Christ and walking with Him in a living faith. If we do that, we will have a blessed relationship with our spouse.

Paul's teachings in verses twenty-two through twenty-four were not the accepted standards of his day, nor are they in ours. He calls for a new type of fellowship, and for new relationships.

We have considered the verse, *Wives . . . unto your own husbands as unto the Lord.* Now it is time to turn our attention to *Husbands, love your wives.*

Paul was direct and to the point, yet he did not stop there. He did not let them use their own imaginations as to how they were to love their wives, nor did he let them use the existing moral attitudes, the street talk, or the language of the day. Paul was also very specific. He told them how they were to love their wives. They were to do so as Christ loved the church and as Christ gave Himself for the church to sanctify it and cleanse it. They were to present it so that it does not have a spot or wrinkle; to have it holy and without blemish; to love their wives as themselves; and to nourish and cherish them forever. Husbands: think, think, think as to how you are to love your wives! These are specific commands, not mere suggestions.

As if that is not enough Paul adds to it saying, *For we are members of His body* [Eph. 5:30]. Paul wants the husbands to remember they are members of Christ's body. They are to love their wives according to His teachings and His example, just as their wives are to do regarding their husbands.

What type of love are husbands to practice toward their wives? Paul says that the love with which husbands are to embrace their wives is no ordinary love. Therefore, he relates it to the love Christ has for His church. Love is to be the controlling factor of the husband for his wife.

Someone may observe that the Apostle does not command wives to love their husbands. His letter contains the essence of his teaching, but it is not a detailed treatise on marriage. Though he does not command the wives to love their husbands, it is rather implicit in his statement, *Wives, submit yourselves unto your own husbands, as unto the Lord* [Eph. 5:22].

The Apostle is concerned with harmony in marriage as well as peace and unity. Therefore, he stresses the primary requirements for both husbands and wives, and uses Christ and the church as the model from which they are to learn and to practice. Yes, Scripture says, *the husband is the head of the wife, . . .* [Eph. 5:23] but it also commands the husband to love his wife as Christ loves the church. What kind of love is that? Certainly, it is not tyrannical or demanding or self-centered.

First, it is a sacrificial love. It is not a selfish love. These words have a real impact when we carefully consider them, and seek to practice them. The emphasis of Christ's love was what He could give His Bride, what He could bestow upon her, how He could lift her up, and how He could bless her. He denied Himself, He suffered, He gave all that He had and was, and He held nothing back!

Husbands, love your wives according to Christ's way and example. When husbands willingly obey this command, then there is no hesitation, not the slightest problem, with wives submitting themselves unto their own husbands with joy and delight.

Such harmony between a husband and wife is a wonderful ideal and very desirable, but it may seem to be an unreachable goal. It is dependent upon what each partner may do and will do for the other, and on their relationship to the Lord Jesus Christ. Also, by realizing what Christ will do for them.

Probably the most beautiful description of the husband's love for his wife is the following description by the eminent scholar and theologian, Chrysostom, when he proclaimed, "Hast thou seen the measure of obedience? Hear also the measure of love. Wouldst thou that thy wife shouldst obey thee as the Church doth Christ? Have care thyself for her as Christ for the Church. And if it be needful that thou shouldst give thy life for her, or be cut to pieces a thousand times, or endure anything whatever, refuse it not . . . He brought the Church to his feet by his great care, not by threats nor fear nor any such things; so do thou conduct thyself towards thy wife." Thus, Chrysostom penetratingly describes what a husband's love for his wife should be. He could not be more direct. Husbands, take note.

Scripture says, the *husband is the head of the wife,* . . . [Eph. 5:23] but it also says that the husband must love his wife as Christ loves the church. That is a love that does only what is best for his bride. Oh, that every marriage that is about to begin or that is continuing would hear and understand the Lord's teaching as contained in Ephesians and the New Testament! The focal point of these marriages should be the Lord Jesus Christ, not the husband or the wife.

Yes, the husband's love for his wife is to be a sacrificial love. It is also to be a purifying love. As Barclay notes, "Christ cleansed and consecrated the Church by the washing of water . . . " A husband is to love his wife in such a way that he will help to cleanse her. His love will be an up-building one, not one that tears down, abuses, or destroys. It is a love that refines a person's character and strengthens it. Certainly, it does not weaken it.

Further, it is a love that is the fruit of the Spirit. *But the fruit of the Spirit is love, joy, peace, long-suffering, gentleness* (kindness), *goodness, faith* (faithfulness), *Meekness, temperance* (self-control): *against such there is no law* [Gal. 5:22–23]. Grasp how the Apostle Paul logically proceeds from one point to another.

You will recall the eighteenth verse says, *And be not drunk with wine, wherein is excess* (dissipation); *but be filled with the Spirit* [Eph. 5:18]. Husbands and wives are to be filled with the Holy Spirit. The first fruit of the Spirit is love. If a husband is not filled with the Spirit then how can he love his wife as Christ loves the church? One of the ways a husband shows whether or not he is filled with the Spirit is by how he treats his wife.

A husband's love is to be a caring love. A primary example is the dialogue between Peter and the Lord Jesus after the Resurrection. Jesus asked Peter three times, *Lovest thou me?* The first two times Peter responded, *Yea, Lord; thou knowest that I love* (have affection for) *thee.* Jesus replied on the two occasions, *Feed my lambs* (and) *Feed my sheep.* A third time Jesus asks, *Simon, . . . lovest thou* (have affection for) *me? Peter was grieved because he said unto him a third time, . . . Lovest thou* (have affection for) *me? And he said unto him, Lord, thou knowest all things; thou knowest that I love* (have affection for) *thee. Jesus saith unto him, Feed my sheep* [Selections from John 21:15–17].

The word for *love* used in this account of our Lord's conversation with Peter is *phileō*. It has a different meaning than the word *agape*. It means "to have a tender affection" or "to be fond of." It means a love that values and esteems another person. It is a love that is unselfish and ready to serve rather than to be served. It contains the thought of cherishing the object of that love above and beyond everything else. This type of love is marked by a constancy of affection and fondness.

A caring love is not for the purpose of extracting service or comfort but to cherish the one he or she loves. A caring love is not one that merely expects the wife to cook, clean, wash, shop, and rear children. A caring love follows the example of Christ watching over His church. It is a love that feeds the lambs and the sheep.

Christ's love for His church is an unbreakable love. A husband's love for his wife should be the same. They have become one; they are united.

A husband would not think of dismembering his own body. Therefore, he should not think of separating his wife from himself.

What factors contribute to the development and continuation of an unbreakable love? Undoubtedly two people have been attracted to each other. There is nothing in Scripture that says there should not be a physical attraction between a man and woman. Both the man and woman who become husband and wife are initially attracted to one another. Probably for physical reasons, but it is God who gives these gifts. There is nothing wrong with them. The Bible does not do away with natural elements or attractions. Even though we are members of Christ's body, we should feel an attraction to the one we are going to marry or to whom we have been married.

In addition, the two people should be fond of each other, they should be attracted to each other, and they should have the same interests. Whether the interests come naturally or are created, they occur because of the desire to please the other person. There should not be fundamental differences between a husband and wife. If there are, there will not be harmony, but there will be trouble. It is important that the husband and wife be attracted to each other and be fond of each other.

The essential element is that the two people become and remain members of Christ's body. Christ can and does make a difference in a marriage. There may be some happy marriages based upon being attracted and fond of one another, but above and beyond that there is a love blessed by God that has its foundation in Christ Jesus. It is a love that sanctifies them and gives them a special glory.

Probably the best description of love is in Paul's letter to the Corinthians where he says, under the influence of the Holy Spirit,

> *Charity* (Love) *suffereth long, and is kind; charity envieth not; charity vaunteth not* (does not brag on) *itself, is not puffed* (arrogant) *up,*
> *Doth not behave itself unseemly* (rudely), *seeketh not her own, is not easily provoked, thinketh no evil* (keeps no account of evil);
> *Rejoiceth not in iniquity, but rejoiceth in the truth;*
> *Beareth all things, believeth all things, hopeth all things, endureth all things.*
> *Charity never faileth* [1 Cor. 13:4–8].

> *And now abideth faith, hope, charity, these three; but the greatest of these is charity* (love) [1 Cor. 13:13].

What type of love is this? It is a love that is in the Lord Jesus Christ. The husband and wife are to continually remember that there are three partners to the marriage, not just two. So often when this twenty-fifth verse is read or heard people stop with the first four words, *Husbands, love your wives, . . .* Less frequently the phrase is added, *even as Christ also loved the Church.* Even less are the words added *and gave himself for it.* The whole sentence must be considered and taken in context. It reads, *Husbands, love your wives, even as Christ also loved the church, and gave himself for it* [Eph. 5:25].

Why does the Apostle do this? According to Martyn Lloyd-Jones, "First, he wants everyone of us to know Christ's great love to us. He wants us to know the truth about Christ and ourselves, and our relationship to Him."

How can a husband know full well how to love His wife unless He knows about Christ's love and His relationship with His bride, the church? It is a question to ponder. Of course, some people do not want to deal with it. They ask, what does doctrine have to do with marriage? Others say to learn about Christ and His church takes time and effort. Or they say we have our own ideas about marriage; we see it on television, in the movies, and if we do not like it, we can leave it.

Christ cannot and would not leave His church. A husband is to know the New Testament teaching about Christ and His church, and he is to apply it to his marriage.

What does this teach us about Christ's love for His church? You and I are members of His church. Do we always obey Him? Do we always please Him? Are we always worthy of His love? Are we perfect in thought, word, and deed? Have we been cleansed of every spot and wrinkle? Here we are with all our deficiencies, shortcomings, and other negatives, yet He loves us.

> *Husbands, love your wives, even as Christ loved the church* [Eph. 5:25].

Then, for appropriate emphasis, Paul added as part of the same sentence,

> *. . . and gave himself for it;*
> *That he might sanctify* (set it apart) *and cleanse it with the washing of water by the word,*
> *That he might present it to himself a glorious church, not having spot, or wrinkle, or any such thing; but that it should be holy and without blemish* [Eph. 5:25–27].

Note Christ gave Himself for her. A husband is to give himself for his wife. He is to be concerned about her, her well-being, her growth and development. He wants her to be perfect. He wants to show her off. He wants her to be respected, liked, and admired. Christ gave Himself willingly, deliberately, joyfully for His Bride. A husband is to give himself the same way for his wife.

What great principles should characterize a husband's love for his wife?

This love of which the Apostle speaks, the love which Christ has for His church, is not self-centered. It does not think of self. It is entirely directed to the other person.

Marriage is not 50/50. It is 100/100 plus another 100 for the Lord Jesus Christ.

May God bless unto us a real and practical understanding of this verse. May it become part and parcel of our daily life.

> *Husbands, love your wives, even as Christ also loved the church, and gave himself or it* [Eph. 5:25].

In closing, there is a final word for husbands to ponder and to do for themselves and then for their wives. "*Husbands*, put your ear close to this bit of God's Word; and get the full force of these words. Yours is the submission of love which partakes of both the nature and manner of Christ's love for the Church, His Bride. Christ loved with a love that was utterly selfless and self-sacrificing. He loved, not thinking of what He could *get*, but of what he could *give*. And He gave all that He is and has; He gave Himself unto the uttermost, even of death. Christian husband, 'love your wife, *even as*.' Then subjection to you on the wife's part will be only a joy and a delight. Then she will reverence you for what you truly are," as forcefully, yet beautifully described by Ruth Paxson.

Amen!

18

Marriage: the Husband and Wife Relationship

> *Nevertheless let every one of you in particular so love his wife even as himself; and the wife see that she reverence* (respects) *her husband* [Eph. 5:33].

Examining the Lord Jesus Christ and His Bride, the church, as well as the relationship between a husband and wife, is beneficial to knowing Christ and to having a blessed, joyful marriage. We are to keep in the forefront of our minds the Apostle's commands to *be filled with the Spirit;* and *Submitting* (subjecting) *yourselves one to another in the fear* (reverence) *of God* [Eph. 5:18, 21]. Paul concludes this section with the statement, *Nevertheless let everyone of you in particular so love his wife even as himself; and the wife see that she reverence* (respects) *her husband* [Eph. 5:33].

These exhortations form the foundation for hearing, understanding, and applying the truths contained in the Apostle's exposition on Christ and His church as it pertains to the marriage relationship between a husband and wife.

Paul always provides building blocks. He proceeds in a constructive, orderly manner. Why does he provide such detail? Why does he describe the relationship between Christ and the church and then emphasize marriage, the bond between one man and one woman? Why does he do these things?

First, to make us stop and think and to realize there is something meaningful and valuable in these relationships. They are not to be taken for granted. They are not to be dismissed by merely acknowledging that they exist or that an event has occurred. They are to be studied, extra effort is to be exerted, and both thought and action are required by the different parties.

There may be exceptions, but primarily real success in the Christian life requires thinking or, more appropriately, studying, understanding, and applying these teachings. Real success as members of Christ's body does not happen automatically. Not anymore than a beautiful rose garden, or a concert pianist, or gourmet cook happens automatically.

Unfortunately, there is a belief that if a person makes a profession of faith, or joins a church, or attends worship services that things happen automatically; that they will live happily ever after; and that the preacher will be their intermediary.

The apostles spent three years with the Master. They asked questions, they listened, they walked and talked with Him, they tried to obey Him; then they denied Him and were absent in His hour of need.

Why were the New Testament Epistles ever written? To teach us! To get us to think! To get us to understand! To work things out! For us to know Christ is not as easy "as falling off a log." It requires instruction and learning. It requires support and care. It requires forgiving and denying oneself. It requires recognizing that at best you are no more than one-half of a whole.

Why do marriages fail? Why do members of a church fade away or only participate on the surface? The Apostle Paul offers an excellent description of the reasons, saying,

> *But ye have not so learned Christ;*
> *If so be that ye have heard him, and have been taught by him, as the truth is in Jesus:*
> *That ye put off concerning the former conversation* (conduct) *the old man, which is corrupt according to the deceitful lusts;*
> *And be renewed in the spirit of your mind;*
> *And that ye put on the new, which after God is created in righteousness and true holiness* [Eph. 4:20–24].

As members of Christ's body, we are to think on these things and to act accordingly.

Second, our conception of Christ and the church, as well as marriage, should be very positive. The approach to and the view of marriage regarding the responsibilities of both husband and wife should be based upon the teachings contained in Scripture. It is not always easy, but it is to be the light that guides their path. Married couples, regardless of their ages or the length of their marriage, should ask,

> Am I aware of these teachings?
> Am I governed by them?
> Are we increasing in knowledge and understanding?
> Are we thinking and learning about our responsibilities
>   to each other?
> Is the Lord Jesus Christ the true head of our relationship?

The marriage between members of Christ's body should grow, develop, and mature. And like our relationship to Christ, it should become more wonderful as the years go by.

Third, the Apostle wants us to realize that the primary obstacle to a successful, positive relationship with the Lord Jesus Christ is the same one that has a negative impact on a successful marriage, namely self with all its derivatives, manifestations, vices, and vulgarities. Because self wants things for itself. One of the unfortunate things about this is that the desires of self are more evident in others, at least to ourselves, than they are in our own being. We have that wonderful, dangerous, self-serving trait known as rationalization. It works most effectively and ingeniously when self is involved. Think about it, observe yourself and others, and see how deceptively rationalization works.

Undoubtedly, the Apostle Paul recognized this, because he introduces this section by admonishing us to *be filled with the Spirit;* and *Submitting* (subjecting) *yourselves one to another in the fear* (reverence) *of God* [Eph. 5:18, 21]. These basic principles are commands and we are to adhere to them. They are for each of us, not for someone else.

Paul reminds both husbands and wives as to what they are to do. He tells the husbands what they are to do, not as a group or collection of people, but as individuals. He says to them, *let everyone of you in particular so love his wife even as himself* [Eph. 5:33]. No husband is omitted. It applies to each and every one, from the newly wed to those celebrating their golden wedding anniversaries and beyond.

Paul said previously, *So ought men to love their* (own) *wives as their own bodies* [Eph. 5:28]. The Apostle is not repeating himself, but he is expanding upon his earlier statement. He says that each husband ought to love his wife as his own body, or as part of his own body. He is to love his wife as part of himself, as his own arms, legs, head, heart, and mind, not as something that does not belong to his own body.

What does it mean that "Every husband is to love his wife as part of his own body?" It means that they are more than partners. They are halves of the same entity. The husband is not to think of himself as a single entity or an individual.

Each husband is to always include his wife in his thinking. He is no longer a separate unit. He does not operate or have his being apart from his other half. His wife is to be involved in all his desires. Once a man becomes a husband, he is no longer a single entity operating on his own and independently of anyone else.

The husband is not to be selfish or primarily concerned with himself. Of course, neither is the wife to be selfish or self-centered. Both the husband and wife must be ever watchful and alert to the wiles of self-rationalization and Satan. Both are to remind themselves to think, govern, and control their relationships according to Scripture.

What should a husband do or not do regarding his wife? Certainly, he is not to abuse her. Men may abuse their own bodies by over-indulging themselves, but they should not do so. Also, they should not abuse, gratify, or over-indulge their wives. If they do, then there will be a breakdown in the relationship.

Each husband is to show concern and care for his wife. He is to involve her and do things with her. A husband and wife are to do things together.

A husband is not to neglect his wife. He is to nourish and cherish her. If he does, then it will be impossible to neglect her. When the husband nourishes and cherishes his wife, there is much more involved than providing for the physical desires and comforts of life or satisfying tangible needs. This means that there is: nourishing and cherishing of the mind; spiritual development and growth; maturing in the Lord Jesus Christ; and enhancing and enriching the marriage itself.

In addition, there should be dialogue between the husband and wife on all matters. They should talk. They should share. As stated earlier, there should be hearing, thinking, understanding, and applying. This is true of our relationship with the Lord Jesus Christ as well as between the husband and wife.

The husband has another responsibility towards his wife. He is to protect her. He is to protect her from her weaknesses. He is neither to condemn her frailties, nor to berate her. He is to strengthen and support her. He is to help turn the weaknesses into strengths.

What did Christ do with His disciples? What does Christ do with the members of His body? He gets them to listen, think, understand, and practice. This is true of the so-called normal maladies, that may beset her, his wife. The husband is to protect her, to nourish and cherish her, and she is to know that he will.

While the husband is protecting, nourishing, and cherishing his wife, he is also to build her up. He is to prepare her for the times she may have to do things by herself. Recall that the Apostle said, *I THEREFORE, the prisoner of the Lord, beseech you that ye walk worthy of the vocation* (calling) *wherewith ye are called* [Eph. 4:1].

What should the husband do to show that he understands Paul's exhortation in the following? *Nevertheless let every one of you in particular so love his wife even as himself,* . . . or as we probably more accurately interpret the statement, "Let each particular husband love his wife as his own body or as part of his own body."

Paul calls us to be something, to do something. Then he proceeds to describe the characteristics of this walk: unity, holiness, love, light, wisdom, praise, and harmony.

This portion of Chapter 5 and the first several verses of Chapter 6 are devoted to harmony. Harmony in marriage is based upon the example of the Lord Jesus Christ and His bride, the church. Before the Apostle discusses harmony, he presents the ingredients that must precede it. They are unity, holiness, love, light, wisdom, and praise. There is to be a unity in our walk with Christ. There is to be a unity between a husband and a wife. There is unity between the Lord Jesus Christ and the true members of His body.

When these characteristics are present, then self with all its deficiencies fades into the background. Individual rights and asserting them are not as important as they once seemed. Therefore, clashes, discord, and separation are not prevalent.

Consider, *and the wife see that she reverence* (respects) *her husband.* The Greek word for *reverence* in this verse actually means "reverential fear" or "deference." This means either respectful or courteous regard for another's wishes, or yielding to another's judgment or preference out of respect and reverence.

The church is to yield unto Christ. In the same manner, the wife is to yield to her husband. However, the husband is to conduct himself in such a way that the wife will willingly submit to him as she willingly submits to Christ.

Peter reminds the hearers of the example of pious women who sought the blessings of the Spirit and were subject unto their husbands. Also, Peter reminds them of Sarah, who called Abraham lord because she knew that the Lord God had so commanded her.

Peter describes in his first letter what the wives and husbands are to do in their marriage relationship. He informs the hearers that

> *Even as Sarah obeyed Abraham, calling him lord: whose daughters ye are, as long as ye do well, and are not afraid with any amazement* (terror).
> *Likewise, ye husbands, dwell with them according to knowledge* (with understanding), *giving honor unto the wife, as unto the weaker vessel, and as being heirs together of the grace of life; that your prayers be not hindered* [1 Pet. 3:6–7].

Peter wants the husbands to be prudent in discharging their responsibilities as head of the family. The husbands are to "honor their wives for nothing destroys the fellowship of life more than contempt, and we cannot really love any but those whom we esteem, so that love must be connected with respect," as stated justifiably by John Calvin.

Then individuals begin to think, to understand, and to practice. Unity is formed. It develops and grows. There is unity with Christ. There is unity with each other in Christ. The fundamental principle in our relationship with the Lord Jesus Christ is unity.

The same principle is central in the marriage relationship between a husband and wife.

> *For we are members of his body, of his flesh, and of his bones.*
> *FOR THIS CAUSE SHALL A MAN LEAVE HIS FATHER AND MOTHER, AND SHALL BE JOINED UNTO HIS WIFE, AND THEY TWO SHALL BE ONE FLESH* [Eph. 5:30–31].

When the walk begins in unity, then it can flower into holiness, love, light, wisdom, praise, and harmony.

When studying Scripture, there is a tendency to jump ahead or to skip over words. Consequently, we deprive ourselves of learning certain truths. The words *leave* and *join* are significant. They impact upon the basic earthly entity—the family.

A man has been a member of one family unit as a son. Then one event changes his relationship, his duties, and responsibilities. He becomes the head of a family with different duties and responsibilities. The marriage ceremony becomes a momentous occasion when it is properly understood and interpreted. It impacts equally upon the new husband and the new wife. The new wife has new duties and responsibilities as well as a new relationship.

The marriage relationship is of primary importance and takes precedence over all other human relationships. That is why it is important to know the relationship between Christ and His church and why Paul stresses it. This allows a husband and wife to better understand their relationship and to walk in harmony. Remember, Paul said: *But be filled with the Spirit* . . . *(and) Submitting yourselves one to another in the fear of God* [Eph. 5:18b, 21].

Husbands are to love their wives and treat them honorably and kindly. Why? God favors them to do so. Peter describes the husbands and wives as *being heirs together of the grace of life* [1 Pet. 3:7]. The Greek word for *heirs* in this verse means, "one receiving a lot with another." The husband and wife receive it together. "God bestows the same grace alike on husbands and wives; he invites them to seek an equality in them, and we know that those graces which wives share with their husbands are manifold," as Calvin appropriately describes God's grace in the marriage relationship.

Why does Scripture say a man should leave his father and mother, but it does not say the same about the wife? Prior to the marriage, the husband was paying deference to his parents; but after the marriage, he becomes head of a new family. Likewise, prior to the marriage, the wife was paying deference to her parents. However, after the marriage, she is to pay deference to her husband. When the marriage relationship is understood according to Scripture and on the basis of the Lord Jesus Christ and His church, then there can be unity and harmony. When it is not understood and practiced by the husband and wife and the parents involved, then there will be disunity and disharmony. Peer pressure has been evident through the ages. Peter said to the women, *Even as Sarah obeyed Abraham, calling him lord: whose daughters ye are, as long as ye do well, and are not afraid with any amazement* (terror) [1 Pet. 3:6].

What does this mean? Peter says to the wives who are members of Christ's body, do as the Master would have you to do, and do it according to the will of God. He tells them that the non-Christian women will make fun of them, taunt them, rebuke them, tell them they are being foolish, and that they should assert their rights and do their thing. Peter says do not pay any attention to those comments, but focus upon the will of God and the teachings of Scripture. Realize what you are to do and let your conduct and behavior reflect that you are walking with the Lord Jesus Christ and no one else but Him and Him alone.

These teachings about marriage are addressed to whom? To the members of Christ's body. To those *being filled with the Spirit* [Eph. 5:18, 21] and to those *submitting yourselves one to another in the fear of God* [Eph. 5:18, 21]. They are not addressed to those outside Christ's body.

These teachings are meant for us individually. They are provided for our benefit, so that our lives may be filled with joy, so that we might have life and have it more abundantly. They are provided so that we will stop and think; learn, understand, and practice; have a positive approach to marriage as well as to the Lord Jesus Christ and His church; and recognize the primary obstacle to either a successful marriage or a positive relationship with the Lord Jesus Christ is self with all its foibles, including self-centeredness, self-importance, self-rationalization, and other impediments to a Christcentered life. These teachings are provided so that we may walk in unity, holiness, love, light, wisdom, praise, and harmony.

Lastly, they are provided so that our relationship with the Lord Jesus Christ may grow and enrich our daily living. If a husband and wife are walking with Him and are *joint-heirs of the grace of life*, then their relationship will be blessed.

Remember Christ gave Himself for His church, and that: He died for Her; He nourishes and cherishes Her; He intercedes for Her; He prepares Her; and He watches over Her.

> *Therefore as the church is subject unto Christ, so let the wives be to their own husbands in every thing* [Eph. 5:24].

> *Husbands, love your wives, even as Christ also loved the church, and gave himself for it* [Eph. 5:25].

> *Nevertheless let every one of you in particular so love his wife even as himself; and the wife see that she reverence* (respects) *her husband* [Eph. 5:33].

May God bless the study of His Word. May we do as He would have us to do and *be filled with the Spirit* of Christ as members of His body.

May each husband and wife thank God, through Christ Jesus and the Holy Spirit, for enlightening Paul and revealing to him God's requirements for receiving His manifold blessings in their marriage, and may they be obedient to His commands as they continue receiving His grace upon grace.

Amen!

19

Christ Nourishes and Cherishes

> *So ought men to love their (own) wives as their own bodies. He that loveth his wife loveth himself.*
> *For no man ever yet hated his own flesh; but nourisheth and cherisheth it, even as the Lord the church* [Eph. 5:28–29].

The Apostle in these last eleven verses of the fifth chapter is doing two things: describing what and how the relationship should be between a husband and wife; and the relationship between the Lord Jesus Christ and His Bride, the church, which is to serve as a model for husbands and wives.

We have been considering how the Lord Jesus Christ treats His Bride. How he cares and provides for her, but as we continue examining these eleven verses we are to learn from them and apply the truths contained therein.

There are certain fundamental points to remember as the Word is opened and God's will is revealed. First, the analogy regarding marriage is provided because it is similar to the relationship between the Lord Jesus Christ and His church, and it applies to the marriage relationship between a husband and wife who are members of Christ's body.

Second, the marriage relationship, as well as the parent–child, and employer–employee relationship are not to be the primary focal points. Why? Because they are encumbered by human frailties and deficiencies. The focus is to be upon God's faithfulness and His extreme care in providing a perfect example upon which to base the most meaningful relationships experienced during our lives.

A positive marriage relationship is derived from God's faithfulness, responding to His call and obeying His commandments willingly.

Therefore, we are to apply the teachings contained in the Word to our marriage relationship.

We are to learn and to understand more about God and His Son Jesus Christ. We are to grow in knowledge. Yes, but even more important, we are to become more obedient to His commandments and teachings.

Third, a living, growing, meaningful faith is a basic requirement for developing and enjoying a marriage that is analogous to the relationship between Christ and His church. We are to continuously seek God's blessing upon our marriage and to pray for the enabling grace and power of the Holy Spirit to strengthen us.

What type of faith do we mean? "It is the I–Thou relation, which is what faith in fact is, (it) is by analogy a response to and a taking of responsibility for God's personal relation to man. However, God is the Creator," as proclaimed by Otto Weber. This I–Thou relation requires each individual husband or wife taking responsibility for God's personal relationship with him or her. This relationship includes both positive and negative situations experienced in living our lives, such as acceptance and rejection, obedience and disobedience, liking and disliking, companionship and solitude, and many contrasting similarities. However, there is one significant difference; our primary relationship is to be with God the Father and His Son Christ Jesus. God is the Creator! We are not. He is not only the object of our faith, He is the One who initiates and makes our faith effective. He is both the object and the subject of our faith. Weber states it beautifully and truthfully, saying, "He (God) confronts us as one who can be confused or exchanged with no other." That is so true of both the believer and the nonbeliever.

Even though God confronts us on one side, He does even more. He supports the other side through the Lord Jesus Christ. When considering analogies, remember one thing, there is no way there can be an analogy from the creature back to the Creator. It is only from the Creator to the creature. It is in the Lord Jesus Christ that God the Creator comes to us and dwells among us. Even though He dwells among us, He still remains the Creator.

How is our faith in God the Creator and His Son the Lord Jesus Christ to be expressed? It is to be lived by dependent, obedient behavior. Yes, at times it is very difficult. Nevertheless, it is to be lived, it is to be tried, and it is to be forged, even in the most trying circumstances.

Faith is not just observing certain religious rites or services or performing specific acts. It is living as God through Christ would have us live in the most intimate and demanding relationships of life. It is living as He would have us live in one-on-one situations. Remember, our relationship to Him is one-on-one. We should not lose sight of that.

Our faith is dependent upon the outside call, accepting the Word of the Lord, and being cleansed and sanctified. We are to respond to the outside factors in a positive way. We are to apply the teachings to marriage, to family, to home, and to work.

Each of us has ambitions. There are things we would like to do. The interesting aspect is that the ambitions change as we grow older, our circumstances change, our knowledge increases, and our relationship to God increases or decreases. However, there is one ambition that should remain unchanged and at the top of the list once we recognize it: the goal of our life at the beginning, throughout all our days, and at the end should be to do the will of God, our Father.

What did the Lord Jesus strive to do? *I can of mine own self do nothing: as I hear, I judge: and my judgment is just* (righteous)*; because I seek not mine own will, but the will of the Father which hath sent me* [John 5:30]. Christ's will was to do the will of the Father. He was never discouraged from doing His Father's will, even when He went to Calvary's Hill. That was the pinnacle of obeying the Father. Oswald Chambers vividly describes our Lord's dependence and obedience to His Father when he says, "Nothing ever discouraged our Lord on His way to Jerusalem. He never hurried through certain villages where He was persecuted, or lingered in others where He was blessed. Neither gratitude nor ingratitude turned our Lord one hair's breadth away from His purpose to go up to Jerusalem."

When considering these facts, is it asking too much to obey the Father's will; seek to apply His teachings to marriage, home, and work; or focus on our Father and His Son no matter what joys or sorrows, successes or defeats, triumphs or trials may come our way? It is very difficult to do, but our ambition should be to do the will of our Father. This requires effort, knowledge, and work. We are to walk toward our Jerusalem. The way may be difficult, but the Lord will bless our journey.

Scripture is direct, and to the point in telling husbands how they are to behave toward their wives throughout their marriages as proclaimed in *so ought men to love their* (own) *wives as their own bodies.*

This is a bold statement that is to be heeded by each and every husband, and soon-to-be bridegroom. It is the bedrock of every beautiful, enriching, and loving marriage that grows stronger and stronger throughout the years as it radiates the values of Christ to family and friends.

What do the words *so ought* declare? They are "a divine compulsion that exempts no husband. The divine standard can never be lowered. The "ought" of the wife's loyalty is complemented by the "ought" of the husband's love. "*Men are to love their wives as their own bodies*"—the very highest human standard of which man is capable of reaching, which, when reached, means that the husband loves his wife as he loves himself.

"The husband's headship entails upon him yet one more responsibility: He is to protect and provide for his wife in the same tender and loving way that Christ does for the church," as faithfully expressed by Ruth Paxson.

Our Scripture also reveals truths that we readily acknowledge. Also, it contains a couple that we may gloss over too rapidly. *For no man ever yet hated his own flesh; but nourisheth and cherisheth it, even as the Lord the church* [Eph. 5:29]. Once again, it is important to notice not only the words, but the tense used by the Apostle. He says *nourishes and cherishes*. He does not use the past tense or the future tense. He uses the present tense. The nourishing and cherishing are continuing processes. They keep occurring, occurring, and occurring. Look at these two words. It is interesting to note that the Greek word used for *nourish* appears only this one time in Scripture. It does not just mean to nourish, but "to nourish much."

Therefore, husbands ought "to nourish much" their wives, with an abundance not with just a little or an average amount. Christ nourishes the church with much food and nourishment. Husbands are to do the same with their wives. This nourishment should meet all the needs of one's wife and much more. Paul says, *And he* (himself) *gave some, apostles; and some, prophets; and some, evangelists; and some, pastors and teachers* [Eph. 4:11]. Why did He do this? Paul tells us forthrightly, saying it is:

> *For the perfecting* (equipping) *of the saints, . . .*
> *for the edifying of the body of Christ;*
> *Till we all come in* (into) *the unity of the faith, and of the knowledge of the Son of God, . . .*
> *That we henceforth be no more children, . . . and carried about by every wind of doctrine, . . .* [Eph. 4:12–14].

Christ *nourishes much* the church. Husbands are *to nourish much* their wives.

The Word is given to provide needed spiritual nourishment. There is no excuse for the church to plead that she is ignorant, or underdeveloped, or wasting away. Nor for any of us to say the same thing. Peter says *According as his divine power hath given unto us all things that pertain unto life and godliness, through the knowledge of him that hath called us to glory and virtue* [2 Pet. 1:3]. He also says, *As newborn babes, desire the sincere* (pure) *milk of the word, that ye may grow thereby* [1 Pet. 2:2].

The Lord provides for the *ecclesia*. The husband is to provide for his wife. The question is how are we to make this nourishment available? It is by desiring to study the Word and to attend public worship. These things are not to be done as a matter of duty or performing works, but by wanting to do so and then doing them realizing we cannot grow without receiving the necessary nourishment; and recognizing and accepting that it is God who calls, who separates, who illuminates, and who leads. All these things are available and are to become part of us because it is God's way of nourishing "His people."

What does the word *cherish* mean? It comes from the Greek word *thalpō* which means "to heat," "to soften by heat." Also, it means "to keep warm with a covering." An example is that of a bird keeping its young warm with its feathers. In using this word, Paul means that husbands are to cherish their wives with a tender, warm love and care.

What should be the results of nourishing and cherishing? The individuals receiving these benefits by grace should grow, develop, and prosper in the Lord. When a person is nourished and cherished they should realize they are under the watchful care of the One who is providing for them.

Unfortunately, many of us do not truly realize our Lord's great concern for us individually as well as collectively. It is one thing to accept the fact that, yes, the Lord Jesus Christ loves the church, nourishes her, and cherishes her. It is entirely different to accept the fact that the Lord Jesus Christ loves me, that He nourishes and cherishes me—with all my warts, blemishes, spots, stains, and wrinkles.

Probably the greatest hindrance to accepting and realizing this fact is our lack of knowledge about God and His Son and not knowing Him as we should. It is from having other ambitions and allowing that old *self* to get in the way.

What keeps us from knowing more about Him, from knowing Him better? Television, social activities, business, sports, hobbies, family, and other interests. What is it? Lack of study time? The Word not being presented?

We have heard it said you cannot get some of the people out at night. That is true, you cannot get some out, but you can get others. When you know more about Him, then you want to know more about Him. The more you know, the more you love Him.

Why do we love Him? Because He first loved us! We need to accept that fact and begin to understand it. We need to begin to understand the practical realities of applying His teachings and practicing them in marriage, in the home, and in the workplace.

Too often people stop at the Cross. They come to Good Friday, the suffering, the forgiveness, the death, and the atonement. They come to Easter morning, to the Resurrection, to the fact that He lives. That is where we have a tendency to begin and to end. But that is not where Christ terminates His work. He continues to nourish and cherish us. He continues to sanctify and cleanse us. He continues to wash us.

Why? Paul says, *That he might present it to himself a glorious church, not having spot, or wrinkle, or any such thing; but that it should be holy and without blemish* [Eph. 5:27]. That is the objective, that is the purpose, that is what He is going to do with the church and with you and me.

Actually, for us to receive the full impact of this verse we need to add a word. It should read: "That He Himself might present it to Himself." Martyn Lloyd-Jones says you need "to introduce an additional Himself there," because even analogies need amplification. The Apostle uses the relationship between Christ and the church as an analogy for the husband and wife.

All of us have attended or participated in weddings. One thing always happens, either the father, or a relative, or even a friend, gives the bride to the groom. The bride is presented by someone else. However, not in this instance. Christ Himself will present His bride, the church, and the individuals in it to Himself. This is another way of illustrating that great truth of Scripture: our salvation is the work of the Lord. He will present His bride to Himself.

Why? Because no one else can do it. What is going to happen to the church, to the individuals who are the people of God, when she and they are presented to Christ Himself? What is it going to be like?

First, it will be a glorious church. *Glorious*, in this instance, means "splendid, gorgeous." *Whom he justified, them he also glorified* [Rom. 8:30]. Further, Scripture says,

> *For our conversation* (citizenship) *is in heaven from whence also we look for the Saviour, for the Lord Jesus Christ:*
> *Who shall change our vile body, that it may be fashioned like unto his glorious body, according to the working whereby he is able even to subdue all things unto himself* [Phil. 3:20–21].

Second, it will be without spot or stain. Remember, He is sanctifying, cleansing, and washing it. When He does this, then the most detailed inspection will not reveal the slightest or most minute spot or stain.

Third, it will be without wrinkle. Let's face it, as we get older wrinkles appear. Or if we are sick they will be noticeable. But the Apostle tells us that we will be presented to Christ Himself without a wrinkle to mar our appearance.

Fourth, *that it should be holy and without blemish* [Eph. 5:27]. The purpose of our baptism, the sanctifying, cleansing, and washing is that we may live holy and blameless lives to God. "For Christ washes us, not that we may return to rolling in our pollution, but that we may retain through our life the purity which we have once received," as John Calvin enlightens us.

We are to be holy in the sight of God, not in the eyes of men. Being holy is an ongoing process. It is not to be confused with morality, nor is it to be marked by an absence of a specific sin or sins. What does this mean? Sharing the righteousness of God and obeying His commands. Remember that beautiful verse, *And be ye kind one to another, tenderhearted, forgiving one another, even as God for Christ's sake* (in Christ) *hath forgiven you* [Eph. 4:32]. God is holy! We are to become holy and righteous.

How does this happen? It happens by: knowing Him; learning about Him; and doing His will; walking toward our own Jerusalem; having a personal relationship with Him; exercising dependent behavior; being nourished and cherished; and applying His teachings.

By enumerating these things we are in reality emphasizing a great truth. Our relationship to the Lord Jesus Christ is a continuous process; it is ongoing. It is not a one-time event, nor is it a once-a-week happening. It proceeds day by day. It is a powerful, unyielding force. The following states it very well,

> *Now unto him that is able to do exceeding abundantly above all that we ask or think, according to the power that worketh in us,*
> *Unto him be glory in the church by Christ Jesus throughout all ages, world without end* [Eph. 3:20–21].

Christ is able to do within us.

However, there is an ingredient that we need to provide. We need to examine ourselves. The next time you participate in Holy Communion remember Scripture makes it perfectly clear we are to examine ourselves as we prepare our hearts and our minds to *eat this bread, and drink this cup* [1 Cor. 11:26]. It is important to examine ourselves properly while preparing for this service and being in His presence.

Scripture issues a severe warning to those who partake of the elements in an unworthy manner:

> *For he that eateth and drinketh unworthily* (in an unworthy manner), *eateth and drinketh damnation* (judgment) *to himself, not discerning the Lord's body.*
> *For this cause many are weak and sickly among you, and many sleep* (are dead) [1 Cor. 11:29–30].

People do not examine themselves because they do not realize that they are members of Christ's bride, the church, and that He is going to sanctify, cleanse, and wash the church, which is His bride. Therefore, we are to judge ourselves, or He will do it for us.

> *For if we would judge ourselves, we should not be judged.*
> *But when we are judged, we are chastened of the Lord, that we should not be condemned with the world* [1 Cor. 11:31–32].

For as Paul says, He is going to make her *a glorious church, That it should be holy and without blemish* [Eph. 5:27].

When will it be? It is an ongoing process to prepare the church and the people of God for that day. But that day will come. The Apostle John reveals this truth when he says,

> *And I heard as it were the voice of a great multitude, and as the voice* (sound) *of many waters, and as the voice* (sound) *of mighty thunderings, saying, Alleluia: for the Lord God omnipotent reigneth.*
> *Let us be glad and rejoice, and give honor* (glory) *to him: for the marriage of the Lamb is come, and his wife hath made herself ready.*

> *And to her was granted that she should be arrayed in fine linen, clean and white* (bright)*: for the fine linen is the righteousness* (righteous acts) *of saints.*
> *And he saith unto me, Write, Blessed are they which are called unto the marriage supper of the Lamb. And he* (Christ) *saith unto me, These are the true sayings of God* [Rev. 19:6–9].

The church will be clothed in righteousness. Do you see how Scripture supports Scripture and is tied together by God's truth?

Yes, husbands are to nourish and cherish their wives. Yes, Christ nourishes and cherishes His church. Why?

> *That he* (himself) *might present it to himself a glorious church, not having spot, or wrinkle, or any such thing; but that it should be holy and without blemish* [Eph. 5:27].

Amen!

20

Christ and the Ecclesia

> *Husbands, love your wives, even as Christ also loved the church, and gave himself for it;*
> *That he might sanctify* (set it apart) *and cleanse it with the washing of water by the word*
> *That he might present it to himself a glorious church, not having spot, or wrinkle, or any such thing; but that it should be holy and without blemish* [Eph. 5:25–27].

There is a quotation attributed to Konrad Adenauer which states, "I am determined to know more today than yesterday and to be smarter tomorrow than today." That may not be the exact wording, but it captures the essence of his statement. This should be our motto, especially as it applies to the Lord Jesus Christ, our relationship to Him, and our daily living as members of the community of believers.

We enter into marriage with great anticipation. We look forward to the mountains to be climbed, to the worlds to be conquered, to what we will receive, to what we will get, to benefits, to joys, to satisfaction, and other things that appeal to self. Then what happens? Reality sets in, difficulties occur, and hopefully, we will be pricked by the Holy Spirit and learn that, *Wisdom is the principal thing; therefore get wisdom: and with all thy getting get understanding* [Prov. 4:7]. We are to get understanding and in so doing turn the focus from ourselves to others.

Unfortunately, there is another relationship into which we enter. A relationship with the church. Yes, I said unfortunately. That may surprise or shock you. However, let me explain. It can be that our early recollections, our mindset, our focus is on going to church, attending church, being married in the church, taking the children to church, supporting

Christ and the Ecclesia 157

the church, and inviting people to church. The emphasis becomes directed toward the church.

What is the church? A building? A congregation? A general assembly? It is the *ecclesia*, the called out, the body of Christ, the bride of Christ.

We, you and I, are the church. We have a relationship with one another. It is important; it is vital. It needs to be nourished, cherished, and enhanced. Without the presence of the Lord Jesus Christ, the church is nothing. And I repeat: it is nothing!

That is why I said that unfortunately we enter into a relationship with the church, whereas our relationship is to be with the Lord Jesus Christ, with Him personally. His Word, His Holy Spirit, and His Father. The focus of our relationship is to change from the church to the Lord Jesus Christ. We are to develop, to grow, to mature; and with all of our getting, we are to get understanding.

When doing these things we are to be guided and supported by the Word of God as contained in Scripture, and as it is revealed to us. Why do we have Scripture? So that God may reveal Himself and His Son to us. So that our pathways may be illuminated, our choices may be guided, our weaknesses may be strengthened, and our relationship with the Lord Jesus Christ may be blessed.

Paul and the other writers of the New Testament were used by the Holy Spirit not only to instruct us, but to chastise us and to bring us back to reality. What is more real than husbands and wives? Marriages? Churches? *Nothing should be more real than the Lord Jesus Christ! Nothing was more real to the Apostles, Paul, Peter and John, than Jesus Christ!*

If we do not pursue this relationship where it is and where it exists, if we do not open our hearts and minds to the Word of God, to the teachings of Scripture, then how can this relationship with Christ develop and mature? How can a marriage develop and mature?

Paul feeds us morsel by morsel, sip by sip, so that we may digest and assimilate the nourishment he has provided by the Holy Spirit's guiding hand: we are to study each phrase and verse, because it is provided for our benefit and welfare. Paul said, *Husbands, love your wives, even as Christ also loved the church, and gave himself for it* [Eph. 5:25]. Paul intertwines the exhortation for husbands to love their wives with an illustration of how Christ loved the church. He gave Himself for it!

He writes to believers, not to every resident of Ephesus. He has commanded them to *be filled with the Spirit*. He wants them to be able to apply the teachings of Christ. Therefore, he wants them to understand basic doctrine.

Christ gave Himself for the church, for the called out. This is a fundamental truth. There would not be a church, or a body of believers, if the Lord Jesus had not given Himself. The Apostle states it very succinctly, *For other foundation can no man lay than that* (which) *is laid, which is Jesus Christ* [1 Cor. 3:11]. In addition, he says, *Feed* (Shepherd) *the Church of God, which he* (Christ) *hath purchased with his own blood* [Acts 20:28]. Paul also says, *And the life which I now live in the flesh I live by the faith of* (faith in) *the Son of God, who loved me, and gave himself for me* [Gal. 2:20]. Certainly we should not forget,

> *And walk in love, as* (or even as) *Christ also hath loved us, and hath given himself for us an offering and a sacrifice to God for a sweet-smelling savor* (aroma) [Eph. 5:2].

Here we are in the midst of husbands and wives, love and marriage, and what does the Apostle do? He focuses our attention on the Cross, upon His sacrifice for you and me, and for the church. Our Lord in the night in which He was betrayed prayed to the Father, saying *I pray for them: I pray not for the world, but for them which thou hast given me, for they are thine* [John 17:9].

Calvin and others have stated He died for you and me, and He did not die for anyone else. What were the reasons for His going to the Cross and giving Himself? To redeem us; to redeem His Church.

We are to know and to remember that He is the foundation; no other foundation can be laid; He is the Head of the body; and He is the life-giving component and ingredient. We become members of Christ's body, the church, by the fact that Christ went to the Cross, shed His blood, and died. And in this way He redeemed us. It is an old, old story. How true are the words of that great hymn by Katherine Hankey,

> Tell me the old, old story of unseen things above,
> Of Jesus and His glory, of Jesus and His love,
> Tell me the story simply, as to a little child,
> For I am weak and weary, and helpless and defiled.
>
> Tell me the story slowly, that I may take it in,
> That wonderful redemption, God's remedy for sin,

Tell me the story often, for I forget so soon
The early dew of morning has passed away at noon.

Tell me the story softly, with earnest tones and grave;
Remember, I'm the sinner whom Jesus came to save,
Tell me the story always, if you would really be,
In any time of trouble, a comforter to me.

Tell me the same old story when you have cause to fear,
That the world's empty glory is costing me too dear.
Yes, and when that world's glory is dawning on my soul,
Tell me the old, old story: Christ Jesus makes thee whole.

How are we made whole? By becoming members of the invisible, true church, which is the spiritual body of Christ. Christ gave Himself for the church, for the called out. *Husbands, love your wives, even as Christ also loved the church, and gave himself for it* [Eph. 5:25]. There is a question to ponder: what was the state of the church, or the called out, when Christ gave Himself for it? They were sinners. Yes, although they had committed acts and spoken words that they should not have, He took the first step, He initiated the reconciliation, and He forgave them when they repented and accepted Him."

Dare we do less, even when we are upset or emotional? It's a hard lesson to learn. *For when we were yet without strength, in due time* (at the right time) *Christ died for the ungodly* [Rom. 5:6].

According to Calvin, the term *without strength* or "yet weak" means the time prior to being reconciled to God. We are born as children of wrath and remain in that condition until we become partakers of Christ's body by faith. When we were unfit and unworthy to be called the children of God, it was at that time Christ went to the Cross and died. A response in faith to the call of God is the beginning of godliness. Abram and Moses responded in faith when God called them.

> *For when we were yet without strength, in due time* (at the right time) *Christ died for the ungodly.*
> *For scarcely for a righteous man will one die: yet peradventure* (perhaps) *for a good man some would even dare to die.*
> *But God commendeth his* (demonstrates his own) *love toward us, in that, while we were yet sinners, Christ died for us.*
> *Much more then, being* (having been) *now justified by his blood, we shall be saved from wrath through him* [Rom. 5:6–9].

Note some of the other words the Apostle uses: *For scarcely for a righteous man will one die; . . . while we were yet sinners.* These were the conditions under which Christ gave Himself for the church, under which He loved the church and each member.

Does that sound like the conditions under which Prince Charming and Cinderella met and were married? Hardly. *Husbands, love your wives, even as Christ loved the church, and gave himself for it* [Eph. 5:25]. Paul says, *But God commendeth his* (demonstrates his own) *love toward us* [Rom. 5:8]. Even when we were weak and sinners God stood with us. He confirmed and declared His love toward us. Why? Not to give thanks to Him, but to bolster our confidence and security in Him.

There are certain things and people in which we have confidence. Even when situations are not going well, the appearance of someone special or remembering what someone said will bolster our spirits and allow us to proceed with confidence.

What is Paul saying to the husbands and wives? You find yourself in this marriage relationship, and now everything is not coming up roses. There are thorns on the stem, and they hurt. There is black spot on the leaves, and the bushes need tender loving care. The plants are not doing really well, so they need to be fed and watered; they need nourishment. The roses have deficiencies, failures, faults, and shortcomings.

In addition, think of the church, think of husbands and wives. They can talk back, they can be critical, disobedient, they can argue, get their feelings hurt, they can stand on their dignity, they can condemn, and they can pout.

Why does Paul tie all this together: Christ and the church, husbands and wives, teachings and applications, and sinners and saints? Why does He do it? If you are part of the *ecclesia*, you cannot separate them. Paul reminds the Ephesians (and us) that if the Lord Jesus Christ had reacted to the *ecclesia* as we have a tendency to react to one another then the foundation would never have been laid. *Charity* (love) *never faileth* [1 Cor. 13:8]. *And now abideth faith, hope, charity* (love), *these three; but the greatest of these is charity* (love) [1 Cor. 13:13]. Hopefully, you see how intertwined are the teachings of Christ and applying them. You cannot separate them.

Without the Word of God, we would not connect it to Christ giving Himself to be the atonement. We are to consider marriage, the responsibilities of husbands and wives, according to how God reveals Himself.

Christ and the Ecclesia

We are to open Scripture, study it, and apply it. It does not do us any good to keep the book closed, as well as our minds, to these eternal truths. It is revealing and exhilarating to examine Scripture in this way!

There is an observation to make at this juncture. There are people who dislike doctrine unless it is "God is love," and then they only want to know about it according to their own narrow definition, which is usually secular, not spiritual.

There are those who say you cannot get people out at night to study the Bible. Have we gotten to the point where we are tired of hearing about the Cross, forgiveness, the love of Christ, obedience, and reconciliation, or have we really never heard it for the first time? Are we hung up on what we do for Christ instead of what God through Christ has done for us?

There are certain, specific things which should control our hearts and minds. It is interesting that they are all one word: God, Christ, Cross, reconciliation, redemption, faith, commitment, grace, and trust. I am sure you could add a few more to this list.

Here we are in the midst of the second half of Paul's letter, the practical part, and what is the Apostle doing? He is expounding doctrine and tells us if we are filled with the Spirit, we will apply it to our marriages. He reminds us that throughout our marriage journey, the Cross is to go wherever we go and to be wherever we may be.

Paul, in this particular verse [Eph. 5:26], builds upon the previous verses where he exhorts the husbands to do something, relates to the love of Christ, presents doctrine, reminds us of what Christ has done for us, and sets the stage for the following verses:

> *Husbands, love your wives, even as Christ also loved the church, and gave himself for it* (the church),
> *That* (in order that) *he might sanctify* (set it apart) *and cleanse it with the washing of water by the word,*
> *That* (in order that) *he might present it to himself a glorious church, not having spot, or wrinkle, or any such thing; but that it should be holy and without blemish* [Eph. 5:25–27]

What do we have in this particular portion of Scripture? Husbands and wives in marriage? Yes, but we have much more.

We have the atonement, justification by faith, sanctification, and baptism. Some people believe you can separate these events or developments. Others believe that all of them are not necessary, that you only have to be baptized, or forgiven, or justified. However, that is not the case. They are all interrelated. They all must be addressed and accepted.

Christ giving Himself for us is not the end, it is only the beginning. Note what it does for baptism, for fulfilling prophecy, for establishing the teachings of Christ, and for bringing us into a right relationship with God. *Who gave himself for us, that he might redeem us from all iniquity, and purify unto himself a peculiar* (his own special) *people, zealous of good works* [Titus 2:14].

He gave Himself that we might have new life, that we might be released from the bondage of sin, that we might be His possession, and that we might be zealous for good works. Jesus prays in His High Priestly Prayer, *for their sakes I sanctify myself, that they also might be sanctified through the truth* [John 17:19].

As Calvin notes, "these words" explain that sanctification flows from Christ, and is accomplished by teaching the Gospel and obeying Christ's commands. It is because Christ obeyed the Father that His holiness comes to us, and we become partakers of it. He presents us to the Father as part of His own person, *which after God is created in righteousness and true holiness* [Eph. 4:24].

Therefore, you cannot stop with justification. Why? Because He is going to sanctify and cleanse the church. He is the one who is going to do it. It is not something that we decide to do or that we are able to do by ourselves.

Scripture teaches that it is Christ who sanctifies. That He has set His heart and His affection upon the church, despite her condition, and has reconciled her to God. He has taken her infirmities upon Himself. He has justified her. But that is not enough, nor is it the end of the story. He wants her to be a glorious church and to present her to Himself without a spot, wrinkle, or blemish.

Christ giving Himself for the church is only the first step. He has plans, and He will move forward step by step. Consider one of the ways by which the Lord shows His love for us as we proceed through the process of sanctification:

> MY SON, DESPISE NOT THOU THE CHASTENING (DISCIPLINE) OF THE LORD, NOR FAINT (BE DISCOURAGED) WHEN THOU ART REBUKED OF HIM,
> FOR WHOM THE LORD LOVETH HE CHASTENETH (DISCIPLINES)...

> *If ye endure chastening* (discipline), *God dealeth with you as with sons . . .*
>
> *But if ye be without chastisement . . . then are ye bastards* (illegitimate), *and not sons . . .*
>
> *Now no chastening* (discipline) *for the present seemeth to be joyous, but grievous: nevertheless afterward it yieldeth the peaceable fruit of righteousness unto them which are exercised* (trained) *thereby* [Heb. 12:5–8, 11].

Verse 6 says, *FOR WHOM THE LORD LOVETH HE CHASTENETH (DISCIPLINES) AND SCOURGETH EVERY SON WHOM HE RECEIVETH.* Although He died for us, He will continue the process of sanctification within us. He will sanctify and cleanse us one way or another. If we are His and do not submit to His teachings and become obedient unto Him, then He will try another way.

He will not allow us to remain in a condition that is outside of Himself. He will not allow us to remain where we are. He will motivate us, He will push and shove us, He will wash us, He will cleanse us, and He will do whatever is necessary for us to progress along "Sanctification Road."

It is important to understand that sanctification is something the Lord Jesus Christ does to us and for us. However, we are to obey Him and follow Him wherever He leads us. We are to do our part.

God's purpose is to scourge us and to chasten us with the rods of His love. Calvin states with penetrating honesty that "Everyone who knows and is persuaded that he is chastised by God ought at once to advance to this realization that it happens because he is loved by God." This is difficult to accept and to realize. However, as Calvin further notes "When believers find God in the midst of their punishments, they have a sure pledge of His loving kindness" and his concern for their salvation. The word *sanctify* means "to set apart."

Remember Peter's words,

> *But ye are a chosen generation, a royal priesthood, a holy nation, a peculiar* (his own special) *people; that ye should show forth* (proclaim) *the praises of him who hath called you out of darkness into his marvellous light:*
>
> *Which in time past were not a people, but are now the people of God* [1 Pet. 2:9–10a].

He reminds us that Moses called the people *a holy nation, a priestly kingdom and God's peculiar people.* He is also saying these titles now belong to us. We are *the called out, the ecclesia*. We have new responsibilities, a new life, and a new way of living with all its duties, responsibilities, and joy.

The husbands and wives in marriage have a new way of living. Neither the husband nor wife is free to do as he or she may wish. They have new responsibilities; they live for each other; and they are to think, act, and do for each other according to the teachings of Scripture. The example is Christ Himself and how He gave Himself for the church in order that husbands and wives should give themselves for each other.

In closing, are we determined to know more today than yesterday, and to be smarter tomorrow? With all our getting, are we getting understanding? Are we aware of the fact that it is Christ who separated us, who called us out? Do we realize and accept the fact that our relationship is with the Lord Jesus Christ? Do we want to be sanctified, and do we know that He is the One doing it? Are we aware of the fact that He gave Himself for us? Are we willing to obey His commands? Are we willing to practice them? Are we willing to accept and practice the duties and responsibilities that have been given to us?

These are questions to ask and to examine when studying the phrase, *and gave himself for it; That he might sanctify* (set it apart) *and cleanse it* [Eph. 5:25–26]. We can obey, accept, and practice His commands through the strength of His power and might in the time of need and temptation. We are to remember this truth as we continue "Walking with Jesus."

Amen!

21

The Mystery

> *This is a great mystery: but I speak concerning Christ and the church.*
> *Nevertheless let every one of you in particular so love his wife even as himself; and the wife see that she reverence* (respects) *her husband* [Eph. 5:32–33].

The Apostle Paul has much to say about the Lord Jesus Christ and the church in the closing verses of Chapter 5. His premise is that if we do not understand the true relationship between Christ and His bride then we cannot fathom the marriage relationship between a man and woman. The mystical union between Christ and the church needs to be probed, it needs to be grasped, and it needs to be applied.

Analogies, with which we are familiar, help to grasp and assimilate divine teachings. However, when everything is said and done, it is being enlightened by the Holy Spirit and understanding the teachings of God and Christ that enable us to appreciate and accept the truths presented for our edification and guidance.

The twenty-first through the thirty-first verses in Chapter 5 of Ephesians describe the relationship between Christ and the church, as well as between husband and wife, then the thirty-second verse says, *This is a great mystery: but I speak concerning Christ and the church* [Eph. 5:32]. Yes, it is. Therefore, this statement needs to be examined prayerfully, so we understand it properly.

The Greek word for *mystery* is *mustērion*. It means, "that which is known only to the initiated." In this instance, it is known only by divine revelation, and in a manner and time appointed by God. The Holy Spirit needs to enlighten the initiated.

Mystery, in this context, does not mean that it cannot be understood. It means that those seeking and receiving the Holy Spirit's illumination will discover that it is both accessible and intelligible. God's plan is for the members of Christ's body to unravel the mystery through the Holy Spirit.

Scripture concisely states,

> *But God hath revealed them unto us by his Spirit; for the Spirit searcheth all things, yea, the deep things of God.*
>
> *Now we have received, not the spirit of the world, but the Spirit which is of God; that we might know the things that are freely given to us of God.*
>
> *Which things also we speak, not in the words which man's wisdom teacheth, but which the Holy Ghost teacheth, comparing spiritual things with spiritual.*
>
> *But the natural man receiveth not the things of the Spirit of God: for they are foolishness unto him: neither can he know them, because they are spiritually discerned* [1 Cor. 2:10, 12–14].

It is important to know God, to know the Lord Jesus Christ, and to know the will of God if we want to understand the teachings contained in both the Old and New Testaments. If we are His disciples, we are to know Him, obey Him, and do His will.

Spiritual truths are revealed to those initiated into the faith, into the body of Christ. Then they are able to obtain and possess knowledge of God, His purposes, will, and commands through Christ and the Holy Spirit. Those who are not initiated are unable to grasp the truths revealed.

"The word *mystery* in the thirty-second verse has been interpreted by the Roman Catholics as "sacrament." Therefore, they read it as "This is a great sacrament," instead of *This is a great mystery*. Therefore, from this interpretation, they state that marriage is a sacrament and one of the seven they recognize. The Reformed faith recognizes only two sacraments: Baptism and the Lord's Supper," to quote and paraphrase Martyn Lloyd-Jones.

The thirty-second verse is definite and must be considered in its entirety. It says, *This is a great mystery: but I speak concerning Christ and the church* [Eph. 5:32]. Paul "concludes with wonder at the spiritual union between Christ and the Church. For he exclaims that this is a great mystery," as John Calvin properly interpreted.

Paul tried, under the influence of the Holy Spirit, to inform the Ephesians about Christ and the church, and about husbands and wives in marriage. Although, he has done an excellent job in describing these relationships he realizes some things are ineffable; that his lack of knowledge or ignorance does not detract from the majesty and reality of God's teaching; that there are those who refuse to accept certain truths, because it is beyond their capacity to grasp them; although some things are beyond us, this does not mean that we discard what we cannot grasp; and despite our shortcomings, or our inability to grasp certain teachings, we are to persist in seeking to know Him, the living Christ. What can we do about this teaching? We can ignore it and not try to understand it. Or we can say it is too difficult or requires too much time. However, that is to forget the Apostle's prayer *That the eyes of your understanding being enlightened* [Eph. 1:18]. "The mere fact that there are difficulties in Scripture does not mean that we should bypass them," according to Martyn Lloyd-Jones. Both the easy and difficult passages are provided for our instruction and benefit. We are to learn from them.

Recall what Paul says, *And he gave some, apostles; and some, prophets; and some, evangelists; and some, pastors and teachers* [Eph. 4:11]. Why? *For the perfecting* (equipping) *of the saints, for the work of the ministry, for the edifying of the body of Christ* [Eph. 4:12]. When we understand the Apostle's teachings about Christ and the church, and about husbands and wives, we have a better understanding of both, and receive enrichment and nourishment from them.

Second, we can eliminate the *mystery* and pretend it never existed. However, that should not be done because the Apostle deliberately states, *This is a great mystery: but I speak concerning Christ and the church* [Eph. 5:32].

Third, we may generate too much detail in attempting to examine this teaching. Therefore, what should we do? We should strive to understand the teachings contained in the twenty-first through the thirty-first verses of Chapter 5. We should pray that the Holy Spirit will reveal the essence of these words while realizing there may be certain truths we do not fully understand at this time, but may in the future.

What does the Apostle say about the relationship between Christ and the church?

> *So ought men to love* (own) *their wives as their own bodies. He that loveth his wife loveth himself.*
>
> *For no man ever yet hated his own flesh; but nourisheth and cherisheth it, even as the Lord the church:*
>
> *For we are members of his body, of his flesh, and of his bones* [Eph. 5:28–30].

Paul reveals that the relationship between these entities is much more than an external one. It is an intimate, special relationship whereby each entity is an integral part of the other one. Though each one maintains his or her identity there is a sense in which the two become one.

It is more than an external relationship. It is deeper and more abiding than that. The church is part of Christ. *And hath put all things under his feet, and gave him to be the head over all things to the church* [Eph. 1:22].

When considering this great mystery it is appropriate to return to Genesis and recall what happened.

> . . . but for Adam there was not found a help meet for (helper comparable to) him.
> And the Lord God caused a deep sleep to fall upon Adam, and he slept: and he took one of his ribs, and closed up the flesh instead thereof;
> And the rib, which the Lord God had taken from man, made he (built he into) a woman, and brought her unto the man.
> And Adam said, This is now bone of my bones, and flesh of my flesh: she shall be called Woman, because she was taken out of Man.
> Therefore shall a man leave his father and his mother, and shall cleave (be joined) unto his wife: and they shall be one flesh [Gen. 2:20–24].

The Apostle Paul quotes these verses when he says, *For we are members of his body, of his flesh, and of his bones* [Eph. 5:30].

When reading these verses in Genesis we should ask: what is God trying to tell us? We need to look for the eternal purposes of God in presenting, preserving, and revealing His sacred truth. He brought forth the woman out of man for a purpose: having both the male and female come from the same origin. God created human nature in Adam. Then He formed Eve out of Adam. In this way the whole human race originates from the same source. *So God created man in his own image, in the image of God created he him; male and female created he them* [Gen. 1:27].

It was in this way that "Adam was taught to recognize himself in his wife, . . . and Eve, in her turn, to submit herself willingly to her husband, . . . But if the two sexes had proceeded from different sources there would have been occasions either of mutual contempt, or envy, or contentions," according to John Calvin's enlightened understanding.

Of course, there may be other explanations about man being created, such as evolution, which does not come from Scripture. However, as members of Christ's body, we are to seek the truth revealed in God's Word.

A logical explanation is that God prepared Adam when He took from him the rib that would bring forth a woman, man's helpmate. Why was it done in this way? One reason being for Adam, or man, to embrace with more care and love that which is part of himself. *For no man ever yet hated his own flesh; but nourisheth and cherisheth it, even as the Lord the church* [Eph. 5:29]. Adam may have lost part of himself, but his gain was infinitely greater and of far more value. He received a faithful companion for life. He had a helpmate.

Adam had been incomplete, now he was complete. Whether we know it or not, when we are without Christ we are incomplete. When we are in Him, all His graces are available to us.

God informed Adam as to what He had done. He wanted Adam to know what had happened so that they would be more closely bound together by the bond between them. *But for Adam there was not found a help meet for* (helper comparable to) *him* [Gen. 2:20]. This reveals that something had been lacking in his existence. However, because of God's action Adam now had a helpmate that would satisfy his needs. The helpmate is *bone of my bones, and flesh of my flesh* [Gen. 2:23].

Adam's statement bears witness to God's wisdom not only in creating man, but in bringing forth woman, and in sanctifying marriage between one man and one woman. This is a testimony to God's eternal wisdom. The Apostle says, *For no man ever yet hated his own flesh; but nourisheth and cherisheth it, even as the Lord the church: For we are members of his body, of his flesh, and of his bones* [Eph. 5:29-30]. Paul does not leave the statement alone by saying that we are members of His body, the church. He goes further. He goes back to the beginning. He says as members of the church, or as the called out, we are flesh of His flesh and bone of His bones. How this happens we do not know, but it happens. *This is a great mystery* [Eph. 5:32].

A body is a vital organic entity, and it is marked by its unity. It is not something that is put together with parts that do not fit or that are out of place. The Apostle does not say the Lord Jesus Christ has taken our flesh and bones. However, he says that we are members of His body and that we are flesh of His flesh and bone of His bone. We have seen how woman, Eve, the bride of man, Adam, came into being.

How did the church come into being? A deep sleep came upon Christ when He spent three days in the tomb. The church was taken out of Him. The woman was taken out of Adam's side. The second Adam had a wounded, bleeding side and out of it came the church. That is how she came into being. She is flesh of his flesh, bone of his bones. *This is a great mystery* [Eph. 5:32]. The Apostle emphasizes, in these verses, that we are part of Christ's body and nature. Scripture says, *So ought men to love their* (own) *wives as their own bodies. He that loveth his wife loveth himself* [Eph. 5:28]. It also says, *For no man ever yet hated his own flesh; but nourisheth it and cherisheth it, even as the Lord the church* [Eph. 5:29]. The body is part of man. He pays attention to his body and to himself. What he does for his body, he does for himself. He cannot separate the two. They are not separate entities.

That is the relationship between Christ and the church. What He does for the church, He does for Himself. Therefore, what the husband does for himself, he should do for his bride. We are partakers of what the Lord Jesus Christ does. *Whereby are given unto us exceeding great and precious promises: that by these ye might be partakers of the divine nature, having escaped the corruption that is in the world through lust* [2 Pet. 1:4].

What impact does being members of His body have upon Christ? The Lord Jesus Christ is perfect and complete as the Son of God. *For in him dwelleth all the fullness of the Godhead bodily* [Col. 2:9]. Nothing is lacking.

The Mediator Christ is not complete and full without the church. Yes, this is a mystery. Christ the Mediator will not be complete and full until the whole church, each and every last member, has been brought in. Then the two shall become one.

This is a great mystery. Think back: Adam was incomplete without Eve. So God brought forth Eve and in a sense this made the fullness of Adam. This is what the Apostle says about the church with respect to Christ.

> And hath put all things under his feet, and gave him to be the head over all things to the church,
> Which is his body, the fullness of him that filleth all in all [Eph. 1:22–23].

Therefore, it can be said, "the church is the *fullness* of Christ." Adam and Eve became one.

> *And Adam said, this is now bone of my bones, and flesh of my flesh: she shall be called Woman, because she was taken out of Man.*
> *Therefore shall a man leave his father and his mother, and shall cleave* (be joined) *unto his wife: and they shall be one flesh* [Gen. 2:23–24].

The Lord Jesus Christ left the courts of heaven. He took upon Himself the nature of man, yet he still remained the blessed Son of God. *This is a great mystery.* We do not understand it fully. He returned to heaven. When He did, He did not leave His body behind.

> *For we are members of his body, of his flesh, and of his bones. FOR THIS CAUSE SHALL A MAN LEAVE HIS FATHER AND MOTHER, AND SHALL BE JOINED UNTO HIS WIFE, AND THEY TWO SHALL BE ONE FLESH* [Eph. 5:30–31].

Then the Apostle adds,

> *This is a great mystery: but I speak concerning Christ and the church* [Eph. 5:32].

Christ left His Father in Heaven to be joined to His Bride, the church. The two became one. The church, the called out, are members of His body, of his flesh, and of his bones. God created Adam. Out of Adam He brought forth Eve. Adam said, *This is now bone of my bones, and flesh of my flesh* [Gen 2:23]. A man leaves HIS FATHER AND MOTHER, AND SHALL BE JOINED UNTO HIS WIFE, AND THEY TWO SHALL BE ONE FLESH. *This is a great mystery: but I speak concerning Christ and the church* [Eph. 5:31–32].

We are members of the church, the called out, the body of Christ. We are joined to Him. We share His human nature. How did He make this a reality? He left His Father, He came into the world, He went to Calvary's Hill, He bled on His side, He went into a deep sleep, He brought forth the church, He joined Himself to His Bride, and He gave Himself for her.

> *This is a great mystery* [Eph. 5:32].

> *Husbands, love your wives, even as Christ also loved the church, and gave himself for it* [Eph. 5:25].

When we partake of the Lord's Supper, we are in the presence of our Lord Jesus Christ. He is in our midst. We meet Him with all our deficiencies, frailties, and weaknesses. We are to obey the command, *This do in remembrance of me* [Luke 22:19b]. This command does not mean "in memory of." It does mean an affectionate call to obey the Person Himself Christ Jesus.

There needs to be an awakening of our minds to the presence of Christ, to the reality of being members of His body, to confessing our sins, to the need for forgiveness, and to accepting with humility and confidence His forgiveness of our sins.

> *This is a great mystery: but I speak concerning Christ and the church* [Eph. 5:32].

Amen!

22

Old and New Blessings

Cleansing and Washing By the Word

> *That he might sanctify* (set it apart) *and cleanse it with the washing of water by the word* [Eph. 5:26].

Husbands are to love their wives as Christ loved the church. How did He love the called out? His example was that He gave Himself for her. Why did He do this? Scripture tells us in order that He might *sanctify* her and *cleanse* her with *the washing of water by the word*.

What does this mean? How are we to interpret it? What about cleansing, *the washing of water*, and *by the word*? How are these teachings to be applied? This particular verse says, *That* (in order that) *he might sanctify* (set it apart) *and cleanse it with the washing of water by the word* [Eph. 5:26].

As expressed previously, the word *sanctify* means "to set apart." When a man asks a woman to marry him, he sets her apart. When they are united in marriage, they are set apart; the two become one. The word *cleanse* means "to make clean," "to cleanse from the guilt of sin," and *the washing of water by the word*.

When examining this verse we are considering the relationship of Christ to the church as well as that of husband to wife. When doing this, we are to be cognizant of the Old Testament teachings as well as the New Testament ones.

The Old Testament describes the covenant between Yahweh and Israel. Ephesians speaks of Christ's relationship to the called out.

In the Old Testament, the bridegroom pays a price for the bride. Peter reveals that Christ paid a price with His precious blood for His bride, the *ecclesia*. These verses clearly state,

> *Forasmuch as ye know that ye were not redeemed with corruptible* (perishable) *things, as silver and gold, from your vain conversation* (aimless conduct) *received by tradition from your fathers;*
> *But with the precious blood of Christ, as of a lamb without blemish and without spot* [1Pet. 1:18–19].

The Old Testament prophets speak fervently of the covenant between Yahweh and both Israel and Judah. They describe the relationship and the punishment inflicted, but they always exalt their message by declaring the promise of forgiveness and extending an invitation for the unfaithful to return.

Malachi depicts vividly the Lord God's relationship with Israel and Judah, the relationship as between a husband and wife, and the Lord's attitude toward divorce. Hear the words of the Lord in the book of Malachi:

> *Because the Lord hath been witness between thee and the wife of thy youth, . . . is she thy companion, and the wife of thy covenant. And did not he make one? . . . Therefore, take heed to your spirit, and let none deal treacherously against the wife of his youth,*
> *For the Lord, the God of Israel, saith that he hateth putting away* (divorce)*: . . . therefore take heed to your spirit, that ye deal not treacherously* [Mal. 2:14–16].

There is no thought of divorce between Christ and His bride. There should be no thought of divorce between a husband and wife if the marriage foundation is built on that solid rock, the Lord Jesus Christ. The relationship should look forward to the promises available from God through His Son. The husband and wife should seek those blessings together.

In the Old Testament, the primary purpose of a marriage and in determining whether it was blessed or not was the bringing forth of children. However, the Messiah changed the emphasis. If the husband and wife are new creatures in Christ, then the primary objective is not producing children: it is not physical; it is developing, nourishing, and enriching the intimate relationship between the two who have become one, and it is subordinating their own desires in order to show forth the love of God through the Lord Jesus Christ.

As Markus Barth points out, "The Old Testament contains precedents for Eph. 5:25–27 that are indispensable tools for understanding this text." However, we must realize that the Apostle's teaching in

Ephesians is to be understood in the light of Christ's covenant with the called out people of God, the *ecclesia*.

Christ's love for the church is such that it incorporates the will, the power, the patience, the understanding, the strength, the wisdom, and the knowledge to make her perfect. His love is a working love. It feeds, it waters, it nourishes the church. Also, His love rebukes, chastises, and even scourges the church when it is necessary. Christ loves the church for her sake, not His.

This description should provide an understanding of the love and the great esteem with which God the Father and Christ the Son look upon the church—the people of God. Earlier it was noted that Christ gave Himself in order that He might cleanse the church, cleanse it from the guilt of sin. The wording in this verse indicates that it is a continuous process. He knows the need of the *ecclesia*, and He meets that need.

Why? So that He might not only cleanse her, but also present her to Himself without spot, wrinkle, or blemish. He wants those called out to be perfect, to be delivered fully and completely from sin no matter what shape or form it takes. We need to also remember that the New Testament never stops at just cleansing us from the guilt of sin, but it also cleanses us from the power and pollution of sin.

Earlier in Ephesians it says,

> *AND you hath he quickened (made alive) who were dead in trespasses and sins;*
>
> *Wherein in time past ye walked according to the course* (age) *of this world, . . . the spirit that now worketh in the children of disobedience:*
>
> *We all had our conversation* (conducted ourselves) *in times past in the lusts of our flesh, . . . and of the mind; and were by nature the children of wrath . . .*
>
> *But God, who is rich in mercy, for his great love wherewith he loved us,*
>
> *Even when we were dead in sins, hath quickened* (made us alive) *us together with Christ, (by grace ye are* (have been) *saved;)*
>
> *And hath raised us up together, and made us sit together in heavenly places in Christ Jesus:*
>
> *That in the ages to come he might shew the exceeding riches of his grace in his kindness toward us through* (in) *Christ Jesus* [Eph. 2:1–7].

He cleanses us from the guilt, power, and pollution of sin. How is this done? Paul says, *with the washing of water by the word.*

What does this mean? What should we consider? This is not the easiest passage to examine, but we must consider it and pray for illumination. The Old and New Testaments help us understand the Apostle's words. The Old Testament says, *And the Lord said unto Moses, Go unto the people, and sanctify* (consecrate) *them today and tomorrow, and let them wash their clothes, And be ready against the third day: for the third day the Lord will come down in the sight of all the people upon Mount Sinai* [Exod. 19:10–11]. In these two verses, the people prepare themselves by washing their garments.

Ezekiel records that God said to the people in Jerusalem, *Then washed I thee with water; yea, I thoroughly washed away thy blood from thee, and I anointed thee with oil* [Ezek. 16:9]. Yes, Yahweh washed his bride with water. In Ephesians, the Messiah washes His bride, the church, with water. God says to the Israelites,

> *Then will I sprinkle clean water upon you, and ye shall be clean:*
> . . .
> *A new heart also will I give you, and a new spirit will I put within you: . . . and I will give you a heart of flesh.*
> *And I will put my spirit within you, and cause you to walk in my statutes, and ye shall keep my judgments, and do them* [Ezek. 36:25–27].

Paul says Christ will cleanse the church *with the washing of water.* What else does the New Testament say? *. . . but the water that I shall give him shall be in him a well* (fountain) *of water springing up into everlasting life* [John 4:14]. Jesus says,

> *He that believeth on me, as the scripture hath said, out of his belly* (heart) *shall flow rivers of living water.*
> *(But this spake he of the Spirit, which they that believe on Him should receive: for the Holy Ghost was not yet given; because that Jesus was not yet glorified.)*
> [John 7:38–39]

"Most likely the 'water' signifies the 'Spirit' with whom only the coming Messiah can baptize," according to Markus Barth. The words *to cleanse* or *to make clean* describe the gift of the Spirit.

Most authorities believe that the phrase *with the washing of water* refers to baptism. Think, who were the people to whom Paul was writing? Probably they were recent converts or people who had accepted Christ in their adult years. Therefore, they were baptized after hearing and believing the Gospel. Consequently, baptism was something they could understand as cleansing them, washing them, delivering them, and preparing them for their tasks as members of Christ's body. Paul says to the Ephesians,

> *That ye put off . . . the old man*
> *And be renewed in the spirit of your mind;*
> *. . . put on the new man, which after God is created in righteousness and true holiness* [Eph. 4:22–24].

Peter says,

> *In the days of Noah, . . . eight souls were saved by water.*
> *Whereunto even baptism doth also now save us . . . by the resurrection of Jesus Christ* [1 Pet. 3:20–21].

In baptism, we are to appropriate the blessings available to us through the Lord Jesus Christ. "Baptism is a figure, . . . of what the Lord Jesus Christ does for us in the process of sanctification," as proclaimed by Martyn Lloyd-Jones.

It does nothing in and of itself other than to represent what Christ has done for us to seal it in our hearts and minds, and to claim His blessings. Baptism is not "an expression of our faith in God or our love to Him"; it is "the expression of a Divine thought," it is "the symbol of a Divine act," as described by R.W. Dale.

A person is not changed just because he or she is baptized. During earlier periods in the church, people spoke about baptism cleansing men, women, and children from sin and regenerating them because they knew that the rite itself was only a symbol of the fact that it is the Spirit of God that really cleanses and regenerates a person. They were well aware of the fact that all baptized people were not cleansed and regenerated.

Unless the Spirit illuminates, unless the Spirit acts, nothing happens. If the Word of God falls on deaf ears, then nothing happens. The same is true of the Sacrament of Baptism. It is also true of the Lord's Supper.

Administering baptism to a person declares that the Lord Jesus Christ has atoned for his or her sins by going to the Cross, shedding His blood, dying, and rising from the dead on the third day. Also, that that person is blessed with all the spiritual blessings of Christ Jesus. However, baptism does not make these things happen.

Baptism does not confer the blessings of Christ, but declares that they belong to him or her and that they will receive them if their faith is real and genuine. We do not become Christ's inheritance because we are baptized; however, we are baptized because we are Christ's inheritance.

What does baptism represent? First, by the grace of God and through our faith in the Lord Jesus Christ, we have been washed from the guilt of sin. When we think of baptism or participate in the Sacrament of Baptism we should think of the Holy Spirit descending upon our Lord in the form of a dove. Also, of the Holy Spirit entering into us so that the work and process of sanctification may proceed. How does the work and process of sanctification proceed with a person, a class, a congregation, or a church? *By the Word!* The act of baptism occurs one time, but the sanctifying and cleansing processes go on day by day, month by month, and year by year. It is accomplished *by the Word*.

What does Scripture say about the Word and how it works through a believer? *Wherefore lay apart all filthiness and superfluity* (abundance) *of naughtiness* (wickedness), *and receive with meekness the engrafted* (implanted) *word, which is able to save your souls* [Jas. 1:21]. In Scripture, *meekness* does not mean weakness or cowardliness. The Greek word *praútes* is not easily interpreted into English. It is not only a gentleness of mind and heart, but also a resoluteness towards God and His commandments and adhering to them. It is a disposition that accepts God's dealings with us as being good for our welfare. It is closely linked to humility. A humble heart does not fight, struggle, and contend with God. *Of his own will begat he us with the word of truth, that we should be a kind of firstfruits of his creatures* [Jas. 1:18]. The first fruits are love, joy, peace, long-suffering, gentleness, faith, meekness, and temperance as noted in Galatians. In addition, Scripture reveals that we are

> *Born again, not of corruptible* (perishable) *seed, but of incorruptible* (imperishable), *by the word of God, which liveth and abideth forever* [1 Pet. 1:23].

> *For this cause also thank we God without ceasing, because, when ye received the word of God which ye heard of us, ye received* (welcomed) *it not as the word of men, but as it is in truth, the word of God, which effectually* (effectively) *worketh also in you that believe* [1 Thess. 2:13].

What does our Lord say about the Word? Jesus says,

> *If ye continue* (abide) *in my word, then are ye my disciples indeed;*
> *And ye shall know the truth, and the truth shall make you free* [John 8:31–32].
>
> *Now ye are clean through* (because of) *the word which I have spoken unto you* [John 15:3].

Jesus prays in His high priestly prayer,

> *Sanctify them* (Set them apart) *through thy truth: thy word is truth.*
> *As thou hast sent me into the world, even so have I also sent them into the world.*
> *And for their sakes I sanctify myself, that they also might be sanctified through the truth* [John 17:17–19].

What truth is used to sanctify? The Word! What is the Word that sanctifies? Is it a special formula? Is it a special act? Is it administering a sacrament? Is it saying, "I believe?" Is it blindly accepting by faith? Is it trusting and obeying? No! It is not any one or all of these things!

What sanctifies us, and teaches us about sanctification? It is the whole of Scripture. It is working with it, probing it, asking why, understanding it, and applying it.

Consider this letter to the Ephesians. Paul was writing to believers, to the called out. He reminds them of that in the first chapter. Why is he writing to them? So that they will grow in grace, mature in faith, rid themselves of the guilt, power, and pollution of sin, and walk in unity and harmony with the Lord Jesus Christ. Paul wants them (and us) to be holy and perfect.

The entire Epistle to the Ephesians is about sanctification. The Word that sanctifies and cleanses is the fullness of Scripture. It is the great doctrine taught throughout the Bible. It is not to be ignored. It is to be studied and applied.

Where does the Bible start teaching about sanctification? Where is the emphasis? With the individual? That you can be happy and enjoy life? That you can overcome problems, defeats, and obstacles? Is that where sanctification begins? No! No! No! It begins with God. Not with you or me. It begins with the nature and character of God as exemplified in that beautiful, meaningful hymn by Reginald Heber.

> *Holy, Holy, Holy! Lord God Almighty!*
> *Early in the morning our song shall rise to thee;*
> *Holy, Holy, Holy! merciful and mighty!*
> *God in three persons, blessed Trinity!*
>
> *Holy, Holy, Holy! All the saints adore Thee,*
> *Casting down their golden crowns around the glassy sea;*
> *Cherubim and seraphim falling down before thee,*
> *Who wert, and art, and ever-more shalt be.*
>
> *Holy, Holy, Holy! Though the darkness hide Thee,*
> *Though the eye of sinful man thy glory may not see,*
> *Only Thou art holy; there is none beside Thee*
> *Perfect in power, in love, and purity.*
>
> *Holy, Holy, Holy! Lord God Almighty!*
> *All thy works shall praise Thy name, in earth and sky and sea;*
> *Holy, Holy, Holy! Merciful and mighty!*
> *God in three persons, blessed Trinity!*

Why is there so much failure, sin, and disobedience in individual lives? Because people do not really know the Lord God Almighty. They do not really know the Lord Jesus Christ, the Word, and the Holy Spirit. This applies to those who may call themselves Christians, as well as those who do not darken the doorway to a church or ever open a Bible.

It is the people who have sought God, who want to know Him, who want to walk with Him, who want to grow in grace, and mature in the faith. What do we need in order to do this? An experience, a particular act? No! What do we really need? "It is this knowledge of God, of the attributes of God, His glory, His ineffability, His holiness, His almightiness, His eternity, His omniscience, His omnipresence," as stated forcefully and clearly by Martyn Lloyd-Jones. That is what we really need!

When we know these things, and know that no matter what we are doing or saying He is aware of it, that is when our lives are transformed. When we really grasp and know the truths contained in the two hymns, *"Holy! Holy! Holy! Lord God Almighty!"* and *"How Great Thou Art"* written by Carl Bobert our hearts will be filled with joy and thanksgiving. The latter hymn expresses it beautifully, unequivocally, and forcefully:

O Lord my God, when I in awesome wonder,
Consider all the worlds Thy hands have made,
I see the stars, I hear the rolling thunder,
Thy power throughout the universe displayed.

When through the woods and forest glades I wander
And hear the birds sing sweetly in the trees,
When I look down from lofty mountain grandeur
And hear the brook and feel the gentle breeze.

And when I think that God, His Son not sparing
Sent Him to die, I scarce can take it in,
That on the Cross, my burden gladly bearing,
He bled and died to take away our sin.

When Christ shall come with shout of acclamation
And take me home, what joy shall fill my heart!
Then shall I bow in humble adoration
And there proclaim my God, how great Thou art.

The Word, both in the Old Testament and the New Testament, teaches sanctification. But it starts with doctrine, with the teachings of Christ. It starts with God, with walking with Jesus, with knowing the Word. The Word is essential, but it needs to be the Word of God, revealing His being, nature, and character.

How do you start teaching sanctification? Paul states it so beautifully,

> *Blessed be the God and Father of Our Lord Jesus Christ, who hath blessed us with all spiritual blessings in heavenly places in Christ:*
> *According as he hath chosen us in him before the foundation of the world, that we should be holy and without blame before him in love* [Eph. 1:3-4].

How is the sanctification process carried out? By the Lord Jesus Christ, through the Holy Spirit, and the Word. Jesus prayed,

> *Sanctify them* (Set them apart) *through thy truth: thy word is truth* [John 17:17].

Can we pray for less?
Amen!

Outline Questions

Chapter 1

BE FOLLOWERS OF GOD

> BE ye therefore followers of God, as dear children;
> And walk in love, as Christ also hath loved us, and hath given himself for us an offering and a sacrifice to God for a sweet-smelling savor (aroma) [Eph. 5:1–2].

What does the command *Be ye imitators of God* mean?

What did Paul say to the Ephesian elders at Miletus?

What does Christ want from you as expressed by Paul?

How are we to know God?

What does Jesus say about imitating God?

Why are we to be imitators of God?

How are we to know God?

What does Paul reveal in these important verses?

Why are we to be imitators of God?

What new commandment did Christ give His disciples regarding how they are to conduct themselves?

Why did Christ give this new commandment?

How are we to live as imitators of God?

Chapter 2

GOD'S LOVE

> And walk in love, as Christ also hath loved us, and hath given himself for us an offering and a sacrifice to God for a sweet-smelling savor (aroma) [Eph. 5:2].

What is your reaction to *And walk in love*?

What is love?

How is the word *love* used in this verse?

What type of love did Jesus reveal?

Why is the word love used regarding God's commandments?

How is God's love revealed?

What does God's love seek?

What is meant by *and hath given himself for us*?

What is meant by *an offering and a sacrifice to God*?

What is meant by *for a sweet-smelling savor*?

Was our Lord Jesus active or passive?

How are we to conduct ourselves when attacked by evil forces and practices?

Chapter 3

WALKING IN THE LIGHT

> *But fornication, and all uncleanness, or covetousness, let it not be once named among you, as becometh saints;*
> *Neither filthiness, nor foolish talking, nor jesting, which are not convenient: but rather giving of thanks.*
> *For this ye know, that no whoremonger, nor unclean person, nor covetous man, who is an idolater, hath any inheritance in the kingdom of Christ and of God* [Eph. 5:3–5].

What is it like to walk with Jesus?

What happened at the transfiguration?

What does God want us to do regarding His Son?

What did Jesus do after the transfiguration?

How are we to conduct ourselves as members of Christ's body?

What negative injunctions does Paul state?

What are the positive injunctions?

Why does Paul stress these negative and positive injunctions?

To whom was Paul speaking?

Why are knowledgeable and committed people essential for conducting the affairs of the church?

What is to be our relationship to God and to the Gospel?

How are we to walk willingly in the presence of God?

Chapter 4

NO INHERITANCE IN GOD'S KINGDOM

> For this ye know, that no whoremonger, nor unclean person, nor covetous man, who is an idolater, hath any inheritance in the kingdom of Christ and of God [Eph. 5:5].

What traits did Paul exhibit as an editor and writer?

What does Paul want us to know about the kingdom of God?

What motivating factors does Paul present?

What groups does Paul link together?

What is God's attitude toward sin?

What warnings does Paul give to the saints?

What is meant by the *kingdom of Christ*?

Who will not have an inheritance in Christ's kingdom?

Who will have an inheritance in Christ's kingdom?

Why are we to know Scripture and its teachings?

How are we to respond to these teachings?

Chapter 5

GOD'S WRATH

> Let no man deceive you with vain words: for because of these things cometh the wrath of God upon the children of disobedience.
> Be not ye therefore partakers with them.
> For ye were sometimes (once) darkness, but now are ye light in the Lord: walk as children of light:
> (For the fruit of the Spirit is in all goodness and righteousness and truth;)
> Proving what is acceptable unto the Lord.
> And have no fellowship with the unfruitful works of darkness, but rather reprove (expose) them.
> For it is a shame even to speak of those things which are done of them in secret.
> But all things that are reproved are made manifest by the light: for whatsoever doth make manifest is light.
> Wherefore he saith, Awake thou that sleepest, and arise from the dead, and Christ shall give thee light [Eph. 5:6–14].

Why is our behavior important?

When do people encounter temptations?

What happens when we listen to vain or empty words?

What does walking in unity, love, and light require?

What is the difference between a religion and living faith?

What emphasis has been placed on man during the past one hundred years?

What does Scripture say about the wrath of God?

Who has taught and preached about the wrath of God?

How does God's wrath differ from man's?

When is the wrath of God exhibited?

Why is a religion easier than a living faith?

What does the first chapter of Romans say regarding God's wrath?

How do people exhibit a hatred of God's righteousness?

What are we to do with respect to obeying Paul's teachings in these verses?

Chapter 6

CHILDREN OF LIGHT

Be not ye therefore partakers with them.
For ye were sometimes (once) *darkness, but now are ye light in the Lord: walk as children of light* [Eph. 5:7–8].

What did Abram do after God made His covenant with him?

What happens when you live a life of faith?

Who is the great enemy of the life of faith in God?

Why did the apostles continually stress personal conduct?

What does the New Testament teach regarding sanctification?

How do we come to a living faith?

How are we to walk as children of light?

What is the difference between light and darkness?

What does it mean to enter the kingdom of God?

For what did the Protestant reformers note and state the church should be known?

How do we become light?

What happened to Paul when he saw the light?

When is a person capable of receiving the Gospel?

Chapter 7

KNOWING THE WILL OF GOD

> *For ye were sometimes* (once) *darkness, but now are ye light in the Lord: walk as children of light:*
> *(For the fruit of the Spirit is in all goodness and righteousness and truth;)*
> *Proving what is acceptable unto the Lord.*
> *And have no fellowship with the unfruitful works of darkness, but rather reprove* (expose) *them* [Eph. 5:8–11].

What does maturing in love require?

What are we to know regarding God's will for us?

Why are we to know the scriptural teachings regarding darkness?

Why does Jesus use strong words in Matthew, Chapter 23, when addressing the ministers of the day, the Pharisees, and the scribes?

Why does God tell us the things we are not to do?

How do we determine if something is darkness?

Why are we not to have fellowship with the works of darkness?

What impacts a person's behavior and attitude toward life?

What does Paul forbid under the influence of the Lord Jesus?

What does the Spirit produce?

What does righteousness produce?

Why do people continue in sin and darkness?

What is demanded by the command *And have no fellowship with the unfruitful works of darkness*?

Chapter 8

WHAT IS ACCEPTABLE

> *For ye were sometimes* (once) *darkness, but now are ye light in the Lord: walk as children of light:*
> *(For the fruit of the Spirit is in all goodness and righteousness and truth;)*
> *Proving what is acceptable unto the Lord* [Eph. 5:8–10].

What does Paul admonish us to do?

How are the unfruitful works to be made visible?

How does the light manifest itself?

How do we come to know God and the Lord Jesus?

Who can know God?

What affect did the light of Christ have upon Paul?

What happens when we *walk as children of light*?

What are the characteristics of the fruit of light?

What does the New Testament emphasize about each of us?

What is more important than sacrifices and doing works?

What does Paul mean by *all goodness, righteousness, and truth*?

What proves we are members of Christ's body?

What *is acceptable unto the Lord*?

Chapter 9

NOT AS FOOLS, BUT AS WISE

See then that ye walk circumspectly (carefully), *not as fools, but as wise,*
Redeeming the time, because the days are evil.
Wherefore be ye not unwise, but understanding what the will of the Lord is.
And be not drunk with wine, wherein is excess (dissipation); *but be filled with the Spirit;*
Speaking to yourselves in psalms and hymns and spiritual songs, singing and making melody in your heart to the Lord;
Giving thanks always for all things unto God and the Father in the name of our Lord Jesus Christ;
Submitting yourselves one to another in the fear of God [Eph. 5:15–21].

What is meant by *See then*?

What does Paul want from the Ephesian followers and us?

What key points are we to consider?

What are we to know as members of Christ's body?

Why are we to take heed?

Why are we to be careful about every step we take as members of Christ's body?

What does Bishop Moule tell us?

What does Paul mean by *Walk . . . not as fools, but as wise*?

What are the characteristics of the fool?

What are the characteristics of the wise person?

How does one walk as a wise person?

What are the two types of wisdom revealed in Scripture?

What is the wisdom of God as revealed in Christ?

Chapter 10

WALKING CIRCUMSPECTLY

> *See then that ye walk circumspectly* (carefully), *not as fools, but as wise,* . . . [Eph. 5:15].

What is wisdom?

What is true of the person who is a member of Christ's body?

What qualities does Paul want us to possess?

What is meant by *redeeming the time*?

What does walking circumspectly require?

Why are we to redeem the time?

What does the First Psalm say we are to do about redeeming time?

What does it mean to be in a right relationship with Christ?

What does Paul mean when he says to the Romans, *put ye on the Lord Jesus Christ*?

Why are we to *walk circumspectly* (carefully)?

Where are we to lay up our treasures?

What are we to do when God calls?

What is the real test in our Christian walk?

What is required to know and to understand the will of God?

Chapter 11

THE REALITY OF THE SPIRIT

> *And be not drunk with wine, wherein is excess* (dissipation); *but be filled with the Spirit;*
> *Speaking to yourselves in psalms and hymns and spiritual songs, singing and making melody in your heart to the Lord;*
> *Giving thanks always for all things unto God and the Father in the name of our Lord Jesus Christ;*
> *Submitting yourselves one to another in the fear of God* [Eph. 5:18–21].

Why does Paul admonish us to be *filled with the Spirit*?

What does Paul want for Christ's followers?

What is the contrast between being filled with wine or the Spirit?

Why does Paul emphasize being filled with the Spirit and the fullness of God?

What type of preaching has been a curse?

What are the characteristics of the life filled with the Spirit?

What type of life is filled with the Spirit?

What does the Holy Spirit do to the mind and intellect?

What two commands, one positive and one negative, are not optional for us to obey, but obligatory?

Chapter 12

BEING FILLED WITH THE SPIRIT

> *And be not drunk with wine, wherein is excess* (dissipation); *but be filled with the Spirit* [Eph. 5:18].

How is one to feed the church of God?

How does Paul say we are to conduct ourselves?

When can you share the life of the kingdom of God?

To whom did Christ present His teachings, and to whom were the apostles writing?

What does Scripture say about the person outside the kingdom of God?

What does the New Testament say about the Holy Spirit and being filled with His Spirit?

How do we become a member of Christ's body?

What is the difference between being baptized with the Spirit and being *filled with the Spirit*?

How can we be under the influence of the Holy Spirit and controlled by Him?

How do we have fellowship with the Holy Spirit?

What does fellowship with the Holy Spirit require?

Chapter 13

GIVING THANKS ALWAYS

> *Speaking to yourselves in psalms and hymns and spiritual songs, singing and making melody in your heart to the Lord;*
> *Giving thanks always for all things unto God and the Father in the name of our Lord Jesus Christ* [Eph. 5:19–20].

How did Paul communicate with the Ephesians and now with us?

What are we to do when hearing or reading Scripture?

What did the early followers do after having their hearts pricked?

What significant observation can be made about "the church" during the past two thousand years?

What happened to the early church?

What does the true church require?

For what was the early church known?

How did the early church members praise God and give thanks?

What new meanings did Christ bring to the Eucharist?

What did the early disciples and followers realize about the Lord's Supper?

What else should be noted about the Lord's Supper?

Chapter 14

WALKING IN HARMONY

> *Submitting yourselves one to another in the fear of God* [Eph. 5:21].

What do we desire as we walk along life's pathway?

What should we exhibit to reveal we are walking harmoniously and are *filled with the Spirit*?

How are we to submit ourselves *in the fear of* (Christ)?

What inhibits our relationship with Christ compared to the first century Christians, early reformers, covenanters, and Puritans?

What Christlike attributes are we to exhibit?

What does Peter exhort one to do, especially elders and pastors, regarding certain vices?

How are elders and pastors to tend to their flocks?

To whom was Paul writing when he said, *Submitting yourselves one to another in the fear of* (Christ)?

To whom would Paul never submit himself?

What does the Apostle John say about those who do not bring Christ's doctrine to us?

Why is there tough talk in the scriptures?

How are we to submit ourselves one to another *in the fear of Christ*?

Chapter 15

A RELATIONSHIP AS THAT OF CHRIST TO THE CHURCH

> *Wives, submit yourselves unto your own husbands, as unto the Lord.*
> *For the husband is the head of the wife, even as Christ is the head of the church: and he is the saviour of the body* [Eph. 5:22–23].

What does Paul present to the members of Christ's body before discussing marriage?

What are our daily lives to reflect?

What knowledge and understanding are we to seek continually?

To whom is the Apostle Paul writing in these verses?

What phases in our walk with Christ are we to desire?

How much more meddling can Paul do than to focus on marriage?

What does Paul emphasize in describing marriage?

Who supports the exhortations proclaimed by Paul?

Whose teachings does Paul present?

What happens when the church ignores Christ's teachings?

How does Ruth Paxson describe marriage?

What truths does Paul want to convey to husbands and wives regarding marriage?

What is the Christian view of marriage?

Chapter 16

WIVES ... UNTO YOUR OWN HUSBANDS

> *Wives, submit yourselves unto your own husbands, as unto the Lord* [Eph. 5:22].

Why does Paul provide instruction for our family relationships?

How are we to submit ourselves to God?

What should we bear in mind when considering the relationship between the husband and wife?

How is the wife to submit herself unto her own husband?

How does Ruth Paxson describe the wife's subjection to her husband?

How are the truths regarding marriage to be applied?

What becomes evident of the marriage state when studying Scripture?

What do we learn from the teachings in Genesis?

How are the husband and wife to complement one another?

What significant event occurred in the garden of Eden as recorded in the third chapter of Genesis?

What three things does Paul utilize in writing his letters?

What is *not* meant by *wives, submit yourselves unto your own husbands*?

Chapter 17

HUSBANDS, LOVE YOUR WIVES

Husbands, love your wives, even as Christ also loved the church, and gave himself for it;

That he might sanctify and cleanse it with the washing of water by the word,

That he might present it to himself a glorious church, not having spot, or wrinkle, or any such thing; but that it should be holy and without blemish.

So ought men to love their wives as their own bodies. He that loveth his wife loveth himself.

For no man ever yet hated his own flesh; but nourisheth and cherisheth it, even as the Lord the church:

For we are members of his body, of his flesh, and of his bones.

FOR THIS CAUSE SHALL A MAN LEAVE HIS FATHER AND MOTHER, AND SHALL BE JOINED UNTO HIS WIFE, AND THEY TWO SHALL BE ONE FLESH.

This is a great mystery: but I speak concerning Christ and the church.

Nevertheless let every one of you in particular so love his wife even as himself; and the wife see that she reverence (respects) her husband [Eph. 5:25–33].

What was the status of wives in the Greek and Roman societies two thousand years ago?

What knowledge caused Paul to write to the Ephesians?

What was Paul's direct command to husbands?

How does Paul tell husbands to love their wives?

What type of love are husbands to practice toward their wives?

How does Chrysostom describe a husband's love for his wife?

What are to be the six specific characteristics of a husband's love for his wife?

Why does Paul describe what a husband's love is to be for his wife?

What did Christ do for His bride, the church?

What does Ruth Paxson say to husbands regarding, *put your ear close to this bit of God's Word?*

Chapter 18

MARRIAGE: THE HUSBAND AND WIFE RELATIONSHIP

> *Husbands, love your wives, even as Christ also loved the church, and gave himself for it;*
> *That he might sanctify and cleanse it with the washing of water by the word,*
> *That he might present it to himself a glorious church, not having spot, or wrinkle, or any such thing; but that it should be holy and without blemish* [Eph. 5:25–27].

Where is our focus to be with respect to the church?

Why do we have the scriptures?

How did the Holy Spirit use Paul and the other New Testament writers?

What makes the church a living reality?

Where does Paul focus our attention?

How are we made whole as individuals?

What was the state of the church when Christ gave Himself for it?

What is Paul saying to husbands and wives?

Why does Paul compare husbands and wives with Christ and the church?

Why did Christ give Himself?

What do we have in these verses in addition to husbands and wives and marriage?

What do husbands and wives have in their marriage?

What questions are we to ask ourselves when considering (Christ) *gave himself for it; That he might sanctify and cleanse it*?

Chapter 19

CHRIST NOURISHES AND CHERISHES

> *So ought men to love their wives as their own bodies. He that loveth his wife loveth himself.*
> *For no man ever yet hated his own flesh; but nourisheth and cherisheth it, even as the Lord the church* [Eph. 5:28–29].

Why is the relationship between Christ and His bride, the church, to serve as a model for husbands and wives?

What does Otto Weber say regarding the type of faith we are to have?

What should be our primary ambition or objective?

Why does Paul say a husband is to nourish and cherish his wife?

What should be the results of nourishing and cherishing?

What is the greatest hindrance to accepting God and the Lord Jesus?

What keeps us from knowing more about Christ?

What will it be like when Christ presents the church and the various individuals to Himself?

How are we to become holy and righteous?

What is to be our relationship with the Lord Jesus Christ?

When will the church be glorious?

What are husbands to do for their wives?

Chapter 20

CHRIST AND THE ECCLESIA

> *Nevertheless let every one of you in particular so love his wife even as himself; and the wife see that she reverence* (respects) *her husband* [Eph. 5:33].

What commands of Paul's are we to bear in mind?

Why does Paul describe the relationship between Christ and His church, then emphasize the importance of marriage and the responsibilities of husbands and wives?

Why is it that studying, understanding, and applying these teachings is required for real success in the Christian life and marriage?

Why were the New Testament Epistles written?

What should serve as the basis of marriage for each husband and wife?

What is a primary obstacle to a successful, positive marriage relationship?

What is a husband to do and not to do regarding his wife?

What is the basis for harmony in marriage?

When does Paul discuss harmony?

Why is there to be unity between a husband and wife?

Why does Scripture say a man should leave his father and mother but not say the same about the wife?

To whom are these teachings about marriage addressed?

What did Christ do for His bride, the church?

Chapter 21

THE MYSTERY

> *That he might sanctify and cleanse it with the washing of water by the word,* ... [Eph. 5:26].

Why are we to be cleansed *with the washing of water by the word*?

What does the Old Testament teach about marriage and God's covenant with Israel?

Why should there be no thought of divorce between Christ and His bride?

What does Christ do with His church and with us?

What did God do with Jerusalem and the Israelites as revealed in Ezekiel?

What does the New Testament say about water and cleansing?

What is baptism?

Outline Questions 225

What does baptism represent?

What does the Lord Jesus say about the Word?

What is the Word that sanctifies?

Where does sanctification begin?

Why is there so much failure, sin, and disobedience in individual lives?

What do we need to do in order to grow in grace and mature in the faith?

What does the hymn "How Great Thou Art" say regarding God's attributes and ineffability?

How is the sanctification process carried out?

Chapter 22

OLD AND NEW BLESSINGS

> *This is a great mystery: but I speak concerning Christ and the church.*
> *Nevertheless let every one of you in particular so love his wife even as himself; and the wife see the she reverence* (respects) *her husband* [Eph. 5:32–33].

What is the great mystery Paul presents to the faithful followers in Ephesus?

What can we do in order to understand the true relationship between Christ and His bride and to fathom the marriage relationship between a man and woman?

What does Paul say about the relationship between Christ and the church?

Why is it important to know God, Christ, and the will of God?

Why was Eve formed out of Adam?

Why should we pray for the Holy Spirit to reveal God's truth to us?

Why are we to seek to know the truth as revealed by God?

Why should a husband do for his wife what he does for himself?

How did the church become the fullness of Christ?

Bibliography

Barth, Markus. *Ephesians 1-3*. Garden City, NY: Doubleday & Company, Inc., 1974.

Calvin, John. *Calvin's New Testament Commentaries*. Grand Rapids, MI: William. B. Eerdmans Publishing Company, 1959, 1960, 1961, 1963, 1965, 1972, 1973.

———. *Calvin's Sermons on The Epistle to the Ephesians*. Carlisle, PA: The Banner of Truth Trust, 1973.

———. *Institutes of the Christian Religion*. Philadelphia, PA: The Westminster Press.

Chambers, Oswald. *My Utmost for His Highest*. New York, NY: Dodd, Mead & Company.

Holy Bible. *The King James Study Bible*. Nashville, TN: Thomas Nelson, Inc., 1988.

Lloyd-Jones, Martyn. *Darkness and Light*. Grand Rapids, MI: Baker Book House, 1982.

———. Life in the Spirit. Grand Rapids, MI: Baker Book House, 1974, 1981.

Paxson, Ruth. *The Wealth, Walk and Warfare of the Christian*. London and Edinburgh: Oliphants, Ltd., 1941.

Presbyterian Hymnal. Louisville, KY: Westminster/John Knox Press, 1990.

Vine, W. E. *Vine's Expository Dictionary of New Testament Words*. McLean, VA: MacDonald Publishing Company.

Weber, Otto. *Foundations of Dogmatics. Volumes 1 & 2*. Grand Rapids, MI: William B. Eerdmans Publishing Company, 1981, 1983

Index of Scripture References
Volume Six

OLD TESTAMENT

Genesis

1:2–4	46
1:27	168
2:7	125
2:18	125
2:20	169
2:20–24	168
2:23	169, 171
2:23–24	171
2:24	119, 125
3:1	108
3:6	108, 126
3:16	125–126
8:21	14
13:9	39, 40, 46

Exodus

19:10–11	176

Joshua

24:15	94

Psalms

1:1	76
1:5–6	76
14:1	49
23:1–6	122
111:10	68
112:7	79

Proverbs

4:7	156
9:10	68
13:15	35
15:33	68
23:7	50

Ecclesiastes

2:14	49

Ezekiel

16:9	176
36:25–27	176

Hosea

13:9	36

Micah

6:6–8	60

Malachi

2:14–16	174

NEW TESTAMENT

Matthew

3:15	61
5:6	61

Matthew–continued

5:14	46
5:14–16	42
5:16	7
5:20	61
5:44–45	4
5:46–47	7–8
5:48	7
6:19–21	76
7:21	30
7:23	31
7:24	30
17:5	10, 17
21:32	61
23:3	51
23:3–5a	109
23:13–15	51
23:14	51
23:23–31	51–52
23:33	52
23:37	52

Mark

6:2	69
8:36	50

Luke

4:1	93
9:16	102
12:19–20	53
15:13	84
17:20–21	28
22:19b	171–172

John

1:5	42
1:18	69
3:19	50
3:19–21	22
3:21	22
3:34	93
4:14	176
5:30	149
7:38–39	176
8:12	42
8:31–32	42, 179
10:11	13
13:34	6, 10
13:35	7
14:6	41
14:18	94
15:3	179
16:10	61
16:22b	86
17:3	56
17:9	158
17:17	31, 42, 181
17:17–19	179
17:19	162
17:21	32–33
18:36	27
21:15–17	134

Acts

1:8	92
2:4	82
2:37	96
2:44	97
2:46–47	98
2:47	98
3:19	90
4:32	98
9:4	46
9:5	46
9:15	92
9:17–19	92–93
13:8	93
13:9	93
13:10	93
13:52	93
19:2	88
20:28	88, 158

Scripture Index 233

Romans

1:16–17	22
1:18	36
1:21	36
1:22	36
1:23	36
1:24	36
1:25	36
1:28	37
1:29	37
1:30	37
1:31	38
1:32	38
3:25–26	60–61
5:6	159
5:6–9	159
5:8	160
6:20–23	52
6:21	53
8:30	30, 153
8:38–39	10
12:2	79
13:10	11
13:11–14	77
13:14	77

1 Corinthians

1:18	70
1:20–21	70
1:23	70
1:25–27	71
1:30	31, 71
2:6	70
2:10	71, 166
2:12–14	166
2:13–14	71
2:14–16	57
3:11	158
6:9–10	29
6:11	29
6:19	94
10:31	63, 123
11:11	127
11:26	154
11:29–30	154
11:31–32	154
13:4–8	135
13:8	160
13:13	135, 160
15:33–34	29

2 Corinthians

5:17	6
5:21	14
6:14–17	29–30
8:9	13
13:14	94

Galatians

2:20	158
3:28	127
5:21	50
5:22–23	111, 134
6:8	12
6:9	12
6:10	12

Ephesians

1:1	117
1:3–4	181
1:4	19
1:5	5
1:13	92
1:17	68
1:18	167
1:22	168
1:22–23	170
2:1–7	175
2:10	5–6
2:19	44
2:20–22	110
3:19	83
3:20–21	154

Ephesians–continued

4:1	81, 106, 142
4:3	33
4:11	150, 167
4:12	167
4:12–14	150
4:13	25, 65, 83
4:20	25, 65
4:20–24	139
4:21	111
4:22–24	177
4:23	25
4:24	65, 162
4:30	19, 92
4:32	5, 12, 65, 153
5:1–2	1, 47, 184
5:2	5, 8, 9, 65, 158, 186
5:3–5	16, 18, 188
5:5	21, 24, 190
5:6	32, 34, 47
5:6–14	192
5:7–8	39, 194
5:8	42, 44, 62, 65, 66
5:8–9	55
5:8–10	58, 198
5:8–11	196
5:9	60
5:10	56, 62, 63
5:11	47, 55, 65
5:12	47
5:13–14	55
5:14	56
5:15	67, 72, 202
5:15–17	64
5:15–21	200
5:16	73, 74
5:17	65, 72, 79
5:18	88, 95, 106, 107, 134, 138, 140, 145, 206
5:18b	144
5:18–21	81, 112–113, 204
5:19–20	95, 208
5:19–21	107
5:21	105, 106, 107, 110, 117, 119, 121, 138, 140, 144, 145, 210
5:22	121, 132, 214
5:22–23	112, 212
5:22–33	115
5:23	123, 124, 132, 133
5:23–25	123–124
5:24	123, 145
5:25	136, 137, 145, 157, 159, 160, 171
5:25–26	130, 164
5:25–27	136, 156, 161, 218
5:25–28	124
5:25–33	216
5:26	161, 173, 224
5:27	152, 153, 154, 155
5:28	140, 170
5:28–29	147, 220
5:28–30	167
5:29	150, 169, 170
5:29–30	169
5:30	132, 168
5:30–31	143, 171
5:31–32	171
5:32	165, 166, 167, 169, 170, 171, 172
5:32–33	165, 226
5:33	116, 138, 140, 145, 222
6:12	21

Philippians

1:27	74
2:6	13
2:9–11	27
3:20–21	153
4:6	100
4:4–7	86

Colossians

1:13	27

1:15–18	69
2:7	100
2:9	170
3:16	99
3:16–17	99

1 Thessalonians

2:12	27
2:13	178
3:12	10
5:18	100

2 Thessalonians

1:8	38

1 Timothy

2:13–15	126

2 Timothy

1:7	73, 84

Titus

2:14	19, 162

Hebrews

5:13	61
12:5–8	162–163
12:6–8	35
12:11	163

James

1:5	68
1:18	178
1:21	178
3:17	68

1 Peter

1:8	86
1:18–19	174
1:23	178
2:2	151
2:9–10a	163
2:11–12	76
2:24	14
3:6	144
3:6–7	143
3:7	144
3:15	58
3:20–21	177
4:2	74
4:5	74
5:2–3	109
5:5–8	109

2 Peter

1:1	61
1:3	151
1:4	170
3:14–18	127

1 John

1:6–10	30
2:5	11
3:1–3	78
3:3	31
4:7–10	11
4:8	10
5:2	11

2 John

1:10–11	110

Revelation

19:6–9	154–155

www.ingramcontent.com/pod-product-compliance
Lightning Source LLC
Chambersburg PA
CBHW051634230426
43669CB00013B/2297